10-95
Walden's
1.98

★ BETTER HOMES AND GARDENS® ★

HERITAGE OF AMERICA COOKBOOK

D0201952

BETTER HOMES AND GARDENS® BOOKS
Des Moines

BETTER HOMES AND GARDENS BOOKS®
An Imprint of Meredith® Books

President, Book Group: Joseph J. Ward
Vice President and Editorial Director: Elizabeth P. Rice
Executive Editor: Connie Schrader
Art Director: Ernest Shelton
Test Kitchen Director: Sharon Stilwell

HERITAGE OF AMERICA
COOKBOOK

Project Managers/Editors: Jennifer Darling and Shelli McConnell
Project Art Director/Designer: Lynda Haupert

©Copyright 1993 by Meredith
Corporation, Des Moines, Iowa.
All Rights Reserved.
Printed in China
First Edition. Printing Number and
Year: 5 4 3 2 1 97 96 95 94 93
Library of Congress Catalog Card
Number: 93-78517
ISBN: 0-696-02051-3

Co-Produced by Weldon Owen Inc.
President: John Owen
Publisher: Jane Fraser
Editorial Assistant: Jan Hughes
Production: James Obata,
Stephanie Sherman

Manufactured by Mandarin Offset,
Hong Kong

Our seal assures you that every recipe in the *Heritage of America Cookbook* has
been tested in the Better Homes and Gardens® Test Kitchen. This means that each
recipe is practical and reliable, and meets our high standards of taste appeal.
We guarantee your satisfaction with this book for as long as you own it.

WE CARE!

All of us at Better Homes and Gardens® Books are dedicated to providing
you with the information and ideas you need to create tasty foods. We
welcome your comments and suggestions. Write us at: Better Homes and Gardens®
Books, Cookbook Editorial Department, RW-240,
1716 Locust St., Des Moines, IA 50309-3023

If you would like to order additional copies of any of our books,
call 1-800-678-2803 or check with your local bookstore.

Shown on cover: Apple-Cherry Pie (see recipe page 212)

Preface

⁓

 he Kitchen Companion provides you with all
of the recipes from the Better Homes and Gardens®
Heritage of America Cookbook in an easy-to-use
format. While you use your full-color cookbook to
read and enjoy, you can cook from this handy
volume of recipes.

Contents

⁓

Flavors of New England

Rhode Island

CLAMBAKE

Colonists cooked clams, lobsters, and oysters in rock-lined pits on the beach, a technique that hasn't changed much in three centuries. The modern clambake has expanded the menu to include chicken, corn, potatoes, and fish. This version bakes on a grill.

16 large *or* 20 small clams in shells
4 9-ounce frozen lobster tails, thawed
4 cups parsley sprigs
4 large fresh ears of corn, halved, *or* 8 small ears of corn
Clarified Butter

Thoroughly wash, drain, and rinse clams in salt water (⅓ cup salt to 1 gallon water) three times. With kitchen shears, cut down both undersides of lobster tails; pull off thin underside membranes.

Tear off eight 2½-foot lengths of wide, heavy foil. Use 2 pieces of foil for each packet. Place *1 cup* parsley in center of each packet. Arrange one lobster tail, four large clams, and the corn on top of bed of parsley. Repeat with remaining ingredients. Drizzle Clarified Butter evenly over lobster, clams, and corn in the packets. Sprinkle lightly with salt. Seal tightly.

Place packets, seam side up, on grill directly over coals. Cover and grill over *medium-hot* coals for 20 to 25 minutes or till lobster is bright red and cooked and clams are opened. (Discard any unopened clams.) To serve, remove lobster, clams, and corn from packets to serving plates. Spoon juices over the seafood and corn. Serves 4.

Clarified Butter: In a saucepan melt ½ cup *butter* without stirring. When the butter is completely melted, slowly pour the clear, oily, top layer into a dish. Discard the milky layer left in the pan.

Nutrition information per serving: 500 calories, 35 g protein, 31 g carbohydrate, 28 g total fat (16 g saturated), 169 mg cholesterol, 852 mg sodium, 1,138 mg potassium

Maine

BOILED LOBSTER

Lobster was so plentiful in the earliest days of this country, that some settlers eventually refused to eat it. In fact, a group of Maine colonists called a strike in 1608 to protest the monotony of their diet: lobster, lobster, and more lobster.

6 cups water
1½ teaspoons salt
4 6-ounce lobster tails
Clarified Butter
(see recipe, above)

In a 3-quart saucepan bring water and salt to boiling. Add lobster tails; return to boiling. Simmer, uncovered, for 6 to 10 minutes or till shells turn bright red and meat is opaque; drain. Serve with Clarified Butter. Makes 4 servings.

Nutrition information per serving: 295 calories, 17 g protein, 1 g carbohydrate, 24 g total fat (15 g saturated), 124 mg cholesterol, 529 mg sodium, 289 mg potassium

STEAMED CLAMS WITH HORSERADISH-DILL SAUCE

"Clams should boil about fifteen minutes in their own water; no other need be added, except a spoonful to keep the bottom shells from burning." These simple directions appeared in The American Frugal Housewife, *a cookbook by a Boston woman named Child. The year was 1836, so it couldn't have been Julia; in fact, it was Lydia Maria Child.*

24 live clams
12 quarts cold water
1 cup salt
1 8-ounce carton dairy sour cream
2 tablespoons snipped fresh chives
1 tablespoon milk
1 tablespoon snipped fresh dill *or* 1 teaspoon dried dillweed
1 teaspoon prepared horseradish
Snipped fresh chives (optional)

To clean clams, scrub them under cold running water. In a 4-quart Dutch oven combine *4 quarts* of the water and *⅓ cup* of the salt. Add clams and soak for 15 minutes. Drain and rinse. Discard water. Repeat twice. Rinse clams well.

Meanwhile, for sauce, in a small mixing bowl stir together sour cream, chives, milk, dill or dillweed, and horseradish. Cover and chill till serving time. Garnish with snipped fresh chives, if desired.

To steam clams, in the same Dutch oven add water to ½ -inch depth; bring to boiling. Place clams in a steamer basket. Place basket of clams in Dutch oven. Cover and steam for 5 minutes or till clams open. Discard any clams that do not open. Serve with sauce. Makes 8 servings.

Nutrition information per serving: 82 calories, 4 g protein, 2 g carbohydrate, 6 g total fat (3 g saturated), 22 mg cholesterol, 32 mg sodium, 133 mg potassium

New Hampshire

ROASTED CHESTNUTS

"Under the spreading chestnut tree the village smithy stands," wrote Henry Wadsworth Longfellow in 1842. These graceful trees, now diminished in number by disease, once flourished throughout New England. The nuts were roasted and eaten, and the wood was used for building.

Whole fresh chestnuts

Using a sharp knife, cut an X in the flat side of each chestnut. (This allows the shell to peel easily and prevents the nut from exploding during cooking.) Arrange nuts in a single layer in an ungreased baking pan. Bake in a 425° oven for 15 minutes, tossing once or twice. Cool slightly; peel and serve while warm.

Nutrition information per chestnut: 22 calories, 0 g protein, 5 g carbohydrate, 0 g total fat (0 g saturated), 0 mg cholesterol, 0 mg sodium, 53 mg potassium

Maine

LOBSTER RISOTTO

Native Americans taught early New Englanders how to steam the huge lobsters that were so easily pulled from the Atlantic. The region's cooks continue to create new ways to enjoy this favorite shellfish.

½ cup chopped onion
2 cloves garlic, minced
1 tablespoon olive oil *or* cooking oil
1 cup Arborio rice *or* long grain rice
3 cups vegetable broth *or* chicken broth
1 cup bite-size asparagus pieces *or* small broccoli flowerets
12 ounces cooked lobster, cut into bite-size pieces
¼ cup grated Parmesan cheese
3 tablespoons snipped fresh basil *or* parsley

In a medium saucepan cook onion and garlic in hot oil till onion is tender. Stir in rice. Cook and stir for 5 minutes to brown. Meanwhile, in another saucepan bring vegetable or chicken broth to boiling; reduce heat and simmer. Slowly add *1 cup* of the broth to the rice mixture, stirring constantly. Continue to cook and stir till liquid is absorbed. Add *½ cup* broth and the asparagus or broccoli to the rice mixture, stirring constantly. Continue to cook and stir till liquid is absorbed. Add *1 cup* more broth, ½ cup at a time, stirring constantly till the broth has been absorbed. This should take about 15 to 20 minutes.

Stir in the remaining broth. Cook and stir till rice is slightly creamy and just tender. Stir in lobster, Parmesan cheese, and basil or parsley. Heat through. Serve immediately. Makes 4 servings.

Nutrition information per serving: 358 calories, 28 g protein, 43 g carbohydrate, 7 g total fat (2 g saturated), 66 mg cholesterol, 1,025 mg sodium, 654 mg potassium

Massachusetts

BROILED SCROD WITH LEMON BUTTER

Scrod is a young cod, under two pounds. "Scrod are always broiled, spread with butter, and sprinkled with salt and pepper," wrote Bostonian Fannie Farmer in The Boston Cooking-School Cook Book. *The simplest preparation is still the best for this very New England fish.*

1½   **pounds fresh *or* frozen scrod fillets, cut 1 inch thick**
2   **tablespoons butter *or* margarine, melted**

1   **to 2 tablespoons lemon juice**
  Snipped parsley
  Lemon wedges
  Hot boiled potatoes (optional)

Thaw fish fillets, if frozen. Place in a single layer on a greased rack of an unheated broiler pan. Tuck under any thin edges.

Combine butter and lemon juice; brush fillets. Sprinkle with salt and pepper.

Broil fish 4 inches from the heat for 10 to 12 minutes or just till fish begins to flake easily, brushing occasionally with lemon-butter mixture. Brush again before serving. Garnish with parsley and lemon wedges. If desired, serve with hot boiled potatoes. Makes 6 servings.

Nutrition information per serving: 124 calories, 19 g protein, 0 g carbohydrate, 5 g total fat (2 g saturated), 57 mg cholesterol, 150 mg sodium, 219 mg potassium

Maine

SKEWERED SCALLOPS AND SWORDFISH WITH FENNEL

Although best known for lobster, Maine waters are a prime source for large-shell, succulent sea scallops. They're harvested all year, but are abundant in the warm months. Swordfish is strictly a warm-weather catch in New England.

½   pound fresh *or* frozen
     scallops
½   pound fresh *or* frozen
     swordfish steaks, cut
     1 inch thick
1   fennel bulb, trimmed and
     cut into thin wedges
¼   cup olive oil *or* cooking oil
2   tablespoons lime juice *or*
     lemon juice
2   tablespoons finely chopped
     green onion
1   tablespoon snipped fresh
     thyme *or* ½ teaspoon
     dried thyme, crushed
1   teaspoon fennel seed,
     crushed
1   medium red sweet pepper,
     cut into 1-inch squares
8   small fresh mushrooms

Thaw scallops and swordfish, if frozen. Cut swordfish into 1-inch cubes. Cook fennel in boiling water for 4 minutes; drain and cool.

For marinade, in a plastic bag mix oil, lime juice, onion, thyme, fennel seed, and ¼ teaspoon *pepper*. Add scallops, swordfish, fennel, sweet pepper, and mushrooms. Seal bag. Refrigerate 1 hour, turning bag occasionally to distribute the marinade.

Drain fish and vegetables, reserving marinade. On eight 12-inch skewers, alternately thread scallops, swordfish, fennel, sweet pepper, and mushrooms, leaving about ¼ inch between pieces. Place on the greased unheated rack of a broiler pan. Broil 4 inches from the heat for 5 minutes. Turn kabobs over and brush with reserved marinade. Broil 4 to 5 minutes more or till fish flakes easily with a fork and scallops are opaque. Serves 4.

Nutrition information per serving: 273 calories, 22 g protein, 7 g carbohydrate, 18 g total fat (3 g saturated), 38 mg cholesterol, 346 mg sodium, 797 mg potassium

Massachusetts

NEW ENGLAND CLAM CHOWDER

Clam chowder is one of the great dishes of this region, beloved by New Englanders since colonial days. In Moby Dick, Herman Melville *described its satisfactions: "the chowder being surpassingly excellent, we dispatched it with great expedition...."*

1   pint shucked clams *or*
     two 6½-ounce cans
     minced clams
2   slices bacon, halved
2½ cups finely chopped, peeled
     potatoes
1   cup chopped onion
1   teaspoon instant chicken
     bouillon granules

1 teaspoon Worcestershire
   sauce
¼ teaspoon dried thyme,
   crushed
2 cups milk
1 cup half-and-half
2 tablespoons all-purpose
   flour

Chop shucked clams, reserving juice; set clams aside. Strain clam juice to remove bits of shell. (*Or,* drain canned clams, reserving juice.) If necessary, add water to clam juice to equal *1 cup.* Set aside.

In a saucepan cook bacon till crisp. Remove bacon, reserving 1 tablespoon drippings. Drain bacon on paper towels; crumble. Set aside.

In the same saucepan combine reserved bacon drippings, reserved clam juice, potatoes, onion, bouillon granules, Worcestershire sauce, thyme, and ⅛ teaspoon *pepper.* Bring to boiling; reduce heat. Cover and simmer about 10 minutes or till potatoes are tender. With the back of a fork, mash potatoes slightly against the side of the pan.

Combine milk, half-and-half, and flour till smooth. Add to potato mixture. Cook and stir till bubbly. Stir in clams. Return to boiling; reduce heat. Cook 1 to 2 minutes more. Sprinkle with bacon. Serves 4.

Nutrition information per serving: 487 calories, 31 g protein, 43 g carbohydrate, 21 g total fat (11 g saturated), 112 mg cholesterol, 494 mg sodium, 1,276 mg potassium

Vermont

NEW ENGLAND CHEESE SOUP

The Vermont cheese industry dates at least to 1822, when the Crowley Cheese Company opened for business in rural Healdville. The state's justly famous cheddars have been used in soups like this one to satisfy Yankee appetites during the long, dreary New England winters.

½ cup chopped carrot
½ cup sliced celery
½ cup chopped red sweet
   pepper
¼ cup sliced green onion
¼ cup margarine *or* butter
⅓ cup all-purpose flour
½ teaspoon instant chicken
   bouillon granules
¼ teaspoon ground white
   pepper
2½ cups milk
1 cup water
2 cups shredded sharp
   cheddar cheese
   (8 ounces)
2 cups shredded American
   cheese (8 ounces)

In a saucepan cook carrot, celery, sweet pepper, and onion in margarine till tender. Stir in flour, bouillon granules, and white pepper. Add milk and water all at once. Cook and stir till bubbly. Cook and stir 1 minute more. Stir in cheddar cheese and American cheese till cheese melts. Makes 4 servings.

Nutrition information per serving: 697 calories, 34 g protein, 26 g carbohydrate, 51 g total fat (27 g saturated), 125 mg cholesterol, 1,488 mg sodium, 714 mg potassium

Massachusetts

IRISH STEW WITH MINT SOUR CREAM

In the nineteenth century, Boston was the port of entry for untold numbers of European immigrants, particularly from Ireland, who fled poverty and starvation in hope of a better life. This famous meat-and-potato stew fortified the Irish of Boston and was adopted by New England as its own.

12 ounces lean, boneless lamb, cut into 1-inch cubes
2 cups beef broth
¼ teaspoon salt
⅛ teaspoon pepper
1 bay leaf
3 medium potatoes, peeled and cut into 1-inch chunks
2 medium onions, cut into wedges
1½ cups sliced carrots
½ teaspoon dried thyme, crushed
½ teaspoon dried basil, crushed
½ cup cold beer *or* water
2 tablespoons all-purpose flour
⅓ cup dairy sour cream
2 teaspoons snipped fresh mint

In a large saucepan or Dutch oven combine lamb, broth, salt, pepper, and bay leaf. Bring to boiling; reduce heat. Cover and simmer for 30 minutes. Skim fat off meat mixture. Add potatoes, onions, carrots, thyme, and basil. Cover and simmer for 30 minutes more or till vegetables are tender. Discard bay leaf.

In a small bowl stir together beer or water and flour. Stir into meat mixture. Cook and stir till thickened and bubbly. Cook and stir 1 minute more.

To serve, stir together the sour cream and mint. Dollop each serving with sour cream mixture. Makes 4 servings.

Nutrition information per serving:
327 calories, 23 g protein, 35 g carbohydrate, 10 g total fat (4 g saturated), 65 mg cholesterol, 625 mg sodium, 857 mg potassium

Massachusetts

PORTUGUESE SAUSAGE SOUP

Portuguese fishermen and sailors settled in New England coastal towns like New Bedford, Massachusetts, before the Civil War. They brought with them their spicy Iberian cuisine. Sausage soup is one of the best known of these recipes.

4 ounces hot Italian sausage links, sliced ¼ inch thick
4 ounces sweet Italian sausage links, sliced ¼ inch thick
½ cup chopped onion
2 medium potatoes, peeled and sliced
2 14½-ounce cans chicken broth *or* vegetable broth
1 10-ounce package frozen chopped spinach
½ cup beer *or* water
¼ teaspoon pepper

In a large saucepan cook the hot sausage, sweet sausage, and onion till sausage is browned and onion is tender. Drain fat. Add the potatoes, the chicken or vegetable broth, spinach, beer or water, and pepper. Bring to boiling; reduce heat. Cover and simmer about 20 minutes or till potatoes are tender. Makes 6 side-dish servings.

Nutrition information per serving: 163 calories, 10 g protein, 14 g carbohydrate, 7 g total fat (2 g saturated), 18 mg cholesterol, 698 mg sodium, 504 mg potassium

Massachusetts

NEW ENGLAND BOILED DINNER

A dinner of meat and vegetables boiled together became a New England tradition because it "cooked itself." Colonial women would let the combination simmer in an iron pot all day while they went on with other chores.

2 bay leaves
2 tablespoons snipped fresh thyme *or* 2 teaspoons dried thyme, crushed
1 teaspoon whole cloves
½ teaspoon whole black peppercorns
1 3- to 3½-pound corned beef brisket
8 cups water
3 small onions, halved
4 medium carrots *or* parsnips, quartered crosswise
3 small potatoes (about 12 ounces)
3 stalks celery, quartered crosswise
½ of a small head cabbage, cut into 6 wedges
   Mustard Glaze
   Snipped fresh thyme (optional)

For the spice bag*, cut a double thickness of 100 percent cotton cheesecloth into a 6- or 8-inch square. Place bay leaves, thyme, cloves, and peppercorns in the center of the cheesecloth. Bring up the corners and tie with a clean string.

Place corned beef in a 4- to 6-quart Dutch oven. Add spice bag and the water to corned beef. Bring to boiling; reduce heat. Cover and simmer for 2½ hours.

Add onions, carrots or parsnips, potatoes, and celery to corned beef. Return to boiling. Cover and simmer for 10 minutes. Add cabbage wedges; simmer, covered, about 10 minutes more or till meat and vegetables are tender.

Meanwhile, prepare Mustard Glaze. Drain meat and vegetables; discard the spice bag. Arrange meat and vegetables on a serving platter. Spoon Mustard Glaze over meat and vegetables. If desired, garnish with fresh thyme. Slice the corned beef across the grain. Serves 6 to 8.

*Note: If a spice packet is provided with the corned beef, use it instead of the bay leaves, thyme, cloves, and peppercorns.

Mustard Glaze: In a medium saucepan combine ⅔ cup packed *brown sugar*, ½ cup *vinegar*, ½ cup *prepared mustard*, and ½ teaspoon *garlic powder*. Bring to boiling, stirring till sugar dissolves. Cook, uncovered, for 5 minutes. If necessary, beat glaze smooth with a wire whisk or rotary beater. Makes about 1 cup.

Nutrition information per serving: 487 calories, 27 g protein, 39 g carbohydrate, 26 g total fat (8 g saturated), 125 mg cholesterol, 1,755 mg sodium, 752 mg potassium

Massachusetts

RATATOUILLE-TOPPED COD

The codfish is so intertwined with Massachusetts history that it appears on the state seal, and a wooden replica of the "Sacred Cod" has hung in the statehouse since 1784. Of course, Cape Cod got its name because so many of the fish swam in local waters.

1½	cups cubed, peeled eggplant
½	cup chopped green pepper
½	cup chopped red sweet pepper
½	cup chopped yellow sweet pepper
½	cup chopped onion
½	cup sliced zucchini
½	cup sliced mushrooms
3	cloves garlic, minced
2	tablespoons olive oil *or* cooking oil
3	medium tomatoes, seeded and chopped
½	teaspoon salt
1	tablespoon snipped fresh basil *or* ½ teaspoon dried basil, crushed
1½	teaspoons snipped fresh oregano *or* ¼ teaspoon dried oregano, crushed
¼	teaspoon pepper
1	pound cod fillets, cut into 2-inch chunks
¼	cup snipped fresh basil *or* parsley
¼	cup coarsely shredded Parmesan cheese

In a large skillet cook eggplant, green pepper, red sweet pepper, yellow sweet pepper, onion, zucchini, mushrooms, and garlic in hot oil till tender. Stir in the tomatoes, salt, basil, oregano, and pepper. Cook, uncovered, for 15 minutes more, stirring occasionally.

Arrange fish chunks in the bottom of a greased 2-quart rectangular baking dish. Sprinkle lightly with salt and pepper. Spoon vegetable mixture over fish. Cover with foil. Bake in a 450° oven for 15 to 20 minutes or till fish flakes easily with a fork. Remove from oven and sprinkle with the 1/4 cup basil or parsley and Parmesan cheese. Makes 4 servings.

Nutrition information per serving: 225 calories, 24 g protein, 12 g carbohydrate, 10 g total fat (2 g saturated), 52 mg cholesterol, 461 mg sodium, 704 mg potassium

Vermont

MAPLE-GLAZED TURKEY BREAST WITH ORANGE-PARSLEY STUFFING

Americans so appreciated the native wild turkey that Benjamin Franklin wanted to make it, rather than the eagle, the national bird. He described the turkey as "respectable" but dismissed the eagle as a "Bird of bad moral Character."

⅓	cup maple syrup
3	tablespoons Dijon-style mustard
1	tablespoon margarine *or* butter
2	teaspoons Worcestershire sauce
1	4- to 5-pound fresh *or* frozen whole turkey breast with bone, thawed
	Orange-Parsley Stuffing

For glaze, in a small saucepan combine maple syrup, mustard, margarine or butter, and Worcestershire sauce. Cook and stir over medium heat till margarine melts. Set aside.

Rinse turkey; pat dry. Place turkey, skin side up, in a shallow roasting pan. Bake, uncovered, in a 325° oven for 2 to 2½ hours or till a meat thermometer inserted in thickest part registers 170°. Brush with glaze during the last 30 minutes of roasting.

While turkey breast is baking, prepare Orange-Parsley Stuffing. Bake stuffing, uncovered, alongside turkey during the last 50 minutes of roasting or till stuffing is heated through. Makes 8 to 10 servings.

Orange-Parsley Stuffing: In a large mixing bowl combine 10 cups *dry bread cubes;* 1 cup snipped *parsley;* ½ cup chopped *onion;* 4 teaspoons shredded *orange peel;* 2 teaspoons *dried marjoram,* crushed; 1 teaspoon *dried thyme,* crushed; 2 cloves *garlic,* minced; ½ teaspoon *salt;* and ¼ teaspoon *pepper.* Mix well. In a small mixing bowl stir together ¼ cup *margarine or butter,* melted; 2 slightly beaten *eggs;* ⅓ cup *orange juice;* and ½ cup *water.* Toss with bread mixture; if necessary, add more water for desired moistness. Spoon stuffing into a 3-quart casserole. Cover and bake in a 325° oven for 45 to 50 minutes or till heated through. Makes 9½ cups.

For a whole stuffed turkey: Prepare stuffing as directed, *except* do not bake in the 3-quart casserole. Double the amounts for the glaze and prepare as directed.

Rinse one 12- to 14-pound turkey, then pat dry. Season body cavity with salt. Spoon some of the stuffing loosely into neck cavity. Skewer neck skin to back. Spoon more of the stuffing loosely into body cavity. (Do not pack stuffing too tight or it will not get hot enough by the time the turkey is cooked.) Tuck drumsticks under tail skin or tie to tail. Twist wing tips under the back. Transfer any remaining stuffing to a casserole; cover and chill.

Place turkey, breast side up, on a rack in a shallow roasting pan. Insert a meat thermometer into the center of one of the inside thigh muscles. The bulb should not touch the bone. Cover turkey loosely with foil. Roast turkey in a 325° oven for 4½ to 5½ hours or till thermometer registers 180° to 185°. Cut band of skin between legs after 3½ hours. During the last 30 minutes of roasting, uncover turkey and brush turkey with maple glaze.

Bake casserole of stuffing alongside turkey the last 40 to 45 minutes of cooking time. When done, remove turkey from oven; cover. Let turkey stand 20 minutes before carving.

To serve, remove the stuffing from turkey; transfer it to a serving bowl. Carve the turkey and serve warm. Makes 12 to 14 servings.

Nutrition information per serving: 576 calories, 41 g protein, 40 g carbohydrate, 27 g total fat (6 g saturated), 145 mg cholesterol, 782 mg sodium, 514 mg potassium

Connecticut

WHOLE WHEAT POPOVERS WITH SHALLOTS

*In the nineteenth century, glazed
ovenproof pottery molds known
as Boston cups were manufactured for
baking popovers. They resemble what
we would call a custard cup today.*

¼   cup minced shallots
1   tablespoon margarine *or*
      butter
      Shortening *or* nonstick
      spray coating
2   beaten eggs
1   cup milk
⅔   cup all-purpose flour
⅓   cup whole wheat flour
¼   teaspoon salt

In a small skillet or saucepan cook shallots in margarine or butter till tender. Set aside.

Using *½ teaspoon* shortening for each cup, grease the bottom and sides of six 6-ounce custard cups or the cups of a popover pan. Or, spray cups with nonstick coating. Place the custard cups on a 15x10x1-inch baking pan; set aside.

In a mixing bowl combine beaten eggs, milk, and shallot mixture. Add all-purpose flour, whole wheat flour, and salt. Beat with a rotary beater or wire whisk till the mixture is smooth. Fill the greased cups *half* full. Bake in a 400° oven about 40 minutes or till very firm.

Immediately after removal from the oven, prick each popover with a fork to let steam escape. If crisper popovers are desired, return popovers to oven for 5 to 10 minutes more or to desired crispness (be sure the oven is turned off). Serve hot. Makes 6 popovers.

Nutrition information per popover: *140 calories, 6 g protein, 19 g carbohydrate, 5 g total fat (1 g saturated), 74 mg cholesterol, 147 mg sodium, 128 mg potassium*

Massachusetts

CRANBERRY-MAPLE SAUCE

*Not only did Native Americans teach
the Europeans to enjoy the meat of the
wild turkey, but they also showed
them that cranberries could be sweetened
by boiling them with maple syrup, an
approach which inspired the
ultimate creation of cranberry sauce.*

½   cup packed brown sugar
½   cup maple syrup *or*
      maple-flavored syrup
2   cups cranberries (8 ounces)
1   tablespoon shredded orange
      peel *or* lemon peel

In a saucepan mix brown sugar, maple syrup, and *½ cup water*. Bring to boiling, stirring to dissolve sugar. Reduce heat; simmer, uncovered, for 5 minutes, stirring occasionally.

Add cranberries. Return to boiling; reduce heat. Simmer for 3 to 4 minutes or till cranberry skins pop, stirring occasionally. Remove from heat. Stir in orange peel. Serve warm or chilled with roast poultry, pork, or ham. Makes about 1¾ cups.

Nutrition information per tablespoon:
28 calories, 0 g protein, 7 g carbohydrate, 0 g total fat (0 g saturated), 0 mg cholesterol, 1 mg sodium, 26 mg potassium

Maine

CREAM OF BAKED SQUASH AND GARLIC SOUP

The colonists watched Native Americans rotate their crops to avoid depleting the soil. They followed suit: rather than planting only corn in the same field season after season, they alternated it with another vegetable, usually squash.

2   medium acorn squash (about 3 pounds total)
2   to 4 tablespoons maple syrup *or* maple-flavored syrup
4   teaspoons margarine *or* butter

1   head garlic, cloves separated and peeled
1   carrot, cut into 1-inch pieces
1   onion, cut into wedges
4   cups chicken broth
1   cup whipping cream
    Whole *or* snipped fresh basil leaves *or* Italian parsley sprigs (optional)

Cut each squash in half lengthwise. Scoop out and discard seeds. Place squash halves, cut side up, in a shallow roasting pan. Place *one-fourth* of the maple syrup and *1 teaspoon* margarine or butter in the cavity of each squash half. Arrange garlic, carrot, and onion around squash. Pour *2 cups* of the chicken broth in pan; cover tightly with aluminum foil. Bake in a 350° oven for 2 hours or till vegetables are very tender.

Remove pan from oven; let vegetables cool slightly. Scoop pulp from squash shells and stir into vegetable mixture.

Place *half* of the squash mixture in a blender container or food processor bowl. Cover and blend or process till smooth. Repeat with remaining squash mixture. Transfer entire squash mixture to a large-saucepan; stir in remaining chicken broth. Heat and stir till mixture boils. Stir in whipping cream. *Do not boil.* Season to taste with salt and pepper. If desired, garnish each serving with basil or parsley. Makes 6 servings.

Nutrition information per serving:
305 calories, 6 g protein, 32 g carbohydrate, 18 g total fat (10 g saturated), 54 mg cholesterol, 608 mg sodium, 930 mg potassium

Massachusetts

ANADAMA BREAD

Was Anna a lazy wife who forced her fisherman husband to bake his own bread? As he slipped the loaf into the oven, he was said to have muttered, "Anna, damn 'er!" Or at least that's the story repeated most often about this famous recipe.

½   cup cornmeal
⅓   cup packed brown sugar
1   teaspoon salt
1   cup boiling water
⅓   cup cooking oil
4½   to 5 cups all-purpose flour
1   package active dry yeast
1   8¾-ounce can cream-style corn

In a medium bowl stir together the cornmeal, brown sugar, and salt. Stir in the boiling water and oil. Cool mixture till warm (120° to 130°), stirring occasionally (allow approximately 15 to 20 minutes).

In a large mixing bowl stir together *1 cup* of the flour and the yeast. Add cornmeal mixture and cream-style corn. Beat with an electric mixer on low speed for 30 seconds, scraping the sides of the bowl constantly. Beat on high speed for 3 minutes. Using a spoon, stir in as much of the remaining flour as you can. Turn out onto a lightly floured surface. Knead in enough of the remaining flour to make a moderately stiff dough that is smooth and elastic (6 to 8 minutes total).

Shape the dough into a ball. Place in a lightly greased bowl; turn once to grease surface. Cover and let rise in a warm place till double (about 1 hour).

Punch dough down. Turn out onto a lightly floured surface. Divide dough in half. Cover and let rest for 10 minutes. Lightly grease two 1-quart casseroles or a large baking sheet.

Shape each half of the dough into a round loaf. Place loaves in prepared casseroles or 3 inches apart on the baking sheet. Cover and let rise in a warm place till nearly double (about 40 minutes). Bake in a 375° oven about 40 minutes or till bread sounds hollow when lightly tapped. If necessary, loosely cover the bread with foil the last 20 minutes to prevent over-browning. Remove bread from casseroles or baking sheet immediately. Cool on wire racks. Makes 2 loaves (32 servings).

Nutrition information per serving: 104 calories, 2 g protein, 18 g carbohydrate, 2 g total fat (0 g saturated), 0 mg cholesterol, 90 mg sodium, 42 mg potassium

Vermont

MASHED MAPLE SWEET POTATOES

In many areas of New England, maple syrup was often the only sweetener available to the colonists. Two common uses were to dress up sweet potatoes and to add flavor to beans. Today, Vermont leads the country in maple syrup production.

3   medium sweet potatoes, peeled and quartered
¼   cup maple syrup *or* maple-flavored syrup

2 tablespoons margarine *or*
    butter
¼ teaspoon salt
¼ to ⅓ cup half-and-half,
    light cream, or milk

In a medium saucepan cook potatoes, covered, in a small amount of
boiling water for 30 to 35 minutes
or till very tender; drain. Mash with
a potato masher or beat with an
electric mixer on low speed.

Add maple syrup, margarine or
butter, and salt. Gradually beat in
enough half-and-half, light cream,
or milk to make potato mixture light
and fluffy. Pipe or spoon potato
mixture onto serving plates. Makes
6 servings.

Nutrition information per serving:
151 calories, 2 g protein, 25 g carbohydrate, 5
g total fat (1 g saturated), 4 mg cholesterol,
166 mg sodium, 278 mg potassium

Massachusetts

PARKER HOUSE ROLLS

Boston's Parker House was an instant
success when it opened in 1855 because
it introduced a radical concept: diners
could eat there when they pleased, not just
at specified hours. These soft yeast rolls
that look like little purses are
associated with this famous hostelry.

3½ to 4 cups all-purpose flour
1 package active dry yeast
1 cup milk
¼ cup sugar
¼ cup margarine *or* butter
½ teaspoon salt
3 egg yolks
    Melted margarine *or* butter

In a large mixing bowl combine 1½
cups of the flour and the yeast; set
aside. In a medium saucepan heat
and stir the milk, sugar, margarine
or butter, and salt just till warm
(120° to 130°) and margarine
almost melts. Add to the flour mixture. Then add the 3 egg yolks. Beat
with an electric mixer on low to
medium speed for 30 seconds,
scraping the sides of the bowl. Beat
on high speed for 3 minutes. Stir in
as much of the remaining flour as
you can.

On a lightly floured surface,
knead in enough of the remaining
flour to make a moderately stiff
dough that is smooth and elastic
(6 to 8 minutes total). Shape into a
ball. Place in a greased bowl; turn
once to grease surface. Cover; let
rise in a warm place till double
(about 1½ hours).

Lightly grease baking sheets. On
a lightly floured surface, roll dough
to ¼-inch thickness. Cut with a 2½-
inch round biscuit cutter, dipping
the cutter into flour between cuts.
Brush with melted margarine or
butter. To shape, use a wooden
spoon handle to make a slig ht off-
center crease in each round. Fold
large half over small half, overlapping slightly. Press folded edge
firmly. Place 3 inches apart on the
baking sheets. Let rise in a warm
place till nearly double (about 30
minutes).

Bake in a 375° oven for 10 to 12
minutes or till golden. Remove rolls
from baking sheets and cool on a
wire rack. Makes 24 rolls.

Nutrition information per roll: 113
calories, 3 g protein, 17 g carbohydrate, 4 g
total fat (1 g saturated), 27 mg cholesterol,
75 mg sodium, 45 mg potassium

Massachusetts

BOSTON BROWN BREAD

*The Puritans served this steamed bread as a Sabbath dish along with baked beans, an inseparable combination for New Englanders even today.
It is another of those early American "rye 'n' Injun" mixtures: cornmeal, wheat, and rye flours.*

½   cup cornmeal
½   cup whole wheat flour
½   cup rye flour
½   teaspoon baking powder
¼   teaspoon baking soda
¼   teaspoon salt
1   cup buttermilk *or* sour milk
⅓   cup light molasses
2   tablespoons brown sugar
1   tablespoon cooking oil
¼   cup raisins *or* chopped walnuts
     Soft-style cream cheese *or* flavored soft-style cream cheese (optional)

In a large mixing bowl stir together cornmeal, whole wheat flour, rye flour, baking powder, baking soda, and salt.

In a mixing bowl combine buttermilk or sour milk, molasses, brown sugar, and oil. Gradually add milk mixture to flour mixture, stirring just till combined. Stir in raisins or chopped walnuts. Pour into a well-greased 7½x3½x2-inch loaf pan. Grease a piece of foil. Place the foil, greased side down, over the loaf pan. Press foil around edges to seal.

Place loaf pan on a rack in a 4- or 5-quart Dutch oven. Pour hot water into the Dutch oven around the loaf pan till water covers 1 inch of the loaf pan. Bring water to boiling; reduce heat. Cover and simmer for 2 to 2½ hours or till a toothpick inserted in the center comes out clean. Add additional boiling water to the Dutch oven as needed.

Remove loaf pan from the Dutch oven; let stand 10 minutes. Remove bread from the pan. Serve warm. If desired, serve with cream cheese. Makes 1 loaf (14 servings).

Nutrition information per serving: 95 calories, 2 g protein, 19 g carbohydrate, 1 g total fat (0 g saturated), 1 mg cholesterol, 87 mg sodium, 204 mg potassium

Massachusetts

BOSTON BAKED BEANS WITH PANCETTA

While Boston gets the credit for this dish, it was actually popular throughout all the colonies. Since it could be made a day ahead, it was a favorite with those whose religion restricted work on the Sabbath. For a more traditional dish, use salt pork instead of pancetta or bacon.

1   pound dry navy beans *or* dry great northern beans (2⅓ cups)
8   cups cold water
6   ounces pancetta (Italian bacon) *or* bacon, cut up

1 cup chopped onion
¼ cup packed brown sugar
¼ cup molasses
¼ cup maple syrup *or*
    maple-flavored syrup
¼ cup Worcestershire sauce
1 teaspoon dry mustard
½ teaspoon salt
¼ teaspoon pepper
4 ounces pancetta *or* bacon,
    cooked crisp and
    drained (optional)

Rinse beans. In a 4½-quart Dutch oven combine beans and cold water. Bring to boiling; reduce heat. Simmer, uncovered, for 2 minutes. Remove from heat. Cover and let stand for 1 hour. (*Or,* skip boiling the water and soak the beans overnight in a covered pan.) Drain and rinse beans.

In the same pan combine beans and 8 cups *fresh water.* Bring to boiling; reduce heat. Cover and simmer about 1¼ hours or till tender, stirring occasionally. Drain beans, reserving liquid. In the same pan cook the 6 ounces pancetta or bacon over medium heat till slightly crisp. Add onion to bacon and drippings; cook and stir till tender. Add brown sugar. Cook and stir till sugar dissolves. Stir in molasses, maple syrup, Worcestershire sauce, dry mustard, salt, and pepper. Add drained beans and *1 cup* of the reserved bean liquid. If desired, transfer to a bean pot.

Cover and bake in a 300° oven for 2¼ to 2½ hours or to desired consistency, stirring occasionally. If necessary, add additional reserved bean liquid. If desired, sprinkle with cooked pancetta or bacon before serving. Makes 10 to 12 servings.

Nutrition information per serving: 239 calories, 10 g protein, 45 g carbohydrate, 3 g total fat (1 g saturated), 3 mg cholesterol, 241 mg sodium, 635 mg potassium

Maine

CREAMED SUCCOTASH

Following Native American guidelines, the Pilgrims grew beans and corn so that the vines of one plant twined around the stalks of the other for support. The colonists borrowed from the Algonquian word sukquttahash *to give this dish its name.*

1 10-ounce package frozen
    succotash
1 tablespoon margarine *or*
    butter
1 tablespoon all-purpose flour
¾ teaspoon instant chicken
    bouillon granules
¼ teaspoon onion powder
½ cup milk
    Cracked black pepper

Cook succotash according to package directions; drain. Stir in margarine or butter till melted. Stir in flour, bouillon granules, and onion powder. Add milk all at once. Cook and stir till thickened and bubbly. Cook and stir 1 minute more. Sprinkle with pepper. Makes 3 or 4 servings.

Nutrition information per serving: 154 calories, 6 g protein, 23 g carbohydrate, 6 g total fat (1 g saturated), 3 mg cholesterol, 320 mg sodium, 320 mg potassium

Connecticut

CHEESY CREAMED CORN

Corn graters were folk implements devised to speed up the job of removing the milky pulp from the kernels. With their rows of nails pounded into boards, they looked more like instruments of torture than kitchen helpers.

2 slices bacon, cut up
3 medium ears of fresh corn
   or 1½ cups loose-pack, frozen corn
3 tablespoons water
2 tablespoons finely chopped onion
   Dash pepper
½ of a 3-ounce package cream cheese, cubed
1 tablespoon milk (optional)

In a small saucepan cook bacon till crisp. Remove bacon, reserving *1 tablespoon* drippings in saucepan. Drain the bacon and set it aside.

If using fresh corn, with a sharp knife cut corn from cobs about two-thirds down the kernels; do not scrape cob. (You should have about 1½ cups of corn.) Add the fresh or frozen corn, water, onion, and pepper to the saucepan. Bring just to boiling. Reduce heat. Cover and simmer for 5 to 7 minutes or till corn is crisp-tender.

Add the cream cheese to the undrained corn mixture in the saucepan. Stir over low heat till melted. If necessary, stir in the milk to make corn mixture of desired consistency. Sprinkle with reserved bacon. Makes 4 servings.

Nutrition information per serving: 138 calories, 4 g protein, 11 g carbohydrate, 10 g total fat (4 g saturated), 21 mg cholesterol, 126 mg sodium, 192 mg potassium

Rhode Island

HEARTY CORN CHOWDER

Like settlers in other regions, New Englanders noticed that the Native Americans used fresh corn for its meat and its liquid. Corn, a prime ingredient in substantial soups like this one, both thickened and extended the broth.

6 fresh medium ears of corn
   or 3 cups frozen whole kernel corn, thawed
½ cup chopped onion
½ cup chopped celery
1 tablespoon cooking oil
1 14½-ounce can chicken broth
1 cup cubed, peeled potato
1 cup milk
4 teaspoons all-purpose flour
⅛ teaspoon pepper
   Dash ground red pepper
½ cup diced, fully cooked ham
½ cup shredded sharp cheddar cheese (2 ounces)
2 tablespoons snipped fresh parsley

If using fresh corn, use a sharp knife to cut off just the kernel tips, then scrape the cobs with the dull edge of the knife. (You should have 3 cups corn.)

Place *1¾ cups* corn in a food processor bowl. Cover and process till smooth; set aside.

In a large saucepan cook onion and celery in hot oil till onion is tender but not brown. Stir in chicken broth and potato. Bring to boiling; reduce heat and simmer, covered, for 10 minutes. Stir in the corn purée and the remaining corn. Cook, uncovered, about 10 minutes more or till potato and corn are tender, stirring occasionally.

In a small bowl combine milk, flour, pepper, and ground red pepper; stir into corn mixture. Cook and stir till thickened and bubbly. Cook and stir 1 minute more. Stir in ham and cheese; cook and stir till cheese melts and soup is heated through. Garnish with parsley. Makes 5 servings.

Nutrition information per serving: 274 calories, 14 g protein, 36 g carbohydrate, 10 g total fat (4 g saturated), 23 mg cholesterol, 571 mg sodium, 604 mg potassium

Maine

SPICED BLUEBERRY JAM

Maine is a prime supplier of both wild and cultivated blueberries. Of the two, the wild berry is smaller, with a more intense flavor. It also grows on bushes in mountain areas of New Hampshire and Vermont, there for the picking.

6 **cups blueberries**
2 **tablespoons lemon juice**
½ **teaspoon ground cinnamon**
¼ **teaspoon ground allspice**
   Dash ground cloves
7 **cups sugar**
1 **6-ounce package (2 foil pouches) liquid fruit pectin**

Crush blueberries. (You should have 4½ cups blueberries.) In an 8- or 10-quart kettle combine crushed blueberries, lemon juice, cinnamon, allspice, and cloves. Stir in sugar.

Bring to a full rolling boil, stirring constantly. Stir in pectin. Return to a full rolling boil. Boil hard for 1 minute, stirring constantly. Remove from heat; quickly skim off foam with a metal spoon. Ladle at once into hot, sterilized, half-pint jars, leaving ¼-inch headspace. Adjust lids. Process in a boiling-water canner for 5 minutes. Makes 9 half-pints.

Note: If you would like to use antique canning jars, ladle the hot jam into sterilized, half-pint jars, leaving ¼-inch headspace. Adjust lids; cool and then store in the refrigerator.

Nutrition information per tablespoon: 41 calories, 0 g protein, 11 g carbohydrate, 0 g total fat (0 g saturated), 0 mg cholesterol, 1 mg sodium, 9 mg potassium

Vermont

BEET AND APPLE SALAD

Beets turn up in many New England recipes, including the famous side dishes named after both Harvard and Yale and beet-tinted red flannel hash. Yankees also love apples of all varieties.

3   medium beets (about 1 pound) *or* one 16-ounce can julienne beets, rinsed and drained
3   tablespoons salad oil
3   tablespoons white wine vinegar
1   teaspoon shredded orange peel
2   tablespoons orange juice
2   tablespoons sliced green onion
1   tablespoon snipped fresh mint *or* 1 teaspoon dried mint, crushed
1   teaspoon honey
2   cups torn romaine lettuce
1   coarsely chopped tart green apple (about 1 apple)
    Fresh mint (optional)

In a medium saucepan cook fresh whole beets, covered, in boiling water for 40 to 50 minutes or till tender; drain. Cool slightly; slip off skins and cut into thin strips.

Meanwhile, for dressing, in a screw-top jar combine salad oil, white wine vinegar, orange peel, orange juice, green onion, mint, and honey. Cover and shake well.

In a mixing bowl combine beets and *half* of the dressing. Cover and refrigerate the beet mixture and the remaining dressing 2 to 24 hours.

To serve, in a mixing bowl combine torn romaine and chopped apple. Toss apple mixture with the remaining dressing. Using a slotted spoon, spoon beet mixture over apple mixture. If desired, garnish with fresh mint. Makes 4 servings.

Nutrition information per serving: 136 calories, 1 g protein, 11 g carbohydrate, 10 g total fat (1 g saturated), 0 mg cholesterol, 36 mg sodium, 258 mg potassium

Massachusetts

CRANBERRY-BANANA BREAD WITH ORANGE BUTTER

Cranberries were probably first known as "crane berries" because cranes living near cranberry bogs fed on the fruit. Later they were dubbed "bounce berries" because of the way ripe berries jump if dropped (bruised ones stay put). The marshy waters of Cape Cod are a prime source of this native wetland berry.

1½   cups all-purpose flour
¾   teaspoon ground cinnamon
½   teaspoon baking soda
¼   teaspoon salt
¼   teaspoon ground nutmeg
2   beaten eggs
1   cup sugar
¾   cup coarsely chopped cranberries
⅔   cup mashed ripe banana
¼   cup cooking oil
1   teaspoon finely shredded orange peel
     Orange Butter

In a mixing bowl combine flour, cinnamon, baking soda, salt, and nutmeg. In another bowl stir together eggs, sugar, cranberries, banana, oil, and orange peel. Add to flour mixture, stirring just till combined. Pour batter into a greased 9x5x3-inch loaf pan.

Bake in a 350° oven for 50 to 60 minutes or till a toothpick inserted near the center comes out clean. Cool 10 minutes. Remove from pan; cool on a wire rack. Wrap and store overnight. Serve with Orange Butter. Makes 1 loaf (18 servings).

Orange Butter: In a small mixing bowl beat ½ cup *margarine or butter* with an electric mixer till softened. Add 1 tablespoon *powdered sugar*, 1 teaspoon finely shredded *orange peel*, 1 tablespoon *orange juice*, and 1/4 teaspoon *vanilla*. Beat till smooth.

Nutrition information per serving: 173 calories, 2 g protein, 22 g carbohydrate, 9 g total fat (1 g saturated), 24 mg cholesterol, 103 mg sodium, 53 mg potassium

New Hampshire

BANANA-CINNAMON WAFFLES

In areas where sugar maples grew, colonists made maple syrup according to instructions from local Native Americans. Trees were tapped in the spring when the sap began to rise. Some of the syrup was allowed to crystallize into sugar, while another portion was reserved for maple syrup.

1¾	cups all-purpose flour
1	tablespoon baking powder
¾	teaspoon ground cinnamon
¼	teaspoon salt
2	egg yolks
1½	cups milk
⅔	cup mashed ripe banana
½	cup cooking oil
2	egg whites
	Warm maple syrup *or* maple-flavored syrup

In a large mixing bowl combine flour, baking powder, cinnamon, and salt. In another mixing bowl beat egg yolks slightly; beat in milk, banana, and oil. Add egg yolk mixture to flour mixture all at once. Stir just till combined but still slightly lumpy.

In a medium mixing bowl beat egg whites till stiff peaks form (tips stand straight). Gently fold beaten egg whites into flour-egg yolk mixture, leaving a few fluffs of egg white. *Do not overmix.*

Pour 1 to 1¼ cups batter onto grids of a preheated, lightly greased waffle baker. Close lid quickly; do not open during baking. Bake according to manufacturer's directions. When done, use a fork to lift waffle off grid. Repeat with remaining batter. Keep waffles warm in a 300° oven while cooking remaining waffles. Serve with maple syrup. Makes 4 or 5 waffles.

Nutrition information per waffle: 874 calories, 12 g protein, 137 g carbohydrate, 32 g total fat (6 g saturated), 113 mg cholesterol, 458 mg sodium, 627 mg potassium

RED FLANNEL HASH

*While picturesque — the hash turns
a rich red from the beets — this dish is
strictly utilitarian. Corned beef
left over from Monday's boiled dinner
appeared in Thursday's hash. It is
associated with Vermont, and its famous
native son, Ethan Allen, and his
Green Mountain Boys.*

⅓ cup finely chopped shallots
    or onions
2   tablespoons margarine *or*
    butter
2   cups chopped, cooked
    potatoes *or* loose-pack,
    frozen, hash brown
    potatoes, thawed
1   16-ounce can diced beets,
    drained
1½ cups finely chopped, cooked
    corned beef *or* beef
¼   teaspoon salt
¼   teaspoon pepper
2   tablespoons milk
    Few drops bottled hot
    pepper sauce (optional)

In a large skillet cook shallots or
onions in margarine or butter till
tender. Stir in potatoes, beets, beef,
salt, and pepper. Spread evenly in
skillet. Cook over medium heat for 8
to 10 minutes or till browned on
bottom, turning occasionally. Stir in
milk, and, if desired, hot pepper
sauce. Makes 4 servings.

*Nutrition information per serving:
290 calories, 13 g protein, 22 g carbohydrate,
17 g total fat (5 g saturated), 56 mg cholesterol, 887 mg sodium, 579 mg potassium*

AUTUMN CIDER SYRUP

*In rural New England, especially
Vermont, sweet cider was boiled down
into a syrup for many cooking uses, the
most notable being cider pie.*

2   tablespoons sugar
2   tablespoons brown sugar
¼   teaspoon ground cinnamon
⅛   teaspoon ground nutmeg
    Dash ground cloves
¾   cup apple cider *or* apple
    juice
2   teaspoons lemon juice
¼   cup apple jelly

In a small saucepan stir together
sugar, brown sugar, cinnamon, nutmeg, and cloves. Stir in apple cider
or apple juice and lemon juice.
Cook and stir over medium heat till
sugars dissolve. Stir in apple jelly.
Bring to boiling. Reduce heat and
boil gently, uncovered, about 25
minutes or to desired consistency.
Serve warm with pancakes or waffles. Makes about ⅔ cup.

*Nutrition information per table-
spoon: 39 calories, 0 g protein, 10 g carbohydrate, 0 g total fat (0 g saturated), 0 mg
cholesterol, 3 mg sodium, 30 mg potassium*

Rhode Island

HOT BUTTERED CIDER SIPPER

Most of colonial New England's apple crop went into cider, a very popular beverage. In the early days of this country cider meant hard cider, and every member of the family drank it. Cider mixed with rum was called a stonewall.

1   quart apple cider *or* apple
    juice
3   tablespoons honey
2   tablespoons lemon juice
1   teaspoon whole cloves
1   teaspoon whole allspice
4   inches stick cinnamon,
    broken
¼   to ⅓ cup brandy
3   teaspoons butter *or*
    margarine
    Cinnamon sticks (optional)

In a medium saucepan combine apple cider or apple juice, honey, and lemon juice. For spice bag, place the cloves, allspice, and stick cinnamon in a double thick, 6-inch-square piece of 100 percent cotton cheesecloth. Bring the corners of the cheesecloth together and tie them with a clean string. Add spice bag to cider mixture.

Cover saucepan, and heat cider through but *do not boil.* Discard spice bag and stir in brandy. Ladle the hot cider mixture into mugs; float about *½ teaspoon* butter or margarine atop each serving. If desired, serve the cider with cinnamon sticks as stirrers. Makes 6 (6-ounce) servings.

Nutrition information per serving: 149 calories, 0 g protein, 29 g carbohydrate, 2 g total fat (1 g saturated), 5 mg cholesterol, 25 mg sodium, 210 mg potassium

Massachusetts

CRANBERRY FOOL

Fool, an old English dessert of stewed, puréed fruit and cream, was popular throughout the colonies. One well-known version called for swirling crushed gooseberries through a hearty dollop of whipped cream, or mixing them with a rich custard. The use of cranberries is a New England adaptation.

1½   cups whipping cream
2   tablespoons sugar
1   teaspoon vanilla
1   16-ounce can whole
     cranberry sauce

In a mixing bowl combine whipping cream, sugar, and vanilla. Beat with an electric mixer on medium speed till soft peaks form. Place the cranberry sauce in a large mixing bowl. Using a spatula, gently fold the whipped cream into the cranberry sauce till just combined (the mixture should be red and white). Cover loosely and refrigerate till serving time. To serve, spoon mixture into sherbet dishes, parfait dishes, or wine glasses. Makes 8 servings.

Nutrition information per serving: 252 calories, 1 g protein, 26 g carbohydrate, 17 g total fat (10 g saturated), 61 mg cholesterol, 33 mg sodium, 48 mg potassium

Connecticut

PUMPKIN SHORTCAKE WITH FALL FRUIT MEDLEY

When Benjamin Franklin served as America's representative to France, he was criticized by Connecticut newspapers for his reported extravagance. In reply, Franklin wrote in 1784 that plain Connecticut food like pumpkin, if available to him, would be better than "all the luxuries of Paris."

1¼ cups all-purpose flour
½ cup packed brown sugar
1 teaspoon pumpkin pie spice
½ teaspoon baking powder
½ teaspoon baking soda
⅓ cup buttermilk *or* sour milk
¼ cup shortening, margarine,
   or butter, softened
½ cup canned pumpkin
¼ cup honey
1 egg
½ teaspoon finely shredded
   orange peel
   Fall Fruit Medley
   Pumpkin Cream

In a large mixing bowl combine flour, brown sugar, pumpkin pie spice, baking powder, and baking soda. Add buttermilk or sour milk, shortening, pumpkin, honey, egg, and orange peel. Beat with an electric mixer on low to medium speed till smooth. Pour batter into a greased and floured 8x1½-inch round baking pan.

Bake in a 350° oven for 35 to 40 minutes or till a toothpick inserted near the center comes out clean. Cool in the pan on a wire rack for 10 minutes. Remove cake from pan. Split into 2 layers. Place bottom layer on a serving plate. Spoon *half* of the Fall Fruit Medley over bottom layer of cake. Top with *half* of the Pumpkin Cream. Place remaining cake layer atop and repeat fruit layer. Dollop with remaining Pumpkin Cream. Makes 8 servings.

Fall Fruit Medley: In a large skillet melt 2 tablespoons *margarine or butter.* Stir in ¼ cup packed *brown sugar,* ½ teaspoon ground *cinnamon,* ½ teaspoon finely shredded *orange peel,* and ⅛ teaspoon ground *cloves.* Cook and stir over medium heat till sugar melts and mixture is bubbly. Stir in 1 cup chopped *green apple,* ½ cup *apple cider or apple juice,* and ¼ cup snipped pitted *prunes.* Cook and stir for 5 minutes. Stir in ¼ cup cranberries. Cook and stir till *cranberries* soften and mixture becomes syrupy. Stir in ¼ cup chopped toasted *walnuts or pecans.*

Pumpkin Cream: In a medium mixing bowl beat 1 cup *whipping cream* and 2 tablespoons *sugar* till soft peaks form. Fold in ½ cup canned *pumpkin.*

Nutrition information per serving: 449 calories, 5 g protein, 55 g carbohydrate, 25 g total fat (10 g saturated), 68 mg cholesterol, 130 mg sodium, 230 mg potassium

New Hampshire

CHUNKY APPLESAUCE WITH BRANDY

Apples have always been a favorite fruit of Yankee cooks. They baked them, turned them into pies or pastry-topped slumps and betties, fried them as a side dish, and, of course, cooked them down for applesauce.

1½ pounds cooking apples
    (4 to 5 medium), peeled,
    quartered, and cored
⅓ cup water
3 to 4 tablespoons brown
    sugar
3 tablespoons apple brandy *or*
    apple schnapps
⅛ teaspoon ground cinnamon
    Dash ground nutmeg
2 tablespoons apple brandy *or*
    apple schnapps

In a large saucepan combine apples, water, brown sugar, the 3 tablespoons apple brandy or apple schnapps, cinnamon, and nutmeg. Bring to boiling; reduce heat. Cover and simmer for 8 to 10 minutes or till tender, adding a little more water if necessary.

Remove from heat. Mash with a potato masher or process in a food processor bowl to a chunky purée. Stir in the remaining apple brandy or apple schnapps. Serve warm or chilled; stir before serving. Makes 5 or 6 servings.

Nutrition information per serving: 130 calories, 0 g protein, 25 g carbohydrate, 0 g total fat (0 g saturated), 0 mg cholesterol, 2 mg sodium, 173 mg potassium

Connecticut

CHOCOLATE SNICKERDOODLE DROPS

Several regions claim these crinkle-top sugar-and-spice cookies, but they are as firmly rooted in New England as anywhere else. The addition of chocolate is a modern variation.

½ cup margarine *or* butter
1 cup all-purpose flour
1 cup sugar
⅓ cup unsweetened cocoa
    powder
1 egg
½ teaspoon vanilla
¼ teaspoon baking soda
¼ teaspoon cream of tartar
2 tablespoons sugar
1 teaspoon ground cinnamon

Beat margarine with a mixer on medium to high speed 30 seconds. Add about *half* of the flour, the 1 cup sugar, cocoa powder, egg, vanilla, soda, and cream of tartar. Beat till combined. Stir in remaining flour. Drop by slightly rounded teaspoons 2 inches apart onto an ungreased cookie sheet. Stir together remaining sugar and cinnamon. Sprinkle dough with sugar-cinnamon mixture. Bake in a 375° oven 9 to 11 minutes or till edges are firm. Cool. Makes about 30 cookies.

Nutrition information per cookie: 76 calories, 1 g protein, 11 g carbohydrate, 3 g total fat (1 g saturated), 7 mg cholesterol, 35 mg sodium, 25 mg potassium

Maine

INDIAN PUDDING WITH SWEETENED WHIPPED CREAM

At first, Indian pudding was a plain, stirred cornmeal mush, like Italian polenta. As America left its infancy, it became more elegant. Nineteenth-century cookbooks offered numerous recipes for baked cornmeal puddings with spices, eggs, milk, and sweeteners.

1   cup milk
⅓   cup yellow cornmeal
2   tablespoons margarine *or* butter
⅓   cup molasses
¼   cup sugar
½   teaspoon ground ginger
½   teaspoon ground cinnamon
2   beaten eggs
1½   cups milk
½   cup snipped dried apples *or* mixed dried fruit bits
     Sweetened Whipped Cream
     Ground cinnamon

In a medium saucepan combine the 1 cup milk, cornmeal, and margarine or butter. Bring to boiling, stirring constantly. Reduce heat; cover and cook over low heat for 5 minutes. Remove from heat. Stir in molasses, sugar, ginger, the ½ teaspoon cinnamon, and ¼ teaspoon *salt;* mix well. Combine eggs and the 1½ cups milk; stir into cornmeal mixture. Stir in dried fruit. Transfer mixture to a 1-quart casserole.

Bake, uncovered, in a 325° oven about 1¼ hours or till a knife inserted near the center comes out clean. Serve warm or chilled with Sweetened Whipped Cream; sprinkle with cinnamon. Serves 6.

Sweetened Whipped Cream: In a chilled bowl beat ½ cup *whipping cream* and 1 tablespoon *powdered sugar* with a rotary or electric mixer till soft peaks form.

Nutrition information per serving:
314 calories, 7 g protein, 40 g carbohydrate, 15 g total fat (7 g saturated), 106 mg cholesterol, 215 mg sodium, 495 mg potassium

Connecticut

GINGERBREAD WITH LEMON-BUTTER SAUCE

The earliest forms of gingerbread were made by boiling bread crumbs with honey and ginger to create a thick paste that was pressed into loaves. The first American recipe for a cakelike gingerbread appeared in American Cookery, *written by Amelia Simmons in 1796 and published in Hartford, Connecticut.*

1½   cups all-purpose flour
¼   cup packed dark brown sugar
¾   teaspoon ground cinnamon
¾   teaspoon ground ginger
½   teaspoon baking powder
½   teaspoon baking soda
⅛   teaspoon ground allspice
½   cup shortening
½   cup light molasses
1   egg
¼   cup finely chopped crystallized ginger
     Lemon-Butter Sauce

Mix flour, brown sugar, cinnamon, ginger, baking powder, soda, and allspice. Add shortening, molasses, egg, and ½ cup *water*. Beat with a mixer on low to medium speed till combined. Beat on high speed 2 minutes. Fold in crystallized ginger. Pour into a greased and floured 2-quart square baking dish.

Bake in a 350° oven 35 to 40 minutes or till a toothpick inserted near center comes out clean. Cool 10 minutes. Serve warm with Lemon-Butter Sauce. Serves 9.

Lemon-Butter Sauce: Mix ¼ cup *sugar* and 1 tablespoon *cornstarch;* add ¾ cup *half-and-half or light cream* and 2 tablespoons *butter*. Cook and stir over medium heat till mixture is bubbly. Reduce heat; cook for 1 minute. Remove from heat. Stir in 2 tablespoons finely chopped *crystallized ginger*, ¼ teaspoon finely shredded *lemon peel*, and 3 tablespoons *lemon juice*. Serve warm.

Nutrition information per serving: 345 calories, 4 g protein, 46 g carbohydrate, 17 g total fat (6 g saturated), 38 mg cholesterol, 96 mg sodium, 337 mg potassium

Vermont

DEEP-DISH APPLE PIE WITH CHEDDAR CHEESE CRUST

Apple pie was a fixture on New England breakfast tables. The ultimate was apple pie served with cheddar. As the saying goes, "Apple pie without cheese is like a kiss without a squeeze."

Cheddar Cheese Pastry Crust
½ cup packed brown sugar
2 tablespoons all-purpose flour
½ teaspoon ground cinnamon
7 cups sliced, peeled cooking apples
1 teaspoon finely shredded lemon peel
Vanilla ice cream *or* frozen yogurt (optional)

Prepare Cheddar Cheese Pastry Crust; cover and chill for 30 minutes. Meanwhile, in a large bowl stir together the brown sugar, flour, and cinnamon. Add apples and lemon peel, tossing to coat. Transfer to a 9-inch, deep-dish pie plate, a 10-inch pie plate, or a 1½-quart casserole.

On a lightly floured surface roll chilled pastry into a circle 1 inch larger than the top of pie plate or casserole. Cut slits in pastry. Place pastry atop apple mixture. Seal and flute to rim of pie plate. Cover edges of pie with foil. Place on a baking sheet. Bake in a 375° oven for 25 minutes. Remove foil and bake for 25 to 30 minutes more or till crust is golden and apple mixture is bubbly. Serve warm or cool. If desired, serve with ice cream or frozen yogurt. Makes 8 servings.

Cheddar Cheese Pastry Crust: In a medium mixing bowl combine 1 cup *all-purpose flour* and 2 tablespoons *sugar*. Cut in ½ cup chilled *margarine or butter* till mixture resembles coarse crumbs. Add ½ cup finely shredded sharp cheddar cheese (2 ounces), 1 egg yolk, and 1 tablespoon ice water. Mix just till combined. Form dough into a ball; flatten slightly. Wrap dough in clear plastic wrap and refrigerate for 30 minutes.

Nutrition information per serving: 305 calories, 5 g protein, 40 g carbohydrate, 15 g total fat (4 g saturated), 34 mg cholesterol, 152 mg sodium, 172 mg potassium

New Hampshire

PUMPKIN PIE

For the early colonists the availability of pumpkin often meant the difference between survival and starvation. At first rejected as peasant food, pumpkin became an almost daily staple for settlers in the New World. Was pumpkin pie served at the first Thanksgiving? It's uncertain, but it soon became a colonial favorite.

1   **16-ounce can (1¾ cups) pumpkin***
⅔   **cup sugar**
1   **teaspoon ground cinnamon**
½   **teaspoon ground ginger**
½   **teaspoon ground nutmeg**
3   **eggs**
1   **5-ounce can (⅔ cup) evaporated milk**
½   **cup milk**
    Pastry for Single-Crust Pie (see recipe, right)
    Whipped cream (optional)

For filling, in a large mixing bowl stir together pumpkin, sugar, cinnamon, ginger, and nutmeg. Add eggs. Use a rotary beater or wire whisk to lightly beat till combined. Gradually stir in evaporated milk and milk. Mix well. Set pumpkin mixture aside.

Prepare and roll out Pastry for Single-Crust Pie as directed. Line a 9-inch pie plate with pastry. Trim and crimp the edge of the pastry. With the pie plate on the oven rack, pour the pumpkin filling into the pastry shell.

To prevent overbrowning, cover the edge of the pie with foil. Bake in a 375° oven for 25 minutes. Remove foil. Bake about 25 minutes more or till a knife inserted near the center comes out clean. Completely cool the pie on a wire rack. If desired, serve topped with whipped cream. Store, covered, in the refrigerator. Makes 6 servings.

*Note: To substitute fresh pumpkin for canned pumpkin, cut a medium pumpkin into 5-inch-square pieces. Remove seeds and fibrous strings. Arrange pieces in a single layer, skin side up, in a large shallow baking pan. Cover with foil. Bake in a 375° oven for 1 to 1½ hours or till tender. Scoop pulp from rind. Place part of the pulp at a time in a blender container or food processor bowl. Cover; blend or process till smooth. Place in a cheese-cloth-lined strainer; press out excess liquid. Makes 1¾ cups.

Nutrition information per serving: 357 calories, 8 g protein, 47 g carbohydrate, 16 g total fat (5 g saturated), 116 mg cholesterol, 238 mg sodium, 289 mg potassium

PASTRY FOR SINGLE-CRUST PIE

1¼   **cups all-purpose flour**
¼   **teaspoon salt**
⅓   **cup shortening *or* lard**
3   **to 4 tablespoons cold water**

Mix flour and salt. Cut in shortening or lard till pieces are the size of small peas. Sprinkle 1 tablespoon of the water over part of the mixture; gently toss with a fork. Push to side of bowl. Repeat till all is moistened. Form dough into a ball.

On a lightly floured surface, flatten dough with your hands. Roll out dough from center to edges, forming a circle about 12 inches in diameter. Wrap pastry around a rolling pin. Unroll pastry onto a 9-inch pie plate. Ease pastry into pie plate; do not stretch pastry.

Trim to ½-inch beyond edge of pie plate; fold under extra pastry; flute edge. Do not prick pastry. Bake as directed in individual recipes.

Baked Pastry Shell: Prepare as above, except prick bottom and sides of pastry generously with the tines of a fork. Prick where bottom and sides meet all around pie shell. Bake in a 450° oven for 10 to 12 minutes or till golden. Cool on a wire rack.

Maine

BERRY-APPLE SLUMP

A slump usually consists of dumplings dropped onto hot, sweetened fruit. If you live on Cape Cod, though, a slump is a grunt. Both are cousins to cobblers, betties, and pandowdies, all part of an extended family of whimsically named pastry-topped fruit desserts.

1	**cup water**
1	**cup chopped, peeled cooking apples**
1	**cup fresh *or* frozen blueberries**
¾	**cup cranberries**
⅔	**cup sugar**

¾	**cup all-purpose flour**
¼	**cup sugar**
1	**teaspoon baking powder**
¼	**teaspoon ground cinnamon**
⅛	**teaspoon ground nutmeg**
3	**tablespoons margarine *or* butter**
⅓	**cup milk**
	Half-and-half *or* light cream (optional)

In a 3-quart saucepan combine water, apples, blueberries, cranberries, and the ⅔ cup sugar. Bring to boiling; reduce heat. Cover and simmer for 5 minutes.

Meanwhile, for topping, combine flour, the ¼ cup sugar, baking powder, cinnamon, nutmeg, and ¼ teaspoon *salt*. Cut in margarine or butter till the mixture resembles coarse crumbs. Add milk to flour mixture, stirring just to moisten. Drop topping into 6 mounds atop hot filling. Cover and simmer about 15 minutes or till a toothpick inserted in the topping comes out clean. Serve warm; if desired, top with half-and-half or light cream. Serves 6.

Nutrition information per serving: 366 calories, 7 g protein, 55 g carbohydrate, 14 g total fat (4 g saturated), 111 mg cholesterol, 236 mg sodium, 148 mg potassium

Massachusetts

NEW ENGLAND CHOCOLATE CHIP COOKIES

Ruth Wakefield, proprietor of the Toll House Inn in Whitman, is credited with inventing the chocolate chip in the 1930s. She experimented by chopping up a chocolate bar and blending the bits into her butter drop-cookie batter. When the chocolate bits held their shape during baking, a new industry in chocolate morsels and chocolate-chip cookies was born.

1	cup shortening
2¼	cups all-purpose flour
¾	cup sugar
¾	cup packed brown sugar
2	eggs
1	teaspoon vanilla
1	teaspoon baking soda
1	12-ounce package semisweet chocolate pieces
1	cup chopped walnuts

Beat shortening with a mixer for 30 seconds. Beat in about *half* the flour, the sugars, eggs, vanilla, soda, and ¼ teaspoon *salt*. Beat in remaining flour. Stir in chocolate and nuts. Drop dough by rounded teaspoons 2 inches apart onto an ungreased cookie sheet. Bake in a 350° oven for 10 to 12 minutes or till edges are lightly browned. Makes about 60.

Nutrition information per cookie: 106 calories, 1 g protein, 12 g carbohydrate, 7 g total fat (2 g saturated), 7 mg cholesterol, 26 mg sodium, 42 mg potassium

New Hampshire

CHERRY-RASPBERRY COBBLER

One explanation for the term cobbler *is that the biscuit crust resembles the rounded tops of cobblestones. Raspberries grow wild throughout New England, especially in Vermont and New Hampshire.*

1	cup all-purpose flour
2	tablespoons sugar
1½	teaspoons baking powder
¼	cup margarine *or* butter
⅓	cup sugar
2	tablespoons cornstarch
1	10-ounce package frozen red raspberries, thawed
¼	cup water
1	tablespoon lemon juice
4	cups frozen, unsweetened, pitted, tart red cherries
1	egg
¼	cup milk
1	tablespoon sugar
¼	teaspoon ground cinnamon
½	cup chopped pecans
	Vanilla ice cream, half-and-half, *or* light cream (optional)

For biscuit topping, in a medium mixing bowl stir together the flour, the 2 tablespoons sugar, and baking powder. Cut in margarine or butter till mixture resembles coarse crumbs. Set aside.

For filling, in a medium saucepan combine the ⅓ cup sugar and cornstarch. Add thawed raspberries, water, and lemon juice. Cook and stir till thickened and bubbly. Stir in thawed cherries; cook and stir till bubbly again. Reduce heat and keep filling hot.

In a small bowl use a fork to beat together egg and milk. Add egg mixture all at once to the biscuit topping. Using a fork, stir just till moistened.

Transfer the hot filling to an ungreased 2-quart square baking dish. Immediately drop topping mixture from a teaspoon into small mounds atop filling. Combine the 1 tablespoon sugar and cinnamon; sprinkle over topping. Sprinkle with pecans. Bake, uncovered, in a 400° oven 20 to 25 minutes or till cobbler tests done. If desired, Serve warm with ice cream. Serves 6.

Nutrition information per serving: 402 calories, 6 g protein, 62 g carbohydrate, 16 g total fat (2 g saturated), 36 mg cholesterol, 162 mg sodium, 267 mg potassium

Vermont

MAPLE CRÈME BRÛLÉE

Thomas Jefferson's French chef, Julien, prepared crème brûlée, burnt cream, for him at the White House. A salamander, a heated iron plate that functioned like a broiler, was used to caramelize the sugar on the top. Maple syrup links this version with New England.

2 eggs, slightly beaten
1 egg yolk, slightly beaten
⅓ cup maple syrup *or*
    maple-flavored syrup
1 teaspoon vanilla
1 cup half-and-half
2 tablespoons sugar

Mix eggs, egg yolk, maple syrup, and vanilla. Stir in half-and-half, mix well. Divide mixture among four 6-ounce ramekins or custard cups. Place ramekins in a baking dish. Pour hot water into dish until it reaches halfway up the sides of ramekins. Bake in a 350° oven 35 to 40 minutes or till a knife inserted near the center comes out clean. Remove ramekins from baking dish; cool slightly. Cover with clear plastic wrap; chill at least 2 hours.

Before serving, place sugar in a small skillet. Cook over medium-high heat till sugar begins to melt *(do not stir)*, shaking skillet occasionally to heat sugar evenly. Reduce heat to low; cook till sugar is melted and golden (about 5 minutes). Stir as necessary after sugar begins to melt. Drizzle over brûlée. Serve immediately. Serves 4.

Nutrition information per serving: 224 calories, 6 g protein, 30 g carbohydrate, 11 g total fat (5 g saturated), 182 mg cholesterol, 60 mg sodium, 136 mg potassium

Massachusetts

BOSTON CREAM PIE

This "pie" is actually a cake: two layers of yellow sponge cake with a vanilla custard filling. Boston's Parker House hotel made its version famous by icing the pie with chocolate. Other recipes use powdered sugar instead of chocolate, or raspberry preserves in place of custard which is called Washington pie.

1   cup plus 2 tablespoons
    sifted cake flour *or* 1 cup
    sifted all-purpose flour
⅔   cup sugar
1½ teaspoons baking powder
¼   teaspoon salt
½   cup milk
¼   cup cooking oil
2   egg yolks
1   teaspoon vanilla
2   egg whites
¼   teaspoon cream of tartar
    Vanilla Pudding Filling
    Chocolate Glaze

In a medium mixing bowl combine flour, sugar, baking powder, and salt. Make a well in the center of the flour mixture. Add milk, oil, egg yolks, and vanilla. Beat with an electric mixer on low to medium speed till combined. Then beat on high speed for 3 minutes. Set beaten mixture aside.

Thoroughly wash beaters. In a large mixing bowl beat egg whites and cream of tartar on medium to high speed till stiff peaks form (tips stand straight). Pour the beaten mixture over the egg white mixture and gently fold in.

Gently pour batter into an *ungreased* 9-inch springform pan. Bake in a 350° oven for 25 to 30 minutes or till top springs back when lightly touched. *Immediately* invert the pan on a wire rack. Cool completely. Remove the cake from the pan.

To assemble, cut cake horizontally in half. Place bottom layer on a serving plate or board. Spread Vanilla Pudding Filling on top. Top with second layer. Pour Chocolate Glaze over cake and down sides. Store in refrigerator. Serves 8.

Vanilla Pudding Filling: In a saucepan combine ½ cup *sugar*, 2 tablespoons *all-purpose flour*, 1 tablespoon *cornstarch*, and ⅛ teaspoon *salt*. Stir in 1¼ cups milk. Cook and stir till thickened and bubbly. Reduce heat; cook and stir 2 minutes more. Set aside. In a bowl slightly beat 2 *eggs*. Stir *1 cup* of hot mixture into eggs; transfer entire mixture to the saucepan. Cook and stir 2 minutes more. *Do not boil.* Remove from heat. Stir in 1 tablespoon *margarine or butter* and 1½ teaspoons *vanilla* till combined. Cover surface with plastic wrap; cool. Makes 1¾ cups.

Chocolate Glaze: In a saucepan melt 1 square (1 ounce) *unsweetened chocolate* and 1 tablespoon *margarine or butter* over low heat. Remove from heat. Stir in ¾ cup sifted *powdered sugar* and ½ teaspoon *vanilla* till crumbly. Stir in 2 teaspoons *very hot water.* Stir in 3 to 4 teaspoons additional *hot water,* 1 teaspoon at a time, to a make a glaze of pouring consistency. Makes ½ cup.

Nutrition information per serving: 366 calories, 7 g protein, 55 g carbohydrate, 14 g total fat (4 g saturated), 111 mg cholesterol, 236 mg sodium, 148 mg potassium

Massachusetts

JOE FROGGERS

Are these the first of the giant cookies? Here's the story: Uncle Joe, who lived by a frog pond in Marblehead, made wildly popular molasses cookies that were as big as lily pads. Fishermen would barter for them—offering rum for cookies—because they were good keepers on long sea voyages.

¾ cup **margarine** *or* **butter**
4 cups **all-purpose flour**
1 cup **sugar**
1 cup **molasses**
2 tablespoons **water**
2 tablespoons **rum** *or* **milk**
1½ teaspoons **ground ginger**
1 teaspoon **baking soda**
½ teaspoon **ground cloves**
½ teaspoon **ground nutmeg**
¼ teaspoon **ground allspice**

Beat margarine with a mixer on medium to high speed 30 seconds. Add about *half* of the flour, and all of the remaining ingredients Beat till combined. Stir in remaining flour. Divide dough in half. Cover and chill for at least 3 hours.

On a lightly floured surface, roll *half* of the dough at a time to about ¼-inch thickness. Cut into circles with a floured 4-inch round cookie cutter. Place on a greased cookie sheet. Bake in a 375° oven for 9 to 11 minutes or till edges are firm and bottoms are just lightly browned. Cool on cookie sheet 1 minute. Remove; cool on a wire rack. Makes about 24 cookies.

Nutrition information per cookie: 199 calories, 2 g protein, 34 g carbohydrate, 6 g total fat (1 g saturated), 0 mg cholesterol, 88 mg sodium, 226 mg potassium

Flavors from the Middle Atlantic

New York

BUFFALO CHICKEN WINGS

*Since 1964 Buffalo's Anchor Bar &
Restaurant has been famous for its
deep-fried chicken wings, doused with hot
sauce and cooled with blue cheese
dressing. Buffalo is now firmly fixed on
the culinary map as home to one of
America's premier pub munchies.*

12	chicken wings (2 pounds)
	Cooking oil *or* shortening for deep-fat frying
3	tablespoons margarine *or* butter
½	to 1 2-ounce bottle hot pepper sauce (2 tablespoons to ¼ cup)
	Bottled blue cheese salad dressing
	Celery sticks

Cut off and discard tips of chicken
wings. Cut wings at joints to form
24 pieces. Fry a few wing pieces at
a time in deep hot cooking oil or
shortening (375°) for 8 to 10 minutes or till golden brown. Drain on
paper towels.

In a small saucepan melt margarine or butter. Stir in hot pepper
sauce. Pour mixture over wings,
turning them to coat. Serve wings
with blue cheese dressing and celery sticks. Makes 24 servings.

*Nutrition information per serving:
139 calories, 7 g protein, 1 g carbohydrate,
12 g total fat (3 g saturated), 22 mg cholesterol, 145 mg sodium, 52 mg potassium*

New York

BUCKWHEAT PECAN WAFFLES

*Waffle irons were among the important
household goods carried in Dutch
ships to New Amsterdam. Buckwheat
flourished in the colonies.*

1	cup all-purpose flour
¾	cup buckwheat flour
1	tablespoon baking powder
2	egg yolks
1¾	cups milk
1	tablespoon brown sugar
½	cup margarine *or* butter, melted
1	cup finely chopped pecans
2	egg whites
	Fresh fruit and powdered sugar *or* maple syrup (optional)

In a mixing bowl combine flours
and baking powder. In another
bowl beat egg yolks slightly. Beat
in milk, brown sugar, and melted
margarine or butter. Add egg yolk
mixture and pecans to flour mixture all at once. Stir just till combined but still slightly lumpy.

In a bowl beat egg whites till stiff peaks form (tips stand straight). Gently fold beaten egg whites into flour mixture. *Do not overmix.* Pour about *1 cup* batter onto grids of a preheated, lightly greased waffle baker. Close lid quickly; do not open during baking. Bake according to manufacturer's directions. When done, lift waffle off grid. Repeat with remaining batter.

Serve warm; if desired, top with fresh fruit and powdered sugar or maple syrup. Makes 4 to 5 waffles.

Nutrition information per waffle:
680 calories, 14 g protein, 52 g carbohydrate, 48 g total fat (7 g saturated), 115 mg cholesterol, 515 mg sodium, 424 mg potassium

New York

SCALLOPS WITH FRESH HERB TARTAR SAUCE

Long Island is known for the small, sweet, juicy bay scallops that grow in surrounding shallow waters. Homemade tartar sauce is altogether different — and so much better — than the sauce that comes in a jar.

12 ounces fresh *or* frozen sea scallops
2 tablespoons margarine *or* butter, melted
¼ teaspoon pepper
⅛ teaspoon paprika
⅔ cup mayonnaise *or* salad dressing
1 tablespoon finely chopped onion

½ teaspoon finely shredded lemon peel
2 teaspoons lemon juice
1½ teaspoons snipped fresh dill *or* ½ teaspoon dried dillweed
1½ teaspoons snipped fresh thyme *or* ½ teaspoon dried thyme, crushed
1½ teaspoons snipped fresh parsley *or* ½ teaspoon dried parsley, crushed
Fresh lemon wedges (optional)

Thaw scallops, if frozen. Halve any large scallops. Thread scallops onto four 8- to 10-inch skewers, leaving a ¼-inch space between pieces. Place skewers on the greased unheated rack of a broiler pan.

In a small bowl stir together melted margarine or butter, pepper, and paprika. Brush *half* of the margarine mixture over scallops. Broil about 4 inches from the heat for 8 to 10 minutes or till scallops are opaque, turning and brushing often with the remaining melted margarine mixture. *Or,* place the kabobs on a greased grill rack. Grill, uncovered, directly over *medium* coals for 5 to 8 minutes; turn once. Brush frequently with remaining margarine mixture during the last 2 minutes of grilling.

For the tartar sauce, in a medium bowl stir together mayonnaise or salad dressing, onion, lemon peel, lemon juice, dill, thyme, and parsley. Serve with tartar sauce and, if desired, lemon wedges. Makes 4 servings.

Nutrition information per serving:
404 calories, 13 g protein, 4 g carbohydrate, 38 g total fat (6 g saturated), 47 mg cholesterol, 585 mg sodium, 279 mg potassium

New York

EGGS BENEDICT WITH EASY ORANGE HOLLANDAISE

Delmonico's restaurant catered to Manhattan's elite for almost a century, from 1831 to 1923. Many famous dishes were born in its kitchen, including this one, the result of a request by a Mr. and Mrs. LeGrand Benedict for something new for lunch.

2   English muffins, split
8   slices Canadian-style
    bacon
    Cooking oil *or* shortening
    (optional)
    Water
2   teaspoons instant chicken
    bouillon granules
    (optional)
4   eggs
    Easy Orange Hollandaise
    Orange wedges (optional)

Place muffins and bacon in a single layer on a baking sheet. Bake in a 350° oven 10 to 15 minutes or till muffins are toasted and bacon is hot. Keep warm. If desired, lightly grease a 2-quart saucepan. Add water to half-fill pan; if desired, stir in bouillon granules. Bring water to boiling. Reduce heat to simmering. Break *one* egg into a measuring cup. Carefully slide egg into simmering water. Repeat with remaining eggs. Simmer, uncovered, 3 to 5 minutes or to desired doneness. (*Or*, use an egg poaching pan.)

To serve, top each muffin half with 2 slices of bacon and an egg.

Spoon Easy Orange Hollandaise over eggs. If desired, serve with orange wedges. Makes 4 servings.

Easy Orange Hollandaise: In a small saucepan combine ¼ cup dairy *sour cream*, ¼ cup *mayonnaise or salad dressing*, ½ to 1 teaspoon finely shredded *orange peel*, 1 to 2 tablespoons *orange juice*, and ½ teaspoon *Dijon-style mustard*. Cook and stir over low heat just till warm; do not boil. Makes about ½ cup.

Nutrition information per serving: 364 calories, 21 g protein, 16 g carbohydrate, 24 g total fat (6 g saturated), 256 mg cholesterol, 1,103 mg sodium, 268 mg potassium

Pennsylvania

SCHNITZ UN KNEPP

Few dishes are so locally famous, yet so little known elsewhere, as schnitz un knepp. *It combines two foods, ham and apples, that are staples of Pennsylvania Dutch cooking.* Schnitz *means "sliced, dried apples," and* knepp *is "dumpling."*

1   3-pound smoked pork
      picnic
1   6-ounce package (2 cups)
      dried apples
¼   cup packed brown sugar
1½   cups all-purpose flour
2   teaspoons baking powder
¼   teaspoon salt
1   beaten egg
½   cup milk
2   tablespoons margarine *or*
      butter, melted

Remove skin and fat from outside of smoked pork. Place pork in a Dutch oven; add enough water to cover meat. Bring water to boiling;

reduce heat. Cover and simmer for 30 minutes. Stir in dried apples and brown sugar. Cover; simmer 1 hour more.

Meanwhile, for dumplings, in a bowl stir together flour, baking powder, and salt. In a small bowl combine egg, milk, and melted margarine or butter. Add to flour mixture; stir with a fork just till combined. Drop dough by rounded tablespoonfuls in 10 mounds atop the simmering liquid. Cover; simmer for 20 minutes (do not lift the cover) or till a toothpick inserted into the dumplings comes out clean.

Serve pork on a platter with the dumplings and apples. Spoon a small amount of the remaining liquid over the meat. Makes 8 to 10 servings.

Nutrition information per serving: *390 calories, 32 g protein, 37 g carbohydrate, 12 g total fat (4 g saturated), 82 mg cholesterol, 1,601 mg sodium, 492 mg potassium*

Delaware

ROAST BEEF WITH PEPPERED YORKSHIRE PUDDING

Benjamin Franklin's wife, Deborah, kept him well supplied with food from home during his travels, including roast beef. Like English cooks before them, colonists would roast meat over a dripping pan, then use the fat to make a savory batter pudding like Yorkshire.

1	**4- to 6-pound beef standing rib roast**
4	**eggs**
2	**cups milk**
2	**cups all-purpose flour**
½	**teaspoon coarsely ground pepper**
¼	**teaspoon salt**

Place the meat, fat side up, in a 15 x 10½ x 2-inch roasting pan. Insert a meat thermometer. Roast in a 325° oven for 1¾ to 3 hours for rare (140°), 2¼ to 3¾ hours for medium (160°), or 2¾ to 4¼ hours for well-done (170°).

After removing meat from oven, increase oven temperature to 450°. Transfer meat to a serving platter; cover to keep warm. Measure pan drippings. If necessary, add enough cooking oil to drippings to equal ¼ cup; return to pan.

In a medium mixing bowl combine eggs, milk, flour, pepper, and salt. Beat with an electric mixer or rotary beater till smooth. Stir into drippings in pan. Bake for 20 to 25 minutes or till puffy and golden brown. Cut into squares. Serve at once with roast beef. Makes 12 to 14 servings.

Nutrition information per serving: *328 calories, 29 g protein, 18 g carbohydrate, 15 g total fat (6 g saturated), 142 mg cholesterol, 147 mg sodium, 404 mg potassium*

Pennsylvania

CREAMY NAVY BEAN SOUP WITH PESTO

The Pennsylvania Dutch made the most of what they had. They enjoyed soups, but if only flour and milk were available, that's what they used. When the farms became more productive, the soup pot would reflect the bounty. The addition of pesto adds an Italian twist to this old favorite.

1	pound dry navy beans (2⅓ cups)
6	cups water
4	cups chicken broth
2	cups shredded cabbage
1	cup shredded carrot
1	cup chopped onion
2	cloves garlic, minced
1	teaspoon dried oregano, crushed
½	teaspoon dried marjoram, crushed
2	bay leaves
½	teaspoon salt
¼	teaspoon pepper
2	cups milk
2	tablespoons Homemade Pesto *or* purchased pesto

Rinse beans. In a 4½-quart Dutch oven combine beans and water. Bring to boiling; reduce heat. Simmer for 2 minutes. Remove from heat. Cover and let stand 1 hour. (*Or,* skip boiling the water and soak beans overnight in a covered pan.)

Drain and rinse beans. Return beans to Dutch oven. Add chicken broth, cabbage, carrot, onion, garlic, oregano, marjoram, bay leaves, salt, and pepper. Bring to boiling; reduce heat. Cover and simmer for 2½ to 3 hours or till beans are very tender, stirring occasionally. Discard bay leaves. Mash beans slightly. Stir in milk and heat through. Ladle into soup bowls. Dollop each serving with pesto. Makes 6 servings.

Homemade Pesto: In a blender container or food processor bowl combine 1 cup firmly packed fresh *basil leaves,* ½ cup firmly packed *parsley sprigs* with stems removed, ½ cup grated *Parmesan or Romano cheese,* ¼ cup *pine nuts, walnuts, or almonds,* 1 large clove *garlic,* and ¼ teaspoon *salt.* Cover and blend or process with several on-off turns till a paste forms, stopping the machine several times and scraping the sides.

With the machine running slowly, gradually add ¼ cup *olive oil or cooking oil* and blend or process to the consistency of soft butter. Store in an airtight container. Refrigerate for 1 or 2 days or freeze up to 1 month. Makes about ⅔ cup.

Nutrition information per serving: 385 calories, 24 g protein, 61 g carbohydrate, 6 g total fat (2 g saturated), 7 mg cholesterol, 786 mg sodium, 1,154 mg potassium

New Jersey

INDIVIDUAL BEEF WELLINGTON

The English have relished meat baked in pastry "coffins" since Shakespeare's day. It's a taste they carried with them to the American colonies. Amelia Simmons, in her American Cookery of 1796, recommends Puff Paste No.8 as excellent for meat pies.

½ of a 17½-ounce package
    (1 sheet) frozen puff
    pastry
¼ teaspoon salt
¼ teaspoon pepper
¼ teaspoon dried marjoram,
    crushed
2 beef tenderloin steaks
    (4 to 6 ounces each)
2 tablespoons deli *or* canned
    mushroom pâté *or* liver
    pâté
1 beaten egg white
    Bordelaise Sauce
    (optional)

Thaw pastry according to package directions; set aside. In a small bowl stir together salt, pepper, and marjoram. Rub salt mixture over steaks, coating all sides.

Cut thawed pastry into 2 portions. Spread *1 tablespoon* pâté over one side of each steak. Place a steak, pâté side down, on the center of each portion of pastry. Wrap pastry around meat. Trim excess pastry from ends; seal ends.

Place pastry-wrapped meat, seam sides down, in a greased, shallow baking pan. Brush pastry with beaten egg white. If desired, reroll trimmings to make cutouts. Place cutouts on pastry-wrapped meat. Brush with beaten egg white.

Bake, uncovered, in a 425° oven about 15 minutes or till pastry is golden and meat is medium-rare. If desired, serve with Bordelaise Sauce. Makes 2 servings.

Note: If desired, insert a meat thermometer into pastry-wrapped meat and roast to 140°.

Bordelaise Sauce: In a small saucepan combine ¾ cup *water;* ⅓ cup *dry red wine;* 1 tablespoon finely chopped *shallot or onion;* ½ teaspoon *instant beef bouillon granules;* ¼ teaspoon *dried thyme,* crushed; and 1 *bay leaf.* Bring to boiling; reduce heat. Simmer, uncovered, for 5 to 7 minutes or till mixture is reduced to ¾ cup. Remove bay leaf.

Stir together 2 tablespoons softened *margarine or butter* and 1 tablespoon *all-purpose flour.* Add to wine mixture. Cook and stir till thickened and bubbly. Cook and stir for 1 minute more. Stir in 1½ teaspoons snipped *parsley.* Makes about ¾ cup.

Nutrition information per serving:
743 calories, 36 g protein, 46 g carbohydrate, 45 g total fat (4 g saturated), 122 mg cholesterol, 985 mg sodium, 396 mg potassium

PENNSYLVANIA POT ROAST

In the early days of the Pennsylvania Dutch settlements, pigs were left to forage in the woods. When they were slaughtered, they were tough. Slow-cooked dishes like pot roast tenderized the pork into something very satisfying.

1	2½- to 3-pound boneless pork shoulder roast
2	tablespoons cooking oil
1½	cups beef broth
2	medium leeks, trimmed and cut into 1-inch pieces
1	teaspoon dried basil, crushed
1	teaspoon dried marjoram, crushed
½	teaspoon salt
½	teaspoon pepper
1	bay leaf
1	medium acorn squash
8	small parsnips, quartered
3	medium carrots, sliced
8	ounces fresh mushrooms, sliced
½	cup cold water
¼	cup all-purpose flour

Trim fat from meat. In a 6-quart Dutch oven brown meat on all sides in hot oil. Drain fat. Add beef broth, leeks, basil, marjoram, the ½ teaspoon salt, the ½ teaspoon pepper, and bay leaf. Bring to boiling; reduce heat. Cover and simmer for 1¼ hours.

Cut squash in half lengthwise; discard seeds. Cut each half into 4 pieces. Add squash to meat mixture. Then add parsnips, carrots, and mushrooms. Return to boiling; reduce heat. Cover and simmer for 20 to 25 minutes more or till vegetables and meat are tender. Remove meat and vegetables from Dutch oven; keep warm. Discard bay leaf.

For sauce, skim fat from pan juices. Measure 1½ cups juices. Stir cold water into flour; stir into reserved juices in Dutch oven. Cook and stir till thickened and bubbly. Cook and stir 1 minute more. Season to taste with salt and pepper. Serve sauce with meat and vegetables. Makes 8 servings.

Nutrition information per serving: 410 calories, 38 g protein, 27 g carbohydrate, 17 g total fat (5 g saturated), 122 mg cholesterol, 491 mg sodium, 1,055 mg potassium

PHILADELPHIA CHEESE STEAK SANDWICH

How to make a Philadelphian homesick? Just say "cheese steak." This beef sandwich with cheese and onions on a long roll has been a favorite fast food in the City of Brotherly Love since at least the 1930s.

1	12-ounce boneless beef rib eye steak
2	tablespoons margarine *or* butter
2	medium onions, thinly sliced and separated into rings
1	medium red *or* green sweet pepper, cut into thin strips

4 French rolls *or* hoagie
buns
4 ounces thinly sliced
cheddar cheese

Partially freeze beef. Thinly slice beef across the grain into bite-size strips. In a 10-inch skillet melt margarine or butter; add onions and pepper. Cover and cook over medium-low heat about 10 minutes or till tender, stirring occasionally.

Remove onion-pepper mixture from skillet with a slotted spoon. If necessary, add additional margarine to skillet. Add beef; cook and stir over medium-high heat for 2 to 3 minutes or till done.

To serve, spread rolls open face on a baking sheet. Divide beef and onion-pepper mixture among rolls. Top with cheese. Broil 4 to 5 inches from the heat for 1 to 2 minutes or till cheese is melted. Serve immediately. Makes 4 servings.

Nutrition information per serving: 484 calories, 30 g protein, 34 g carbohydrate, 25 g total fat (10 g saturated), 81 mg cholesterol, 615 mg sodium, 448 mg potassium

CHICKEN À LA KING

Supposedly this creamed chicken dish, served over toast points, was the creation of chef George Greenwald of the Brighton Beach Hotel, who named it after hotel owner E. Clark King III. Other sources say the dish came out of Delmonico's kitchen and was originally "à la Keene," after Jim Keene, a Delmonico's regular.

1½ cups loose-pack frozen
mixed vegetables
1 cup water
1 tablespoon instant chicken
bouillon granules
1 tablespoon white wine
Worcestershire sauce,
dry white wine, *or*
Worcestershire sauce
½ teaspoon dried basil,
crushed
⅛ teaspoon pepper
2 cups milk
½ cup all-purpose flour
2 cups chopped cooked
chicken *or* turkey
4 frozen patty shells, baked
according to package
directions, with tops
removed

In a large saucepan combine the frozen vegetables, water, bouillon granules, Worcestershire sauce or wine, basil, and pepper. Bring mixture to boiling; reduce heat. Cover and simmer for 5 minutes.

Meanwhile, combine milk and flour. Stir into vegetable mixture. Cook and stir till thickened and bub-bly. Cook and stir 1 minute more. Stir in chicken or turkey; heat through.

Serve the chicken mixture in the patty shells. Makes 4 servings.

Nutrition information per serving: 558 calories, 36 g protein, 51 g carbohydrate, 23 g total fat (4 g saturated), 81 mg cholesterol, 1,056 mg sodium, 691 mg potassium

New York

SPICY MANHATTAN CLAM CHOWDER

Is New England's creamy white the only true clam chowder, or is tomato-rich Manhattan red equally worthy? It's an ongoing debate. In an attempt to settle the question, at least in Maine, a state legislator there once introduced a bill that made it illegal to mix clams and tomatoes!

1	pint shucked clams *or* two 6½-ounce cans minced clams
4	slices bacon
1	cup chopped onion
1	cup chopped celery
½	cup chopped green pepper
½	cup chopped red sweet pepper
¼	cup chopped carrots
2	tablespoons chopped shallots
1	16-ounce can tomatoes, cut up
2	cups finely chopped, peeled potatoes
1	cup chicken broth
½	teaspoon dried basil, crushed
⅛	to ¼ teaspoon ground red pepper
⅛	teaspoon ground black pepper
2	tablespoons snipped parsley

Chop shucked clams, reserving juice; set aside. Strain clam juice to remove bits of shell. (*Or*, drain canned clams, reserving juice.) If necessary, add water to reserved juice to equal 1½ cups. Set aside.

In a large saucepan cook bacon till crisp. Remove bacon, reserving *2 tablespoons* drippings. Drain bacon on paper towels; crumble. Set bacon aside.

Cook onion, celery, green pepper, red sweet pepper, carrots, and shallots in reserved bacon drippings till tender. Stir in reserved clam juice, *undrained* tomatoes, potatoes, chicken broth, basil, ground red pepper, and ground black pepper. Bring to boiling; reduce heat. Cover and simmer for 20 to 25 minutes or till vegetables are tender.

Stir in clams. Return to boiling; reduce heat. Cook for 1 to 2 minutes more. Sprinkle each serving with cooked bacon and parsley. Makes 4 main-dish or 6 to 8 side-dish servings.

Nutrition information per main-dish serving: 360 calories, 36 g protein, 40 g carbohydrate, 6 g total fat (2 g saturated), 81 mg cholesterol, 647 mg sodium, 1,627 mg potassium

New York

THREE-PEPPER SLAW

Cabbage for coleslaw, or kool sla *in Dutch, grew in New Amsterdam kitchen gardens. Small, tight heads were preferred for this salad, which was simply dressed with oil, vinegar, salt, and pepper.*

1 medium red sweet pepper, cut into thin strips
1 medium yellow sweet pepper, cut into thin strips
1 medium orange *or* green sweet pepper, cut into thin strips
1 cup shredded cabbage
¼ cup currants *or* raisins
2 green onions, sliced
¼ cup white wine vinegar
3 tablespoons salad oil
2 to 3 tablespoons sugar
 Few dashes bottled hot pepper sauce (optional)

In a large mixing bowl combine red sweet pepper, yellow sweet pepper, orange or green sweet pepper, cabbage, currants or raisins, and green onions.

For dressing, in a screw-top jar combine wine vinegar, oil, sugar, and, if desired, hot pepper sauce. Cover and shake well. Pour the dressing over the pepper mixture, tossing to coat. Cover and chill for 2 to 24 hours. Stir before serving. Makes 4 servings.

Nutrition information per serving:
170 calories, 1 g protein, 20 g carbohydrate, 10 g total fat (1 g saturated), 0 mg cholesterol, 11 mg sodium, 306 mg potassium

New York

WALDORF SALAD

"Oscar of the Waldorf," Oscar Tschirky, was the imperious maître d' at New York's Waldorf-Astoria hotel at the turn of the century. This famous salad, originally a simple mixture of apples, celery, and walnuts in a mayonnaise dressing, was his creation. There have been many variations since.

2 cups chopped apples *or* pears (2 medium)
1½ teaspoons lemon juice
⅓ cup slivered almonds *or* chopped pecans, toasted
¼ cup celery
¼ cup dried red tart cherries *or* raisins
¼ cup seedless grapes, halved
⅓ cup whipping cream
¼ cup mayonnaise *or* salad dressing

In a medium mixing bowl toss chopped apples or pears with lemon juice. Stir in nuts, celery, cherries or raisins, and grapes.

For dressing, in a chilled, small mixing bowl whip the cream to soft peaks. Fold mayonnaise or salad dressing into the whipped cream. Fold dressing into fruit mixture. Cover and chill for 2 to 24 hours. Makes 4 to 6 servings.

Nutrition information per serving:
317 calories, 4 g protein, 24 g carbohydrate, 24 g total fat (7 g saturated), 35 mg cholesterol, 94 mg sodium, 247 mg potassium

New Jersey

HOT CROSS BUNS WITH HAZELNUT ICING

The recipe for this yeast roll, with its distinctive sugar-icing cross, emigrated to America with the English. It is associated with Easter, in particular Good Friday.

1½ cups all-purpose flour
1 package active dry yeast
1 teaspoon ground cinnamon
¾ cup milk
½ cup cooking oil
⅓ cup sugar
½ teaspoon salt
3 eggs
⅔ cup currants *or* raisins
½ cup chopped hazelnuts
    (filberts) (optional)
2¼ to 2¾ cups all-purpose
    flour
1 slightly beaten egg white
    Hazelnut Icing

In a large mixing bowl combine the 1½ cups flour, yeast, and cinnamon. In a small saucepan heat and stir milk, oil, sugar, and salt till warm (120° to 130°). Add to flour mixture along with eggs. Beat with an electric mixer on low speed for 30 seconds, scraping bowl. Beat on high speed for 3 minutes

Using a spoon, stir in currants or raisins, hazelnuts (if desired), and as much of the 2¼ to 2¾ cups flour as you can. Turn out onto a floured surface. Knead in enough remaining flour to make a moderately soft dough (3 to 5 minutes total). Shape into a ball. Place

dough in a greased bowl; turn once to grease surface. Cover and let rise till nearly double (about 1½ hours).

Punch dough down. Turn out onto a floured surface. Cover and let rest 10 minutes. Divide dough into 20 portions; shape each portion into a smooth ball. Place balls 1½ inches apart on a greased baking sheet. Cover and let rise till nearly double (30 to 45 minutes). With a sharp knife, make a shallow crisscross slash across each bun. Brush with egg white. Bake in a 375° oven for 12 to 15 minutes or till golden brown. Cool slightly. Drizzle buns with Hazelnut Icing. Serve warm. Makes 20 buns.

Hazelnut Icing: In a mixing bowl combine 1 cup sifted *powdered sugar*, 1 tablespoon *hazelnut liqueur,* and ¼ teaspoon *vanilla.* Stir in *milk,* 1 teaspoon at a time, till it reaches drizzling consistency.

Nutrition information per bun: 201 calories, 4 g protein, 31 g carbohydrate, 7 g total fat (1 g saturated), 33 mg cholesterol, 71 mg sodium, 92 mg potassium

Pennsylvania

PHILADELPHIA SOFT PRETZELS

Soft pretzels are sold from carts on street corners all over Philadelphia. The only way to eat them, according to locals, is squirted with yellow ballpark mustard. Pretzels are from the Pennsylvania Dutch settlers who learned the art in Germany.

4 to 4½ cups all-purpose
  flour
1 package active dry yeast
1½ cups milk
¼ cup sugar
2 tablespoons cooking oil
1 teaspoon salt
2 tablespoons salt
3 quarts boiling water
1 slightly beaten egg white
1 tablespoon water
  Sesame seed, poppy seed,
  or coarse salt
  Cheddar Sauce (optional)

In a mixer bowl combine *1½ cups* of the flour and the yeast. In a saucepan heat and stir milk, sugar, oil, and the 1 teaspoon salt *just till warm* (120° to 130°). Add to flour mixture. Beat with an electric mixer on low to medium speed 30 seconds, scraping the sides of the bowl. Then beat on high speed for 3 minutes. Using a wooden spoon, stir in as much remaining flour as you can.

Turn dough out onto a lightly floured surface. Knead in enough of remaining flour to make a moderately stiff dough that is smooth and elastic (6 to 8 minutes total). Shape into a ball. Place dough in a greased bowl, turning once to grease the surface. Cover; let dough rise in a warm place till double (about 1¼ hours).

Punch dough down. Turn out onto a lightly floured surface. Cover and let rest for 10 minutes. Meanwhile, grease 2 baking sheets. Roll dough into a 12x10-inch rectangle. Cut into twenty 12x½-inch

strips. Gently pull each strip into a rope about 16 inches long. Shape into pretzels. Place pretzels ½ inch apart on the prepared baking sheets. Bake in a 475° oven for 4 minutes. Remove from oven. Reduce oven temperature to 350°.

Meanwhile, dissolve the 2 tablespoons salt in the boiling water. Reduce heat. Lower 4 or 5 pretzels at a time into simmering water. Simmer for 2 minutes, turning once. Remove with a slotted spoon and drain on paper towels. Leave pretzels on towels only a few seconds; if left too long, they will stick. Then place pretzels ½ inch apart on well-greased baking sheets.

Brush pretzels with a mixture of egg white and the 1 tablespoon water. Lightly sprinkle with sesame seed, poppy seed, or coarse salt. Bake in a 350° oven 20 to 25 minutes or till golden brown. Remove from baking sheet and cool on a wire rack. If desired, serve with Cheddar Sauce. Makes 20 pretzels.

Cheddar Sauce: In a small saucepan melt 1 tablespoon *margarine or butter.* Stir in 4 teaspoons *all-purpose flour* and dash ground *red pepper.* Add ½ cup *milk* all at once. Cook and stir over medium heat till thickened and bubbly. Cook and stir for 1 minute more. Stir in ½ cup shredded *cheddar cheese* till melted. Makes ⅔ cup.

Nutrition information per pretzel:
132 calories, 4 g protein, 23 g carbohydrate, 3 g total fat (0 g saturated), 1 mg cholesterol, 170 mg sodium, 68 mg potassium

Pennsylvania

BUTTERY HOMEMADE NOODLES

*Noodles were a main starch on
Pennsylvania Dutch tables.
They were served boiled and buttered,
fried, steamed, and even
cooked with eggs like a frittata.*

1	egg
¼	teaspoon salt
⅔	cup all-purpose flour
2	14½-ounce cans chicken broth *or* 3½ cups water
1	tablespoon margarine *or* butter, cut up
1	tablespoon snipped parsley

In a medium bowl combine egg and salt. Using a fork, stir in flour. Form the dough into a ball. On a lightly floured surface knead dough for 2 to 3 minutes or till smooth. Cover and let rest 10 minutes.

On a lightly floured surface roll dough into an 18x9-inch rectangle. It may be necessary to allow dough to rest a few minutes between rolls. Dust the top of the dough lightly with flour. Roll up dough, jelly-roll style, from one of the long sides to form an 18-inch roll. Slice the dough crosswise into ¼-inch slices.

Carefully shake out the rings to form noodles. Let stand on a baking sheet about 10 minutes.

In a large saucepan or Dutch oven bring chicken broth or water to boiling. Add noodles. Return to boiling; reduce heat. Simmer for 2 to 3 minutes or till tender; drain. Toss hot noodles with margarine or butter till melted. Sprinkle with parsley and season to taste with salt and pepper. Serve warm. Makes 4 servings.

Nutrition information per serving: *121 calories, 4 g protein, 16 g carbohydrate, 4 g total fat (1 g saturated), 53 mg cholesterol, 307 mg sodium, 29 mg potassium*

Pennsylvania

SWEET-AND-SOUR BEANS AND CARROTS

*A German dish, this vegetable
mixture is more traditionally called
Blindehuhn, or "blind hen," by the
Westphalian immigrants who brought
it to this country. The original
version is a casserole made with green
and white beans, carrots, potatoes,
onions, and apples.*

1	cup chopped carrot
1	9-ounce package frozen cut green beans
2	slices bacon
1	medium onion, sliced
1	apple, peeled, cored, and sliced
2	tablespoons vinegar
1	tablespoon sugar
¼	teaspoon salt

In a saucepan cook the chopped carrot, covered, in small amount boiling salted water till nearly tender, about 10 minutes. Add cut green beans and return to boiling. Cover and cook till the vegetables are tender, about 5 minutes more; drain well.

Meanwhile, in a skillet cook bacon till crisp; drain, reserving *1 tablespoon* drippings. Crumble bacon and set aside. Cook sliced onion in reserved drippings over medium heat till tender but not brown. Add sliced apple, vinegar, sugar, and salt. Cover and cook just till apples are tender, 3 to 4 minutes. Add cooked beans and carrot; heat through. Sprinkle with the bacon. Makes 4 to 6 servings.

Nutrition information per serving:
89 calories, 2 g protein, 17 g carbohydrate, 2 g total fat (1 g saturated), 3 mg cholesterol, 219 mg sodium, 248 mg potassium

BABY CORN RELISH

As early as 1811, Shaker communities were selling a variety of jellies, relishes, sauces, and preserves to their neighbors. Not only were the Shakers superb cooks, but they also devised ingenious inventions like a kernel cutter for corn to lighten household work.

1 cup small cauliflower flowerets
1 15-ounce can baby corn, drained
⅓ cup sugar
1 tablespoon cornstarch
½ cup vinegar
⅓ cup cold water
¼ cup chopped celery
¼ cup chopped green pepper
¼ cup chopped red sweet pepper
2 tablespoons finely chopped onion
1 teaspoon ground turmeric
½ teaspoon dry mustard
¼ teaspoon salt

Cook the cauliflower, covered, in a small amount of boiling water for 6 to 8 minutes or till crisp-tender; drain. Meanwhile, halve the baby corn lengthwise and cut it into 1-inch pieces.

In a saucepan combine sugar and cornstarch. Stir in vinegar and water. Stir in the corn, cauliflower, celery, green pepper, red sweet pepper, onion, turmeric, dry mustard, and salt. Cook and stir till thickened and bubbly. Cook and stir for 2 minutes more; cool.

Cover and store in the refrigerator for up to 4 weeks. Serve with beef, pork, or poultry. Makes about 2½ cups.

Nutrition information per ¼ cup: 45 calories, 1 g protein, 11 g carbohydrate, 0 g total fat (0 g saturated), 0 mg cholesterol, 61 mg sodium, 40 mg potassium

Pennsylvania

CINNAMON ROLLS

Cinnamon is a favored spice in Pennsylvania regional recipes. It appears in all sorts of baked goods, a legacy perhaps from Germany or an influence of the far-reaching Dutch who settled in the Middle Atlantic states. These yeast-leavened cinnamon rolls are usually associated with Philadelphia.

6¼ to 6¾ cups all-purpose flour
2 packages active dry yeast
1½ cups milk
½ cup margarine *or* butter
½ cup sugar
1 teaspoon salt
3 eggs
¾ cup sugar
½ cup margarine *or* butter, softened
4 teaspoons ground cinnamon *or* finely shredded orange peel
2 teaspoons all-purpose flour
¾ cup chopped nuts, miniature semisweet chocolate pieces, *or* raisins (optional)
    Powdered Sugar Glaze

In a large mixing bowl combine 3 *cups* of the flour and the yeast.

In a saucepan heat milk, ½ cup margarine or butter, the ½ cup sugar, and salt just till warm (120° to 130°) and margarine is almost melted, stirring constantly. Add to flour mixture. Add eggs. Beat with an electric mixer on low speed for 30 seconds, scraping sides of bowl constantly. Beat on high speed for 3 minutes. Using a wooden spoon, stir in as much of the remaining flour as you can.

Turn dough out onto a lightly floured surface. Knead in enough of the remaining flour to make a smooth and elastic (6 to 8 minutes total). Shape into a ball. Place in a greased bowl, turning once to grease surface. Cover; let rise in a warm place till double (about 1 hour).

For filling, in a small bowl combine the ¾ cup sugar, the ½ cup margarine or butter, cinnamon or orange peel, and the 2 teaspoons flour; set aside.

Punch dough down; divide in half. Cover and let rest 10 minutes. On a lightly floured surface roll each half of the dough into a 12-inch square.

Spread *half* of the filling over each dough square. If desired, sprinkle with *half* of the nuts, chocolate pieces, or raisins. Roll each square up jelly-roll style; pinch edges to seal. Slice each roll into 8 pieces. Place pieces in two greased 13x9x2-inch baking pans, 12-inch pizza pans, or 9-inch round baking pans.

Cover loosely with clear plastic wrap, leaving room for rolls to rise. Refrigerate 2 to 24 hours. Uncover and let stand at room temperature for 30 minutes. (*Or*, don't chill dough. Instead, cover loosely; let rise in a warm place till nearly double, about 45 minutes). Break any surface bubbles with a greased toothpick.

Bake in a 375° oven for 20 to 25 minutes for 13x9x2-inch baking pans or 12-inch pizza pans, or about 30 minutes for 9-inch round baking pans.If necessary, cover loosely with foil during the last 5 to 10 minutes of baking to prevent overbrowning Remove rolls from pans. Cool slightly. Spread rolls with Powdered Sugar Glaze. Makes 16 rolls.

Powdered Sugar Glaze: In a bowl combine 2 cups sifted *powdered sugar* and ½ teaspoon *vanilla.* Add enough *milk* (2 to 3 tablespoons) to reach drizzling consistency.

Nutrition information per roll: 457 calories, 8 g protein, 69 g carbohydrate, 17 g total fat (3 g saturated), 42 mg cholesterol, 256 mg sodium, 146 mg potassium

Pennsylvania

RHUBARB CHUTNEY

Although rhubarb is nicknamed the "pie plant" because that is one of its most popular uses, it also makes a delicious condiment. Pennsylvania Dutch housewives put up vegetable relishes of all kinds in sterilized jars for later use.

½ cup packed brown sugar
⅓ cup vinegar
¼ cup water
¼ teaspoon salt
¼ teaspoon dry mustard
⅛ teaspoon ground allspice
⅛ teaspoon ground cinnamon
Dash ground cloves
½ cup chopped onion
¼ cup raisins
2 cups chopped rhubarb
¾ cup pitted whole dates, snipped
¼ cup toasted slivered almonds (optional)

In a large saucepan stir together the brown sugar, vinegar, water, salt, dry mustard, allspice, cinnamon, and cloves. Bring to boiling, stirring till sugar dissolves. Boil gently, uncovered, for 5 minutes. Stir in the onion and raisins. Return to boiling; reduce heat. Simmer, covered, for 20 minutes. Add rhubarb and dates and simmer, uncovered, 10 minutes more or till thick, stirring occasionally.

Cool; cover and store in the refrigerator up to 4 weeks. Before serving, if desired, stir in almonds. Serve with pork, poultry, or ham. Makes about 2 cups.

Nutrition information per 2 tablespoons: 108 calories, 0 g protein, 28 g carbohydrate, 0 g total fat (0 g saturated), 0 mg cholesterol, 72 mg sodium, 294 mg potassium

SWEET-AND-SOUR RED CABBAGE WITH PEARS

"Plant cabbage on Friday and lettuce in the dark of the moon." The Pennsylvania Dutch were excellent farmers, but according to their folklore, some precautions were necessary for a successful crop.

1   cup chopped onion
1   clove garlic, minced
1   tablespoon cooking oil
4   cups shredded red cabbage
2   medium pears, peeled and
     coarsely chopped
½   cup mixed dried fruit bits
½   cup dry red wine
⅓   cup red wine vinegar
2   tablespoons brown sugar
1   teaspoon caraway seed
¼   teaspoon salt
¼   teaspoon pepper

In a large skillet cook onion and garlic in oil till tender. Stir in cabbage, pears, mixed dried fruit bits, red wine, wine vinegar, brown sugar, caraway seed, salt, and pepper. Bring to boiling; reduce heat.

Cover and simmer for 30 minutes, stirring occasionally and adding water, if necessary. Makes 6 servings.

Nutrition information per serving: 122 calories, 2 g protein, 22 g carbohydrate, 3 g total fat (0 g saturated), 0 mg cholesterol, 110 mg sodium, 314 mg potassium

VEGETABLES IN SPICY SOUR CREAM

Pennsylvania Dutch tradition insists that each meal include seven sweets and seven sours. The number and variety of these dishes was actually up to the cook, and depended on what else was being served.

½   cup dairy sour cream
1   tablespoon white wine
     vinegar *or* lemon juice
1   teaspoon sugar
½   teaspoon salt
⅛   teaspoon ground red
     pepper
1   small yellow summer
     squash *or* zucchini,
     sliced (1 cup)
½   of a small cucumber,
     halved lengthwise and
     thinly sliced (1 cup)
½   of a small red onion, thinly
     sliced and separated
     into rings
1   medium carrot, cut into
     thin strips
2   tablespoons diced
     pimiento *or* red sweet
     red pepper

In a medium bowl stir together sour cream, vinegar or lemon juice, sugar, salt, and ground red pepper. Add squash, cucumber, red onion, carrot, and pimiento or red sweet pepper; toss to coat. Cover and chill vegetable Mixture for 2 to 24 hours, stirring often.

Stir before serving. Serve with a slotted spoon. Makes 4 servings.

Nutrition information per serving: 78 calories, 2 g protein, 5 g carbohydrate, 6 g total fat (4 g saturated), 13 mg cholesterol, 288 mg sodium, 188 mg potassium

Pennsylvania

LEEK AND WILD MUSHROOM SOUP

Pennsylvania has been a leading mushroom producer since the 1920s. Most of the nation's mushroom crop is grown there in underground caves.

8	ounces Chanterelle mushrooms *or* Cremini mushrooms, sliced (3 cups)
½	cup sliced leeks
1	clove garlic, minced
2	tablespoons margarine *or* butter
1	tablespoon all-purpose flour
⅛	teaspoon pepper
2	cups chicken broth *or* beef broth
1	cup half-and-half, light cream, *or* whole milk
1	tablespoon dry sherry Leek strips

In a large saucepan cook the mushrooms, leeks, and garlic in margarine or butter till leeks and mushrooms are tender. Stir in flour and pepper. Add chicken or beef broth and half-and-half all at once. Cook and stir till slightly thickened and bubbly. Cook and stir for 1 minute more. Stir in sherry; heat through. If desired, garnish with leek strips. Makes 4 to 6 servings.

Nutrition information per serving:
182 calories, 6 g protein, 9 g carbohydrate, 14 g total fat (5 g saturated), 22 mg cholesterol, 466 mg sodium, 427 mg potassium

Delaware

JEWISH FRUIT KUGEL

Kugel *is German for "pudding." Jews from Germany and eastern Europe often serve some type of kugel as part of a holiday meal. It could be sweet, like this one with fruit and noodles, or a savory mixture made with potatoes.*

4	ounces wide noodles
2	beaten eggs
¼	cup sugar
2	tablespoons cooking oil
⅛	teaspoon ground cinnamon
1	medium apple, peeled, cored, and diced
¼	cup dried apricots, chopped
¼	cup raisins

Cook noodles according to package directions; drain well. In a large mixing bowl combine eggs, sugar, cooking oil, and cinnamon; beat well. Stir in apples, apricots, and raisins. Toss fruit mixture with drained noodles. Transfer to a greased 1-quart casserole. Cover and bake, stirring once, in a 350° oven for 30 minutes or till a knife inserted near center comes out clean. Serve hot. Makes 6 servings.

Nutrition information per serving:
212 calories, 5 g protein, 33 g carbohydrate, 7 g total fat (1 g saturated), 101 mg cholesterol, 31 mg sodium, 192 mg potassium

New York

NEW YORK CHEESECAKE

There's nothing "lite" about New York cheesecake. It is a dense, heavy dessert that consists of a lemon-accented cream cheese mixture in a thin pastry crust. (Today, it is commonly served in a graham cracker crust.) When properly made, as it was at Lindy's restaurant in New York City, it is creamy, smooth, and irresistible.

2	cups finely crushed graham cracker crumbs
½	cup margarine *or* butter, melted
5	8-ounce packages cream cheese, softened
1¾	cups sugar
2	tablespoons all-purpose flour
1½	teaspoons vanilla
5	eggs
2	egg yolks
⅓	cup whipping cream
1	teaspoon finely shredded lemon peel

For crust, combine graham cracker crumbs and melted margarine. Stir till well combined. Press onto bottom and about 2½ inches up the sides of a 9x3-inch springform pan.

Mix cream cheese, sugar, flour, and vanilla. Beat with an electric mixer till fluffy. Add eggs and egg yolks, beating on low speed just till combined. Stir in whipping cream and lemon peel. Pour into pan.

Place pan on a shallow baking pan in the oven. Bake in a 325° oven about 1½ hours or till center appears nearly set when shaken.

Cool 15 minutes. Loosen crust from sides of pan. Cool 30 minutes more; remove sides of pan. Cool completely. Chill at least 4 hours. If desired, garnish with fresh berries. Makes 12 to 16 servings.

Nutrition information per serving: 664 calories, 12 g protein, 48 g carbohydrate, 48 g total fat (25 g saturated), 237 mg cholesterol, 494 mg sodium, 153 mg potassium

New York

CRULLERS

The Dutch in New Amsterdam loved krulljes, crispy puffs of fried dough that we know as crullers. One shape, called tangled britches, was made by pulling one end of a strip of dough through a slit cut in the strip's center.

⅓	cup sugar
¼	cup margarine *or* butter
2	eggs
2	tablespoons milk
1¾	cups all-purpose flour
½	teaspoon ground mace *or* nutmeg
¼	teaspoon salt
	Cooking oil *or* shortening for deep-fat frying
	Powdered sugar *or* sugar

In a large mixing bowl beat sugar and margarine or butter with an electric mixer till light and fluffy. Add eggs, one at a time; beat well after each addition. Add milk (batter may appear slightly curdled). Stir together flour, mace or nutmeg, and salt. Stir into the egg mixture. Chill at least 1 hour.

On a well floured surface, gently roll *half* of the dough into a 12x6-inch rectangle. Cut into 2-

inch squares (do not reroll). Repeat with remaining dough. Fry 3 or 4 squares at a time in deep hot fat (365°) about 1 minute on each side or till golden, turning once with a slotted spoon. Drain on paper towels. Repeat with remaining squares of dough. Gently shake warm crullers in a bag with powdered sugar or sugar; cool. Makes 36 crullers.

Nutrition information per cruller: 94 calories, 1 g protein, 9 g carbohydrate, 6 g total fat (1 g saturated), 12 mg cholesterol, 30 mg sodium, 9 mg potassium

New York

BAKED APPLES IN PHYLLO NESTS

Apple orchards flourished in New York and New Jersey in the seventeenth century. The first commercial apple nursery was established on Long Island a hundred years later.

4	medium cooking apples (about 1⅓ pounds)
½	cup raisins *or* mixed dried fruit bits
2	tablespoons brown sugar
½	teaspoon ground cinnamon
¼	teaspoon ground nutmeg
⅓	cup apple juice *or* water
4	sheets frozen phyllo dough (18x14-inch rectangles), thawed
¼	cup margarine *or* butter, melted
	Half-and-half *or* light cream (optional)

If desired, cut a slice off of the stem end of each apple. Then core apples; peel a strip from the top of each. Place apples in a 2-quart casserole. Combine raisins or dried fruit bits, brown sugar, cinnamon, and nutmeg. Spoon mixture into centers of apples. Replace apple slice, if using. Add apple juice or water to dish. Bake, uncovered, in a 350° oven for 45 to 50 minutes or till apples are tender, basting occasionally with the cooking liquid. Remove from oven. Cover with foil to keep warm. Increase oven temperature to 375°.

For nests, unfold phyllo dough; cover with a damp towel or clear plastic wrap. Lay 1 sheet of phyllo dough flat. Brush with some of the melted margarine or butter. Top with another sheet of phyllo dough. Brush with more melted margarine or butter. Add the remaining 2 sheets of dough, making a total of 4 sheets, brushing each sheet with margarine or butter. Cut stack in half lengthwise and crosswise to make 4 smaller stacks.

Place each stack of phyllo dough in a greased 10-ounce custard cup. Place the custard cups on a baking sheet. Bake in the 375° oven for 7 to 10 minutes or till phyllo dough is crisp and golden.

To serve, gently lift each phyllo nest out of custard cups and onto individual dessert plates. Set a baked apple in each nest, spooning apple liquid over apples. If desired, serve with half-and-half or light cream. Makes 4 servings.

Nutrition information per serving: 323 calories, 3 g protein, 55 g carbohydrate, 12 g total fat (2 g saturated), 0 mg cholesterol, 169 mg sodium, 359 mg potassium

New York

DUTCH APPLE CAKE

Both the New Amsterdam Dutch and the Pennsylvania Germans loved apple cakes. This one is probably from New York. A Pennsylvania recipe would use yeast as the leavener, which was kept in a crock above the stove.

2	cups all-purpose flour
1½	cups sugar
1	teaspoon baking powder
1	teaspoon baking soda
1	teaspoon ground cinnamon
¼	teaspoon ground nutmeg
¼	teaspoon ground cloves
¼	teaspoon ground ginger
1	cup applesauce
¼	cup buttermilk
¼	cup margarine *or* butter, softened
¼	cup shortening
½	teaspoon vanilla
3	eggs
2	cups chopped peeled apples
	Apple Brandy Glaze

In a large mixing bowl combine flour, sugar, baking powder, baking soda, cinnamon, nutmeg, cloves, and ginger. Add applesauce, buttermilk, margarine or butter, shortening, and vanilla. Beat with an electric mixer on low to medium speed till combined. Beat 2 minutes on medium to high speed. Add eggs and beat 2 minutes more. Fold in chopped apples.

Pour batter into a greased 13x9x2-inch baking pan. Bake in a 350° oven for 35 to 40 minutes or till a toothpick inserted near the center comes out clean. Cool on a wire rack. Drizzle with Apple Brandy Glaze. Makes 12 servings.

Apple Brandy Glaze: In a small bowl stir together 1 cup sifted *powdered sugar*, 1 tablespoon *apple brandy or apple juice*, and ¼ teaspoon *vanilla*. Stir in additional *apple brandy or apple juice*, 1 teaspoon at a time, till mixture is of drizzling consistency.

Nutrition information per serving: 321 calories, 4 g protein, 55 g carbohydrate, 10 g total fat (2 g saturated), 53 mg cholesterol, 149 mg sodium, 70 mg potassium

Pennsylvania

SHOOFLY PIE

Shoofly pie is perhaps the most famous Pennsylvania Dutch recipe. While there are no firm theories on how the pie got its name, one possibility is that the sweetness of the filling made flies a nuisance.

	Pastry for Single-Crust Pie (see recipe, page 30)
1½	cups all-purpose flour
½	cup sugar
6	tablespoons margarine *or* butter
½	cup molasses
½	cup water
½	teaspoon baking soda

Prepare and roll out pastry. Line a 9-inch pie plate. Line pastry with a double thickness of foil. Bake in a 450° oven for 8 minutes. Remove foil. Bake for 4 to 5 minutes more or till set and dry. Cool pastry on a wire rack.

In a medium mixing bowl stir together flour and sugar. Cut in margarine or butter till the mixture resembles coarse crumbs. Set aside. In another mixing bowl stir together the molasses, water, and baking soda. Pour *one-fourth* of the molasses mixture into pastry shell. Sprinkle with *one-fourth* of the flour mixture. Repeat layers, ending with the flour mixture. Cover edge of pie with foil.

Bake in a 375° oven 15 minutes; remove foil. Bake about 20 minutes more or till a knife inserted near the center comes out clean. Cool on a wire rack. Makes 8 servings.

Nutrition information per serving: 383 calories, 4 g protein, 55 g carbohydrate, 17 g total fat (3 g saturated), 0 mg cholesterol, 254 mg sodium, 345 mg potassium

CHEESE BLINTZES

The traditional filling for a blintz, from the Yiddish blintseh, is either sweetened, spiced farmer cheese and/or fruit. It commonly appears on the menu of Jewish dairy restaurants like Ratner's in New York. The wrapping is somewhat like a French crêpe or Russian blini.

¾ cup all-purpose flour
½ teaspoon salt
1 cup milk
2 eggs

1 12-ounce carton
  dry cottage cheese
  (1½ cups)
1 beaten egg
2 tablespoons sugar
½ teaspoon vanilla
  Dash ground cinnamon
2 tablespoons butter
  Sliced strawberries
  (optional)
  Dairy sour cream
  (optional)

In a bowl mix flour and salt. Combine milk and the 2 eggs; gradually add to the flour mixture, beating till batter is smooth. Pour about 2 tablespoons batter into a hot, lightly greased, 6-inch skillet; quickly swirl skillet to spread batter evenly. Cook over medium heat till pancakes are golden on bottom, 1½ to 2 minutes. Loosen pancakes; turn out onto paper towels. Repeat with the remaining batter, making 12 pancakes.

In a bowl beat cottage cheese, the 1 egg, sugar, vanilla, and cinnamon with electric mixer till nearly smooth. Lay pancakes browned side up; spoon about 2 tablespoons of cheese mixture down centers. Fold in ends and overlap sides over filling. In a 12-inch skillet melt butter; add blintzes, seam side down. Cook over medium heat for 10 minutes, turning once halfway through cooking time. Serve hot; if desired, serve with strawberries and sour cream. Makes 6 servings.

Nutrition information per serving: 195 calories, 12 g protein, 19 g carbohydrate, 7 g total fat (4 g saturated), 122 mg cholesterol, 273 mg sodium, 92 mg potassium

Pennsylvania

FUNNEL CAKES

Deep-fried funnel cakes drizzled with molasses fortified Pennsylvania Dutch farmers in the early morning so they could return to their chores. To create the distinctive spiral, the batter is channeled through a large metal funnel that is slowly swirled over a pan of bubbling hot fat.

2	beaten eggs
1½	cups milk
¼	cup packed brown sugar
2	cups all-purpose flour
1½	teaspoons baking powder
¼	teaspoon salt
2	cups cooking oil
	Powdered sugar *or* Caramel Sauce (optional)

For batter, in a large mixing bowl stir together eggs, milk, and brown sugar. In another bowl combine flour, baking powder, and salt. Add flour mixture to egg mixture. Beat with a rotary beater till smooth.

In an 8-inch skillet heat cooking oil to 360°. Hold a funnel with a ½-inch spout (inside diameter), covering the bottom of the spout with your finger. Pour about *½ cup* of the batter into the funnel. Remove your finger, carefully releasing the batter into the hot oil; start at the center of the skillet and move the funnel in a circular motion to form a spiral. (*Or,* if a funnel is not available, use a small glass measuring cup to carefully pour batter into the hot oil.)

Cook batter about 2½ minutes or till golden brown. Using 2 wide metal spatulas, carefully turn the funnel cake. Cook about 1 minute more or till golden. Remove the funnel cake from the skillet and drain on paper towels. Repeat with the remaining batter.

If desired, sprinkle funnel cakes with powdered sugar or drizzle with Caramel Sauce. Serve warm. Makes 4 or 5 cakes.

Caramel Sauce: In a heavy small saucepan stir together ¼ cup packed *brown sugar* and 1½ teaspoons *cornstarch*. Stir in ¼ cup *milk, half-and-half, or light cream,* 2 tablespoons *water,* and 1 tablespoon *light corn syrup.* Cook and stir till bubbly (mixture may appear curdled). Cook and stir for 2 minutes more. Remove from the heat. Stir in 1 tablespoon *margarine or butter* and ½ teaspoon *vanilla.* Serve warm. Makes about ½ cup.

Nutrition information per cake: 476 calories, 13 g protein, 64 g carbohydrate, 18 g total fat (4 g saturated), 113 mg cholesterol, 334 mg sodium, 239 mg potassium

Delaware

WHOLE WHEAT GINGERBREAD PEOPLE

Since the Middle Ages, European bakers — German, English, Dutch — have been masters at fashioning elaborate images out of flat, rich gingerbread dough. When these groups emigrated to America, the tradition of shaped spice cookies came with them.

1	cup margarine *or* butter
3	cups all-purpose flour
1	cup whole wheat flour
1	cup packed brown sugar
⅓	cup molasses
1	egg
1	tablespoon finely shredded orange peel
2	tablespoons orange juice
2	teaspoons ground cinnamon
1	teaspoon ground ginger
½	teaspoon baking soda
½	teaspoon ground cloves
¼	teaspoon salt
	Creamy Lemon Icing
	Decorative candies

In a large mixing bowl beat margarine or butter with an electric mixer on medium to high speed for 30 seconds. Add about *half* of the all-purpose flour, the whole wheat flour, brown sugar, molasses, egg, orange peel, orange juice, cinna-mon, ginger, baking soda, cloves, and salt. Beat with an electric mixer on medium to high speed till thoroughly combined. Beat or stir in remaining all-purpose flour. Cover and chill for 1 to 2 hours or till firm enough to roll out.

Divide the chilled dough in half. On a lightly floured surface, roll *half* of the dough at a time to ¼-inch thickness. Cut into desired shapes with cookie cutters. Place the shapes 1 inch apart on an ungreased cookie sheet.

Bake in a 375° oven for 8 to 10 min- utes or till edges are firm. Cool on cookie sheet for 1 minute. Remove cookies and cool on a wire rack. Decorate cookies with Creamy Lemon Icing and decora-tive candies. Makes 24 cookies.

Creamy Lemon Icing: In a small mixing bowl beat ¼ cup *short-ening* and ¼ teaspoon *vanilla* with an electric mixer for 30 seconds or till softened. Gradually beat in 1¼ cups sifted *powdered sugar*. Beat in enough *lemon juice* (about 1 table-spoon) till icing is of spreading consistency. If desired, stir in sev-eral drops of *food coloring*.

Nutrition information per cookie: 220 calories, 3 g protein, 30 g carbohydrate, 10 g total fat (2 g saturated), 9 mg choles-terol, 111 mg sodium, 133 mg potassium

Pennsylvania

GINGERSNAP ICE CREAM COOKIES

Like American gingerbread, crinkle-top gingersnaps claim multi-national European ancestry. The Pennsylvania Dutch enjoy them both as a dessert and as a thickener for sauerbraten gravy. These cookies also appear in New England recipe collections.

2¼	cups all-purpose flour
1	cup packed brown sugar
¾	cup shortening *or* cooking oil
¼	cup molasses
1	egg
1	teaspoon baking soda
1	teaspoon ground ginger
½	teaspoon ground cloves
¼	cup sugar
½	cup whipping cream
1	quart vanilla ice cream *or* frozen yogurt
1	teaspoon shredded lemon peel

In a large mixing bowl combine about *half* of the flour, the brown sugar, shortening or oil, molasses, egg, baking soda, ginger, and cloves. Beat with an electric mixer on medium to high speed till thoroughly combined. Beat in the remaining flour.

Shape dough into 2-inch balls. Roll balls in sugar. Place 2 inches apart on an ungreased cookie sheet. Flatten slightly with the bottom of a glass dipped in sugar. Bake in a 375° oven for 10 to 12 minutes or till set and tops are crackled. Cool cookies completely on a wire rack.

For filling, beat the whipping cream with an electric mixer till soft peaks form. Stir the vanilla ice cream or yogurt just to soften; fold in the whipped cream and lemon peel. For each sandwich, quickly spread about ⅓ cup filling onto the bottom side of *one* cookie. Top with another cookie. Immediately place onto a baking sheet in the freezer (keep baking sheet in freezer to prevent sandwiches from softening while assembling the rest). Repeat with remaining cookies and filling. Cover and freeze for 12 to 24 hours. Let stand at room temperature for 10 minutes before serving. Makes 12 sandwiches.

Nutrition information per sandwich: 408 calories, 5 g protein, 49 g carbohydrate, 22 g total fat (9 g saturated), 51 mg cholesterol, 120 mg sodium, 263 mg potassium

Pennsylvania

FUNERAL PIE

It was the custom among the Pennsylvania Dutch to bake this lemony raisin pie, also known as a rosina *(from the German word for raisin) to serve at funerals. Other groups, like the Welsh, Dutch, and English, also reserved special cakes, breads, and cookies for times of mourning.*

3	egg whites
⅔	cup sugar
2	tablespoons cornstarch
2	cups raisins
1⅓	cups cold water
1	teaspoon finely shredded lemon peel *or* orange peel
¼	cup lemon juice *or* orange juice

2 tablespoons margarine *or* butter
Pastry for Single-Crust Pie (see recipe, page 30)
½ teaspoon vanilla
¼ teaspoon cream of tartar
6 tablespooms sugar

Allow egg whites to stand at room temperature for 30 minutes.

In a medium saucepan combine the ⅔ cup sugar and cornstarch. Stir in raisins, cold water, lemon or orange peel, and lemon or orange juice. Cook and stir till thickened and bubbly; cook and stir 2 minutes more. Stir in margarine or butter till margarine melts. Remove from heat. Pour hot filling into pastry shell

For meringue in a medium mixing bowl combine the egg whites, ½ teaspoon vanilla, and cream of tartar. Beat with an electric mixer on medium speed about 1 minute or till soft peaks form (tips curl). Gradually add the remaining sugar, 1 tablespoon at a time, beating on high speed about 4 minutes more or till mixture forms stiff, glossy peaks and sugar dissolves. Immediately spread over pie, carefully sealing to edge of pastry to prevent shrinking. Bake in a 350° oven for 15 minutes or till golden. Cool on a wire rack for 1 hour; chill. Cover and chill to store. Makes 8 servings.

Nutrition information per serving: 385 calories, 4 g protein, 72 g carbohydrate, 11 g total fat (2 g saturated), 0 mg cholesterol, 177 mg sodium, 357 mg potassium

Pennsylvania

FISH HOUSE PUNCH

The Fish House, formally known as The State in Schuylkill, is Philadelphia's oldest and most famous private cooking and eating club. It was chartered in 1732, when America was still an English colony. This punch, the house drink, has been served from the same nine-gallon Lowestoft bowl since 1812.

2 cups water
½ cup sugar
2 cups rum
1 cup brandy
¾ cup lemon juice
½ cup peach brandy
Lemon slices *or* Lemon Ice Ring

In a bowl or pitcher combine water and sugar; stir till sugar dissolves. Stir in rum, brandy, lemon juice, and peach brandy. Cover and chill till serving time. Serve punch in a large pitcher with lemon slices and ice cubes or in a punch bowl with the Lemon Ice Ring. Makes 12 (4-ounce) servings.

Lemon Ice Ring: Line the bottom of a ring mold with sliced *lemons.* Add enough *water* to cover the fruit. Freeze till firm. Then fill the mold with more *water* and freeze till firm.

Nutrition information per serving: 194 calories, 0 g protein, 10 g carbohydrate, 0 g total fat (0 g saturated), 0 mg cholesterol, 1 mg sodium, 20 mg potassium

lavors from the South

Florida

HOT SPINACH AND OYSTER DIP

During the nineteenth century, Americans consumed oysters in amounts almost unimaginable today. Southerners succumbed to oyster fever as much as people anywhere else, perhaps because so many succulent varieties grew in local waters.

¼	cup finely chopped onion
¼	cup chopped red sweet pepper
1	tablespoon margarine *or* butter
1	tablespoon all-purpose flour
¼	teaspoon garlic powder
¼	teaspoon pepper
¼	cup water
1½	cups chopped fresh spinach
1	8-ounce jar cheese spread with jalapeño peppers
1	8-ounce can oysters, drained
	Melba toast rounds, toasted French baguette bread slices, *or* crackers

In a saucepan cook onion and red sweet pepper in hot margarine or butter till tender. Stir in flour, garlic powder, and pepper. Add water. Cook and stir over medium heat till slightly thickened and bubbly. Cook and stir for 1 minute more.

Stir in spinach and cheese. Cook and stir till well blended.

Rinse oysters and drain well; coarsely chop. Stir into cheese mixture; heat through. Transfer to a serving bowl or chafing dish. Serve warm with melba toast rounds, French baguette bread slices, or crackers. Makes 12 servings.

Nutrition information per serving: 78 calories, 5 g protein, 4 g carbohydrate, 5 g total fat (2 g saturated), 21 mg cholesterol, 323 mg sodium, 146 mg potassium

Georgia

SPICY PECANS

Georgia produces one-third of the nation's pecan crop, although the nut isn't native to that state. It did grow wild in other parts of the South and was prized by Native Americans for its flavor and nutrition. The word pecan comes from the Algonquian paccan and the Cree pakan.

1	to 1½ teaspoons chili powder
1	teaspoon curry powder
1	teaspoon garlic salt
¼	teaspoon ground cumin
¼	teaspoon ground ginger
¼	teaspoon ground cinnamon
3	tablespoons olive oil
1	teaspoon Worcestershire sauce
¼	to ½ teaspoon bottled hot pepper sauce
3	cups pecan halves

In a skillet mix chili powder, curry powder, garlic salt, cumin, ginger, and cinnamon. Stir in olive oil, Worcestershire sauce, and hot pepper sauce. Cook and stir over low heat 5 minutes to mellow flavors.

Place pecan halves in a bowl; add the spice mixture. Toss to coat evenly. Spread pecan halves in a single layer on a 15x10x1-inch baking pan. Bake in a 325° oven for 15 minutes, shaking pan occasionally. Cool completely. Makes 3 cups.

Nutrition information per 1/4 cup: 212 calories, 2 g protein, 5 g carbohydrate, 22 g total fat (2 g saturated), 0 mg cholesterol, 153 mg sodium, 121 mg potassium

Louisiana

BOURBON-PECAN PÂTÉ

Although this pâté recipe is contemporary, its combination of French technique and southern tastes—bourbon and pecans—has its roots in Thomas Jefferson's day. Some credit Jefferson's love of French cooking, acquired while he served in Paris as the United States envoy, with adding a French accent to southern cooking.

½   cup finely chopped pecans
2   tablespoons margarine *or* butter
½   pound chicken livers, rinsed and drained
¼   cup finely chopped onion
1   clove garlic, minced
⅓   cup apple juice
½   teaspoon paprika
¼   teaspoon salt
⅛   teaspoon pepper
⅛   teaspoon ground allspice
⅓   cup chicken broth
1   teaspoon unflavored gelatin
2   tablespoons bourbon whiskey
  Parsley
  Toasted pecan halves
  Apple *and/or* pear wedges
  Assorted crackers *or* toasted breads

In a skillet cook the chopped pecans in margarine till golden. Remove pecans; set aside. Add chicken livers, onion, and garlic to skillet. Cook over medium heat till livers are brown and onion is tender. Stir in apple juice, paprika, salt, pepper, and allspice. Reduce heat. Cover; simmer for 3 minutes.

Combine chicken broth and gelatin; let stand for 5 minutes to soften. Stir broth mixture into hot mixture; stir to dissolve gelatin. Remove from heat; stir in bourbon and let mixture cool slightly.

In a blender container or food processor bowl carefully blend or process about half of the liver mixture at a time till smooth. Stir in chopped pecans. Pour into a lightly oiled 2½ to 3 cup mold. Cover and chill for 6 hours or till firm.

Unmold onto platter; garnish with parsley and pecan halves.* Serve with apple and/or pear wedges and crackers or breads. Makes 16 appetizer servings.

*Note: To help unmold the pâté, place the mold in a bowl or sink of warm water just till the edges are loosened from the mold. Invert.

Nutrition information per serving: 70 calories, 3 g protein, 2 g carbohydrate, 5 g total fat (1 g saturated), 67 mg cholesterol, 68 mg sodium, 52 mg potassium

West Virginia

CHUTNEY DIP

Most likely, southern sea captains and spice traders carried home Indian recipes from England for curries and condiments like chutney as part of their exotic cargo.

1   8-ounce carton dairy sour
    cream *or* plain yogurt
¼   teaspoon onion powder
⅛   teaspoon garlic powder
1   teaspoon lemon juice
¼   cup chutney, finely
    snipped
    Snipped chutney
    (optional)

Combine all ingredients. Cover and chill for 1 to 2 hours before serving. If desired, garnish with additional chutney. Serve as a dip with crudités, fruit, melba toast rounds, or crackers. Makes about 1¼ cups.

Nutrition information per table-spoon: *35 calories, 0 g protein, 3 g carbohydrate, 2 g total fat (1 g saturated), 5 mg cholesterol, 39 mg sodium, 17 mg potassium*

Maryland

MARYLAND CRAB CAKES

The blue crabs of Chesapeake Bay are delicate and sweet. A Maryland specialty is panfried patties of crabmeat, bound with breadcrumbs and flavored with lively seasonings. Recipes for crab cakes date back to the eighteenth century.

1   6-ounce package frozen,
    cooked crabmeat *or*
    one 6-ounce can
    crabmeat, drained and
    cartilege removed
1   egg, slightly beaten
2   tablespoons finely
    chopped green onion
2   tablespoons mayonnaise *or*
    salad dressing
1   tablespoon snipped
    parsley
2   teaspoons Dijon-style
    mustard *or* Creole
    mustard
2   teaspoons fresh thyme,
    snipped, *or* ½ teaspoon
    dried thyme, crushed
½   teaspoon white wine
    Worcestershire sauce
½   cup fine dry bread crumbs
¼   cup cornmeal
2   tablespoons cooking oil
    Lemon wedges
    Tartar sauce (optional)

Thaw crab, if frozen; drain. In a mixing bowl combine egg, green onion, mayonnaise, parsley, mustard, thyme, Worcestershire sauce, ⅛ teaspoon *salt*, and ¼ cup of the bread crumbs. Stir in crab; mix well. Shape into four patties about ¾ inch thick.

Combine the remaining bread crumbs and cornmeal. Coat patties with cornmeal mixture. In a large skillet heat oil. Add crab cakes. Cook over medium heat about 3 minutes on each side or till golden and heated through. Add additional oil, if necessary. Serve crab cakes hot with lemon wedges and, if desired, tartar sauce. Serves 4.

Nutrition information per serving: *230 calories, 11 g protein, 12 g carbohydrate, 15 g total fat (2 g saturated), 84 mg cholesterol, 380 mg sodium, 201 mg potassium*

North Carolina

SPICY DOUBLE CHEESE STRAWS

According to North Carolina chef and cookbook author Bill Neal, cheese straws are the penultimate southern cocktail food. Even so, they aren't exclusive to the South. Many regional cookbooks offer recipes for similar paprika- or pepper-spiced pastries, including one that suggests serving them stacked "log-cabin fashion."

1 cup all-purpose flour
¼ teaspoon ground red pepper
1 cup finely shredded cheddar cheese (4 ounces)
¼ cup margarine *or* butter
3 to 5 tablespoons cold water
1 beaten egg
2 tablespoons grated Parmesan cheese

In a large mixing bowl combine flour, red pepper, and ⅛ teaspoon *salt*. Cut in cheddar cheese and margarine or butter till pieces are the size of small peas. Sprinkle *1 tablespoon* of the water over part of the mixture. Gently toss with a fork. Push to side of bowl. Repeat till all of the flour mixture is moistened. Shape dough into a ball.

On a lightly floured surface, flatten dough with your hands. Roll out dough from center to edges, forming a 10-inch square. Brush with egg; sprinkle with Parmesan cheese. Cut dough into 5x½-inch strips. Place strips ½ inch apart on a lightly greased baking sheet. Bake in a 400° oven for 10 to 12 minutes or till golden brown. Makes 40 strips.

Nutrition information per strip: 36 calories, 1 g protein, 2 g carbohydrate, 2 g total fat (1 g saturated), 9 mg cholesterol, 41 mg sodium, 7 mg potassium

Mississippi

CLAM FRITTERS

Fritters are another of those well-loved fried breads characteristic of the region. A hallmark of many southern fritter recipes is the use of cornmeal in the batter.

1 6½-ounce can minced clams
   Milk
1 cup all-purpose flour
¼ cup blue cornmeal
2 teaspoons baking powder
¼ teaspoon salt
1 beaten egg
   Shortening *or* cooking oil for deep-fat frying
   Seafood cocktail sauce (optional)

Drain clams, reserving liquid. Add milk to liquid to equal ⅔ cup. Mix flour, cornmeal, baking powder, and salt. Combine the milk mixture, clams, and egg. Stir into the dry ingredients just till moistened.

Carefully drop by tablespoon into deep, hot fat (365°). Fry 5 or 6 fritters at a time about 2 minutes or till golden brown. Serve immediately with cocktail sauce, if desired. Makes 6 to 8 appetizer servings.

Nutrition information per serving: 162 calories, 8 g protein, 23 g carbohydrate, 4 g total fat (1 g saturated), 47 mg cholesterol, 453 mg sodium, 218 mg potassium

Louisiana

CHICKEN, OYSTER, AND SAUSAGE GUMBO

Gumbo *is from an African word for* okra, *one of the two thickeners used for this Cajun stew. The other is file powder, the invention of Choctaw Indians, who ground it from dried sassafras leaves. Southern purists like Mississippian Craig Claiborne say to use one or the other, never both.*

⅓   cup all-purpose flour
⅓   cup cooking oil
1   large onion, chopped
½   cup chopped green pepper
4   cloves garlic, minced
½   teaspoon ground black
      pepper
¼   teaspoon ground red
      pepper
4   cups hot water
1   pound skinless, boneless
      chicken thighs, cut into
      bite-size pieces
12   ounces andouille *or*
      smoked sausage, cut
      into ½-inch slices and
      halved
1   pint shucked oysters,
      drained
      Hot cooked rice
      Whole okra, split to stem
      (optional)
      Filé powder (optional)

In a heavy 4-quart Dutch oven stir together the flour and oil till smooth. Cook over medium-high heat for 5 minutes, stirring constantly. Reduce heat to medium. Cook and stir constantly about 15 minutes more or till a dark, reddish brown roux is formed.

Stir in the onion, green pepper, garlic, black pepper, and red pepper. Cook and stir over medium heat for 3 to 5 minutes or till vegetables are tender.

Gradually stir the hot water into the vegetable mixture. Stir in chicken. Bring mixture to boiling. Reduce heat. Cover and simmer for 40 minutes.

Stir in the sausage. Cover and simmer about 20 minutes more or till chicken is tender. Remove from heat. Skim off fat.

Rinse oysters and drain well; stir into gumbo. Cover and simmer for 5 to 10 minutes or till the oysters are done and mixture is hot.

Spoon over hot cooked rice and, if desired, garnish with okra. If desired, serve ¼ to ½ teaspoon filé powder to the side of each serving to stir into gumbo. Serves 6.

Nutrition information per serving: 572 calories, 32 g protein, 41 g carbohydrate, 30 g total fat (7 g saturated), 131 mg cholesterol, 549 mg sodium, 481 mg potassium

Louisiana

PO' BOYS

*Submarines, grinders, hoagies, heros —
every part of the country has a version of
a giant sandwich. In New Orleans,
it's the po' boy. Local legend says that
such an oyster-filled loaf was dubbed
la médiatrice (the peacemaker)
because it was used by errant husbands
to appease their angry spouses.*

1	pint shucked oysters *or* ¾ pound fresh *or* frozen peeled and deveined shrimp
½	cup all-purpose flour
½	teaspoon salt
¼	teaspoon pepper
1	beaten egg
¼	cup cooking oil *or* shortening
2	6- or 7-inch-long loaves French bread *or* four 4-inch-long French-style rolls
¼	cup Tartar Sauce, mayonnaise, *or* salad dressing
1	cup shredded lettuce
1	tomato, thinly sliced Bottled hot pepper sauce (optional) Lemon wedges (optional)

Drain oysters. (*Or,* thaw shrimp, if
frozen.) Rinse and pat dry with
paper towels. In a small bowl combine flour, salt, and pepper. Dip
oysters or shrimp into beaten egg,
then coat with flour mixture.

In a large skillet heat oil or
shortening. Add *half* of the oysters
or shrimp in a single layer. Cook
over medium-high heat for 2 to 3
minutes per side or till golden.
Drain on paper towels. Transfer to
a wire rack on a baking sheet.
Keep fried fish warm in a 300°
oven while you cook remaining
seafood and assemble sandwiches.

Slice French bread or rolls in
half horizontally. Place bread or
roll halves on a baking sheet in a
300° oven about 3 minutes or till
heated through.

Spread cut sides of bread with
Tartar Sauce, mayonnaise, or salad
dressing. Arrange lettuce and
tomato slices on bottoms of bread.
Add oysters or shrimp. If desired,
sprinkle with hot pepper sauce and
squeeze lemon juice over oysters or
shrimp. Add bread tops. Makes 4
servings.

Tartar Sauce: In a small mixing
bowl stir together 1 cup *mayonnaise
or salad dressing,* ¼ cup *sweet dill pickle relish,* 1 tablespoon chopped *green
onion,* 1 teaspoon finely shredded
lemon peel, and dash bottled *hot pepper sauce.* Cover and chill at least 2
hours to blend flavors. Makes
about 1⅓ cups.

*Nutrition information per serving:
590 calories, 19 g protein, 63 g carbohydrate,
29 g total fat (5 g saturated), 123 mg cholesterol, 897 mg sodium, 476 mg potassium*

Maryland

PANFRIED SOFT-SHELL CRABS

Chesapeake Bay blue crabs shed their shells and grow new ones more than 20 times during their life span. During the brief stage right after they molt and before their new shells harden, they are completely edible.

4	large *or* 8 small soft-shell blue crabs, cleaned (10 to 12 ounces total)
1	beaten egg
¼	cup milk
¾	cup finely crushed rich round crackers
2	tablespoons all-purpose flour
2	tablespoons grated Parmesan cheese
¼	teaspoon pepper
7	tablespoons cooking oil
	Curly endive (optional)

Rinse crabs; pat dry with paper towels. In a dish mix egg and milk. In another dish mix crushed crackers, flour, Parmesan cheese, and pepper. Dip the crabs into the egg mixture, then roll them in the cracker mixture.

In a 10-inch skillet heat *4 tablespoons* of the oil over medium heat. Add *half* of the crabs, back side down. Fry 3 to 5 minutes or till golden. Turn carefully and fry 3 to 5 minutes more or till golden and crisp. Drain on paper towels. Keep warm in a 300° oven. Repeat. Serve crabs on a platter lined with curly endive, if desired. Makes 4 servings.

Nutrition information per serving: 374 calories, 20 g protein, 8 g carbohydrate, 29 g total fat (5 g saturated), 111 mg cholesterol, 400 mg sodium, 330 mg potassium

Louisiana

CHICKEN AND TASSO JAMBALAYA

Most sources say jambalaya is from jambon, the French word for "ham," an appropriate heritage for a Creole dish, plus the African ya, meaning "rice." Others link it to Spanish paella, which is also appropriate. Creole cooking is a blend of all of these cultures.

1	cup long-grain rice
¾	cup chopped onion
½	cup chopped celery
½	cup chopped green pepper
2	cloves garlic, minced
¼	cup margarine *or* butter
1	16-ounce can tomatoes, cut up
½	of a 6-ounce can (⅓ cup) tomato paste
½	cup chopped tasso *or* smoked sausage
1	teaspoon Creole seasoning *or* Three-Pepper Seasoning
2	whole chicken breasts (about 16 ounces each), skinned, boned, and cut into bite-size pieces
¼	teaspoon bottled hot pepper sauce

Cook rice according to package directions. Set aside.

In a 3-quart saucepan cook onion, celery, green pepper, and garlic in margarine or butter till tender. Stir in the *undrained* tomatoes, tomato paste, tasso or sausage, and seasoning. Bring to boiling. Reduce heat. Cover and simmer 30 minutes.

Stir in chicken and hot pepper sauce. Simmer, covered, about 15 minutes more or till chicken is tender. Stir in rice. Cook, stirring occasionally, till heated through. Makes 6 servings.

Three-Pepper Seasoning: In a tightly covered container combine 2 tablespoons *salt*, 1 tablespoon ground *red pepper*, 1 teaspoon ground *white pepper*, 1 teaspoon *garlic powder*, and 1 teaspoon ground *black pepper*. Makes about ¼ cup seasoning.

Nutrition information per serving: 358 calories, 23 g protein, 34 g carbohydrate, 14 g total fat (3 g saturated), 57 mg cholesterol, 672 mg sodium, 579 mg potassium

Louisiana

CRAWFISH ÉTOUFFÉE

In Louisiana it's crawfish, not crayfish. The latter pronunciation just "won't do," according to famed Cajun chef Paul Prudhomme. In Cajun cooking, étouffée means "smothered in a sauce."

1	pound fresh *or* frozen peeled crawfish tails *or* shrimp
2	large onions, chopped (1½ cups)
1	cup chopped celery
½	cup chopped green pepper

2	cloves garlic, minced
¼	cup cooking oil, margarine, *or* butter
2	tablespoons crawfish fat*, margarine, *or* butter
4	teaspoons cornstarch
1	cup water
½	cup tomato sauce
½	teaspoon salt
¼	to ½ teaspoon ground red pepper
¼	teaspoon ground black pepper
	Hot cooked rice

Thaw crawfish or shrimp, if frozen.

In a heavy, 3-quart saucepan cook onions, celery, green pepper, and garlic, covered, in oil, margarine, or butter about 10 minutes or till tender. Add crawfish fat, margarine, or butter, stirring till melted. Stir in cornstarch.

Stir in crawfish or shrimp, water, tomato sauce, salt, red pepper, and black pepper. Bring mixture to boiling. Reduce heat. Simmer, uncovered, about 5 minutes or till crawfish are tender or shrimp turn pink. Serve with hot cooked rice. Makes 4 servings.

***Note:** The orange fat found in the heads of crawfish adds extra richness and flavor to dishes. Since it's difficult to find crawfish fat outside of southern Louisiana, margarine or butter is a good substitute for the crawfish fat.

Nutrition information per serving: 400 calories, 14 g protein, 41 g carbohydrate, 20 g total fat (3 g saturated), 83 mg cholesterol, 625 mg sodium, 442 mg potassium

Kentucky

KENTUCKY BURGOO

Many traditional recipes for this celebrated Kentucky stew make enough to feed a small town. It has long been standard fare in the South at political rallies and church suppers, and even on Derby Day.

4   cups water
1   16-ounce can tomatoes, cut up
¾   pound boneless beef chuck roast, cut into ¾-inch cubes
2   teaspoons instant chicken bouillon granules
1   pound meaty chicken pieces (breasts, thighs, drumsticks), skinned, if desired
2   cups cubed, peeled potatoes
1   10-ounce package frozen succotash
1   10-ounce package frozen cut okra
1   cup sliced carrots
½   cup chopped onion
2   teaspoons curry powder
1   teaspoon sugar

In a 4½-quart Dutch oven combine the water, *undrained* tomatoes, beef, and chicken bouillon granules. Bring to boiling; reduce heat. Cover and simmer for 30 minutes. Add chicken pieces. Return to boiling; reduce heat. Simmer, covered, about 45 minutes more or till beef and chicken are tender. Remove chicken pieces and set aside.

Stir potatoes, succotash, okra, carrots, onion, curry powder, and sugar into Dutch oven. Return to boiling; reduce heat. Simmer, covered, about 20 minutes or till vegetables are tender.

Meanwhile, when chicken is cool enough to handle, remove meat from bones; discard skin, if any, and bones. Cut the chicken into bite-size pieces. Add chicken pieces to Dutch oven. Cook about 5 minutes more or till the chicken is heated through. Makes 5 or 6 servings.

Nutrition information per serving: 419 calories, 33 g protein, 42 g carbohydrate, 14 g total fat (5 g saturated), 89 mg cholesterol, 629 mg sodium, 1,079 mg potassium

Louisiana

CREOLE SHRIMP AND EGGPLANT

This Creole dish gets a little heat from bottled hot pepper sauce. One of the best known of these sauces is Tabasco, once available only to southern Louisiana cooks. The McIlhenny family has manufactured the product since just after the Civil War.

1   pound fresh *or* frozen peeled and deveined shrimp
1   medium eggplant (about 1 pound)
3   tablespoons all-purpose flour
½   teaspoon salt
¼   teaspoon pepper
2   to 3 tablespoons olive oil

2 cups sliced fresh
mushrooms
2 cloves garlic, minced
1 tablespoon olive oil
1 14½-ounce can stewed
tomatoes
1 tablespoon snipped fresh
oregano *or* 1 teaspoon
dried oregano, crushed
¼ teaspoon bottled hot
pepper sauce
2 tablespoons cornstarch
2 tablespoons water
Fresh oregano (optional)

Thaw shrimp, if frozen. Peel eggplant, if desired. Cut lengthwise into 4 slices. Combine flour, salt, and pepper. Coat eggplant slices with flour mixture. In a 12-inch skillet heat 2 tablespoons olive oil. Cook eggplant slices in hot oil over medium heat for 4 minutes on each side or till tender. (Add remaining 1 tablespoon oil, if necessary.)

Meanwhile, in a medium saucepan cook the mushrooms and garlic in the 1 tablespoon olive oil till tender. Stir in the *undrained* tomatoes, oregano, and hot pepper sauce. Stir together the cornstarch and water; stir into tomato mixture. Add shrimp. Cook and stir till thickened and bubbly. Cook and stir for 2 minutes more or till shrimp are done. Serve tomato mixture over eggplant slices. If desired, garnish with fresh oregano. Serves 4.

Nutrition information per serving:
274 calories, 22 g protein, 22 g carbohydrate, 11 g total fat (2 g saturated), 166 mg cholesterol, 741 mg sodium, 512 mg potassium

Tennessee

HAM WITH RED-EYE GRAVY

Coffee is the surprise ingredient that deepens the color of this whimsically named southern ham gravy to a rich reddish brown.

2 8-ounce slices country-
style ham, cut ¼ inch
thick
2 tablespoons brown sugar
½ cup strong black coffee

In the refrigerator, soak ham in water for several hours or overnight. Drain; pat dry with paper towels.

Trim fat from the ham slices. In a large skillet cook fat trimmings over medium-low heat for 6 to 8 minutes or till crisp. Discard trimmings; reserve *2 tablespoons* drippings in the skillet. Add ham slices to the skillet. Cook over medium heat for 9 to 12 minutes on each side or till brown. Remove ham slices from the skillet, reserving drippings in the skillet. Cover to keep ham warm.

For gravy, stir brown sugar into drippings. Cook over medium heat till sugar dissolves, stirring constantly. Stir in coffee. Boil for 2 to 3 minutes or till gravy is slightly thickened and a rich, reddish brown color, scraping the skillet to loosen any crusty bits. Serve gravy over ham slices. Makes 4 servings.

Nutrition information per serving:
293 calories, 24 g protein, 5 g carbohydrate, 19 g total fat (7 g saturated), 70 mg cholesterol, 1,347 mg sodium, 356 mg potassium

Georgia

BAKED CHICKEN COUNTRY CAPTAIN

A recipe for this chicken curry appeared in Eliza Leslie's New Cookery Book *in 1857. Leslie traced its origins to East India and the British Army. It is also linked to Savannah, Georgia, a seaport where spices were readily available to local cooks.*

2	pounds meaty chicken pieces (breasts, thighs, and drumsticks)
1	large onion, cut into thin wedges
1	small green pepper, cut into 1-inch pieces
2	tablespoons raisins
2	cloves garlic, minced
1	tablespoon cooking oil
1	tablespoon curry powder
1	16-ounce can tomatoes, cut up
½	teaspoon sugar
½	teaspoon salt
½	teaspoon ground mace
¼	teaspoon dried thyme, crushed
2	tablespoons cornstarch
2	tablespoons cold water
3	cups hot cooked rice

If desired, skin chicken. Rinse chicken; pat dry with paper towels. Arrange chicken, onion wedges, green pepper pieces, and raisins in a 2-quart rectangular baking dish.

In a small saucepan cook garlic in hot oil for 1 minute. Add curry powder. Cook and stir for 1 minute more. Stir in the *undrained* tomatoes, sugar, salt, mace, thyme, and ¼ teaspoon *pepper.* Bring to boiling; pour over ingredients in dish.

Cover and bake in a 350° oven about 1 hour or till tender. Using a slotted spoon, transfer chicken, vegetables, and raisins to a platter.

For sauce, measure pan juices; if necessary, add enough water to equal 2 cups. Transfer to a saucepan. In a small bowl combine cornstarch and cold water; add to saucepan. Cook and stir till thickened and bubbly. Cook and stir 2 minutes more.

To serve, spoon chicken, vegetables, and raisins over hot cooked rice. Spoon some of the sauce atop chicken; pass remaining sauce when serving. Makes 4 servings.

Nutrition information per serving: *548 calories, 33 g protein, 62 g carbohydrate, 18 g total fat (4 g saturated), 87 mg cholesterol, 538 mg sodium, 677 mg potassium*

Louisiana

GRILLADES AND GRITS

Without grits, commented the New Orleans Picayune,*"no breakfast in Louisiana is considered complete." Grits served with grillades, meat pounded thin and braised, is a morning institution in that part of the South.*

1	pound veal round steak, cut ½ inch thick
2	tablespoons all-purpose flour
¼	teaspoon salt
¼	teaspoon ground black pepper
⅛	to ¼ teaspoon ground red pepper

1 tablespoon cooking oil
1 8-ounce can stewed
   tomatoes
¾ cup beef broth
1 cup chopped onion
1 green pepper, cut in strips
1 tablespoon water
1 teaspoon cornstarch
2 cups hot cooked grits
   Italian parsley (optional)

Cut meat into 4 serving-size pieces. Trim fat. Combine the flour, salt, black pepper, and red pepper. With a meat mallet, pound meat to ¼-inch thickness, pounding flour mixture into meat. Roll up from a short side. Secure with a wooden toothpick. Repeat with remaining pieces of meat.

In a large skillet brown veal rolls on all sides in hot oil just till nicely browned. Drain fat. Add stewed tomatoes, beef broth, onion, and pepper strips. Cover tightly and cook over low heat about 45 minutes or till meat is tender. Transfer meat to a platter with a slotted spoon; keep warm.

Combine water and cornstarch. Stir into tomato mixture. Cook and stir till slightly thickened and bubbly. Cook and stir for 1 minute more. Serve meat and sauce with hot grits. Garnish with Italian parsley, if desired. Makes 4 servings.

Nutrition information per serving: *286 calories, 29 g protein, 28 g carbohydrate, 7 g total fat (2 g saturated), 88 mg cholesterol, 492 mg sodium, 488 mg potassium*

Kentucky

FRIED GREEN TOMATOES

Early settlers devised many ways to use all the food available to them. In the South, the last tomatoes of the season were picked green, then thickly sliced, dipped in white cornmeal, and fried until golden brown. It's still a popular side dish.

1 pound green tomatoes
   (about 4 tomatoes)
½ cup white cornmeal
¼ cup all-purpose flour
2 tablespoons sesame seed
¼ teaspoon onion salt
⅛ teaspoon pepper
1 beaten egg
2 tablespoons milk
   Cooking oil for frying

Slice tomatoes into ¼-inch-thick slices. In a pie plate or baking dish combine cornmeal, flour, sesame seed, onion salt, and pepper. In a small mixing bowl combine egg and milk. Dip tomato slices into egg mixture, then coat both sides of tomato slices with the cornmeal mixture.

In a heavy large skillet heat about ¼ inch of cooking oil over medium heat. Fry tomato slices in a single layer about 2 minutes on each side or till golden brown. Drain on paper towels. Keep slices warm in a 300° oven while frying remaining tomatoes. Serve immediately. Makes 4 to 6 servings.

Nutrition information per serving: *202 calories, 6 g protein, 16 g carbohydrate, 13 g total fat (2 g saturated), 54 mg cholesterol, 136 mg sodium, 276 mg potassium*

Virginia

BRUNSWICK STEW

Brunswick County, Virginia or Brunswick County, North Carolina? The debate still rages over which state gave this country stew its name, although Virginia usually gets more votes. Originally, squirrel was the meat of choice. Today, chicken or rabbit is considered equally authentic.

2	pounds meaty chicken *or* rabbit pieces, skinned
1½	cups onion, cut in small wedges
4	cloves garlic, minced
1	16-ounce can tomatoes, cut up
1	10-ounce package frozen sliced okra
½	cup chicken broth
1	teaspoon prepared mustard
1	teaspoon Worcestershire sauce
½	teaspoon dried thyme, crushed
¼	teaspoon bottled hot pepper sauce
1	8-ounce can whole kernel corn, drained
1	8-ounce can baby lima beans, drained
½	cup cubed ham
1	12-ounce jar brown gravy

In a 4½ quart Dutch oven combine chicken or rabbit, onion, garlic, tomatoes, okra, chicken broth, mustard, Worcestershire sauce, thyme, ¼ teaspoon *pepper,* and hot pepper sauce. Bring to boiling; reduce heat. Cover and simmer for 30 to 40 minutes or till chicken or rabbit is tender. Add corn, lima beans, and ham. Stir in gravy. Return to boiling; reduce heat. Simmer 5 minutes. Serves 6.

Nutrition information per serving: 359 calories, 40 g protein, 28 g carbohydrate, 10 g total fat (2 g saturated), 100 mg cholesterol, 876 mg sodium, 811 mg potassium

Virginia

SOUTHERN FRIED CHICKEN AND GRAVY

In her 1824 cookbook The Virginia Housewife, *Mary Randolph offered a classically southern recipe for "fried chicken:" Dredge pieces of chicken in seasoned flour and fry in boiling lard until crisp and brown. Randolph then says to add "rich milk" to the drippings, "stew it a little," and pour over the chicken. Other traditional versions mix fine cornmeal with the flour or even dip the chicken in an egg batter.*

2	pounds meaty chicken pieces (breasts, thighs, and drumsticks)
¾	teaspoon poultry seasoning
½	teaspoon salt
⅛	teaspoon ground red pepper
⅛	teaspoon garlic powder (optional)
⅓	cup all-purpose flour*
2	tablespoons cooking oil
2	tablespoons all-purpose flour
¼	teaspoon salt
⅛	teaspoon ground black pepper
1¾	cups milk

If desired, skin chicken. Rinse chicken; pat dry with paper towels. For coating mixture, combine poultry seasoning, the ½ teaspoon salt, red pepper, and, if desired, garlic powder. Divide coating mixture in half. Rub *half* of the coating onto the chicken pieces.

In a plastic bag combine the ⅓ cup flour and remaining coating mixture. Add chicken pieces, a few at a time, shaking to coat.

In a large skillet heat cooking oil; add chicken pieces. Cook, uncovered, over medium heat for 15 minutes, turning pieces to brown evenly. Reduce heat to medium-low. Cook, uncovered, for 35 to 40 minutes more or till chicken is no longer pink, turning once.

Transfer the chicken pieces to a serving platter, reserving *2 tablespoons* drippings. Cover chicken and keep warm.

For gravy, stir the 2 tablespoons flour, the ¼ teaspoon salt, and black pepper into reserved drippings. Add milk all at once. Cook and stir till thickened and bubbly. Cook and stir for 1 to 2 minutes more. Serve gravy with chicken. Makes 4 to 6 servings.

*Note: If desired, substitute ¼ cup *all-purpose flour* and 2 tablespoons fine dry *bread crumbs or yellow cornmeal* for the ⅓ cup all-purpose flour.

Nutrition information per serving:
403 calories, 32 g protein, 16 g carbohydrate, 22 g total fat (6 g saturated), 95 mg cholesterol, 534 mg sodium, 403 mg potassium

Mississippi

CATFISH PECAN

"His meat's as white as snow and makes a good fry," Huck Finn said with relish about the catfish. But until recently, its sweet, firm flesh was appreciated only in the South and Midwest. Now, however, catfish appears on the menus of the trendiest restaurants across the country.

1	to 1¼ pounds catfish fillets (½ to ¾ inch thick)
¼	cup fine dry bread crumbs
2	tablespoons cornmeal
2	tablespoons grated Parmesan cheese
2	tablespoons ground pecans
¼	teaspoon salt
¼	cup all-purpose flour
¼	cup milk
2	to 3 tablespoons cooking oil
⅓	cup chopped pecans

Cut fish into 4 portions. Set aside. In a bowl mix bread crumbs, cornmeal, Parmesan cheese, ground pecans, salt, and ¼ teaspoon *pepper.* Coat each portion of fish with flour, then dip in milk, then coat evenly with crumb mixture.

In a large skillet fry fish in hot oil 4 to 6 minutes on each side or till golden and fish flakes easily with a fork; keep warm.

Remove excess crumbs from skillet. Add additional oil, if necessary. Add pecans. Cook and stir about 2 minutes or till toasted; sprinkle pecans over catfish. Serves 4.

Nutrition information per serving:
353 calories, 24 g protein, 15 g carbohydrate, 22 g total fat (4 g saturated), 65 mg cholesterol, 313 mg sodium, 420 mg potassium

South Carolina

CHEESY CORN AND GRITS

As southern as we may think grits are, they are really a Native American food. It was the Indians who taught settlers to make hominy out of dried kernels of corn, then to grind the hominy into grits. Southern cooks proceeded to devise dozens of ways to enjoy them.

1½ cups water
1 teaspoon instant chicken bouillon granules
½ cup quick-cooking grits
¼ cup finely chopped green onion *or* chives
½ cup shredded cheddar cheese (2 ounces)
2 eggs, slightly beaten
½ cup milk
1 8-ounce can cream-style corn
¼ cup shredded cheddar cheese (1 ounce)

In a medium saucepan bring water and chicken granules to boiling. Gradually stir in grits. Remove from heat. Cover and let stand 5 minutes. Stir in onion and the ½ cup cheese. Stir in eggs, milk, and corn. Transfer to a lightly greased 1-quart casserole.

Bake, uncovered, in a 350° oven for 45 to 50 minutes or till set in center. Sprinkle with the remaining cheese. Let stand 1 to 2 minutes before serving to melt cheese. Makes 4 servings.

Nutrition information per serving: *255 calories, 12 g protein, 28 g carbohydrate, 11 g total fat (6 g saturated), 131 mg cholesterol, 566 mg sodium, 188 mg potassium*

Virginia

BAKED COUNTRY HAM

Good home-cured hams could be found in every colony, but those of Smithfield, Virginia, made from peanut-fattened pigs, were considered perhaps the finest. Their reputation remains stellar today. By law, to be a Smithfield ham, the meat must be cured, smoked, and aged for one year within Smithfield city limits.

1 12- to 14-pound country ham *or* country-style ham
2 teaspoons whole cloves
8 cups apple cider *or* apple juice
½ cup packed brown sugar
2 teaspoons ground cloves
Dry sherry *or* red wine vinegar
Small apples (optional)
Lemon leaves (optional)

Place ham in a large container. Cover with cold water and soak for 16 hours in the refrigerator, changing water once. Pour off water. Scrub ham in warm water with a stiff brush and rinse well. Cut skin from ham and trim off fat. Insert cloves into ham.

Place ham, fat side up, in a large roasting pan. Insert a meat thermometer into the thickest portion of the ham, making sure it doesn't touch fat or bone. Pour apple cider or apple juice over ham.

Bake ham, covered, in a 325° oven for 4 to 4½ hours or till the meat thermometer registers 160°. Drain off pan juices.

For glaze, in a small bowl combine brown sugar and ground

cloves. Add just enough sherry or wine vinegar to make a paste. Spread glaze over fat side of ham.

Bake ham, uncovered, about 30 minutes more or till the meat thermometer registers 170°. Let stand for 15 to 20 minutes before slicing. Transfer to a large platter and garnish with apples and lemon leaves, if desired. Makes 25 to 30 servings.

Nutrition information per serving: 427 calories, 35 g protein, 7 g carbohydrate, 27 g total fat (10 g saturated), 101 mg cholesterol, 1,939 mg sodium, 525 mg potassium

Louisiana

RED BEANS AND RICE

Beans and rice are a famous pair in the South. In New Orleans, the beans are red kidneys, and the dish is traditionally served on Mondays. Louis Armstrong, a New Orleans native son, always signed his letters, "Red beans and ricely yours."

1	cup dry red beans (about 8 ounces)
6½	cups cold water
1	pound meaty smoked pork hocks
2	cups sliced carrots (about 4 carrots)
1	cup sliced celery (about 2 stalks)
½	cup chopped onion
2	cloves garlic, minced
2	bay leaves
1½	teaspoons snipped fresh thyme *or* ½ teaspoon dried thyme, crushed
½	teaspoon bottled hot pepper sauce

4	ounces smoked sausage, chopped (about ¾ cup)
3	cups hot cooked rice Bottled hot pepper sauce (optional) Celery leaves (optional)

Rinse beans. In a Dutch oven or large kettle combine beans and *4 cups* of the water. Bring to boiling; reduce heat. Simmer for 2 minutes. Remove from the heat. Cover; let stand for 1 hour. (Or, soak beans in water overnight in a covered pan.) Drain beans and rinse.

In the same Dutch oven or kettle combine beans, *2½ cups* of the water, pork hocks, carrots, celery, onion, garlic, bay leaves, thyme, and the ½ teaspoon hot pepper sauce. Bring to boiling; reduce heat. Cover; simmer about 2 hours or till beans are tender, stirring occasionally. (Add additional water during cooking, if necessary.)

Discard bay leaves. Remove pork hocks. When pork hocks are cool enough to handle, remove meat from the bones. Cut meat into bite-size pieces. Discard bones. Return meat to bean mixture; add sausage.

Simmer beans and meat, uncovered, about 15 minutes or till a thick gravy forms. (Add water, if necessary, so beans are saucy but not soupy.) Serve over rice. If desired, garnish with celery leaves and pass bottled hot pepper sauce when serving. Makes 5 servings.

Nutrition information per serving: 428 calories, 18 g protein, 67 g carbohydrate, 10 g total fat (3 g saturated), 23 mg cholesterol, 421 mg sodium, 859 mg potassium

Louisiana

PEPPERS AND GRITS

Grits soak up the good flavors of this classic Creole/Cajun mixture of sweet peppers, tomatoes, and onions.

4	slices bacon
¾	cup chopped green pepper
½	cup chopped red sweet pepper
½	cup chopped onion
1	cup quick-cooking grits
¼	teaspoon pepper
¼	teaspoon paprika
⅔	cup chopped, peeled, and seeded tomato

In a large skillet cook bacon till crisp. Drain bacon on paper towels, reserving *2 tablespoons* drippings in skillet. Crumble bacon and set aside. Add green pepper, red sweet pepper, and onion to drippings. Cook about 2 minutes or till vegetables are crisp-tender.

Meanwhile, cook grits according to package directions, adding the salt; keep hot. Sprinkle pepper and paprika over vegetable mixture. Stir in hot grits. Add chopped tomato and bacon; toss to mix. Makes 6 servings.

Nutrition information per serving:
136 calories, 4 g protein, 24 g carbohydrate, 3 g total fat (1 g saturated), 4 mg cholesterol, 70 mg sodium, 160 mg potassium

Maryland

CORN AND CRAB CHOWDER

"Milking" young green ears of corn by scraping the cob was a Native American technique adopted by southern cooks, who used both the whole kernel and its liquid to thicken and flavor chowders and puddings.

2	ears fresh sweet corn *or* 1 cup loose-pack frozen whole kernel corn
2	cups chicken broth
⅓	cup sliced green onion
⅓	cup chopped green pepper
1	teaspoon fines herbes, crushed, *or* ½ teaspoon dried basil, crushed
¼	teaspoon ground white pepper
2	cups milk
2	tablespoons cornstarch
4	ounces process Swiss cheese *or* process Gruyère cheese, shredded (1 cup)
1	6- to 7-ounce can crabmeat, drained, flaked, and cartilage removed, *or* meat from 1 pound cooked crab legs
	Snipped fresh chives (optional)

Cut kernels from ears of corn, scraping ears to remove milky portion also (you should have about 1 cup corn). In a large saucepan combine the fresh or frozen corn, broth, green onion, green pepper, fines herbes, and white pepper. Bring to boiling. Reduce heat. Cover and simmer for 5 minutes.

Stir together the milk and cornstarch. Stir into hot mixture. Cook and stir till thickened and bubbly. Stir in cheese and crab; heat and stir till cheese is melted. Garnish with chives, if desired. Makes 4 main-dish or 8 side-dish servings.

Nutrition information per main-dish serving: 252 calories, 24 g protein, 20 g carbohydrate, 9 g total fat (5 g saturated), 64 mg cholesterol, 985 mg sodium, 627 mg potassium

Corn and Ham Chowder: Prepare as above, *except* use 1 cup chopped *ham* in place of the crabmeat. Makes 4 main-dish or 8 side-dish servings.

Nutrition information per main-dish serving: 277 calories, 26 g protein, 20 g carbohydrate, 10 g total fat (6 g saturated), 50 mg cholesterol, 1,407 mg sodium, 602 mg potassium

Florida

BLACK BEAN SOUP

Black beans reached the American South by traveling north. They were brought to Florida by conquistadores from Spanish settlements in the Caribbean.

1   15-ounce can black beans, drained, *or* ½ cup dry black beans (4 ounces)
2½   cups beef broth
½   cup chopped onion
½   cup chopped celery
½   cup chopped carrot
2   cloves garlic, minced, *or* 1 teaspoon bottled minced garlic
¼   teaspoon dried thyme, crushed
⅛   teaspoon crushed red pepper
⅛   teaspoon ground black pepper
1   tablespoon balsamic vinegar *or* red wine vinegar
½   cup finely chopped ham
3   tablespoons coarsely chopped red onion
3   lemon wedges

In a large saucepan combine beans, broth, onion, celery, carrot, garlic, thyme, red pepper, black pepper, and balsamic vinegar. Bring to boiling; reduce heat. Cover and simmer 20 minutes. Remove about *half* of the hot mixture.

In a blender or food processor carefully blend or process a small amount at a time till nearly smooth. Transfer the entire mixture to saucepan. Stir in ham. Cover and simmer for 5 minutes. Garnish with red onion and serve with lemon wedges. Makes 4 to 6 servings.

Nutrition information per serving: 157 calories, 13 g protein, 23 g carbohydrate, 2 g total fat (1 g saturated), 10 mg cholesterol, 750 mg sodium, 532 mg potassium

South Carolina

HOPPIN JOHN

"Collards for luck, hoppin John for money." Served together, these foods are a New Year's tradition in the Deep South. Hoppin John combines rice, the premier crop of South Carolina's Low Country, and some type of pea, with black-eyed peas the best known.

4	slices bacon
¾	cup chopped onion
½	cup finely chopped green pepper
⅓	cup chopped celery
2	cloves garlic, minced
1	15-ounce can black-eyed peas, drained
½	cup beef broth
½	teaspoon dried thyme, crushed
½	teaspoon dried marjoram, crushed
⅛	teaspoon ground red pepper
2	cups cooked rice
1	medium tomato, cut in wedges, *or* 6 cherry tomatoes, halved
2	tablespoons thinly sliced green onion
	Fresh thyme (optional)
1	bay leaf (optional)

In a large skillet, cook bacon slices till crisp. Drain bacon on paper towels, reserving *2 tablespoons* drippings in skillet. Crumble bacon and set aside. Add onion, green pepper, celery, and garlic to reserved drippings. Cook till nearly tender. Stir in black-eyed peas, beef broth, thyme, marjoram, and red pepper. Stir in cooked rice; heat through.

Garnish with bacon, tomato, green onion and, if desired, the fresh thyme and the bay leaf. Makes 6 servings.

Nutrition information per serving: 188 calories, 8 g protein, 33 g carbohydrate, 3 g total fat (1 g saturated), 4 mg cholesterol, 233 mg sodium, 310 mg potassium

Alabama

BLACK-EYED PEA SALAD

African ingredients and flavors permeate southern cooking. Black-eyed peas, which actually are beans, arrived in the South with the slaves.

2	cups cooked black-eyed peas *or* one 15-ounce can black-eyed peas, rinsed and drained
1½	cups chopped, peeled tomatoes (about 2 tomatoes)
1	cup cooked corn
¼	cup thinly sliced green onion

1 medium jalapeño pepper, seeded and finely chopped
⅓ cup salad oil
2 tablespoons red wine vinegar
2 tablespoons lemon juice
1 tablespoon snipped fresh thyme *or* 1 teaspoon dried thyme, crushed
1 tablespoon Dijon-style mustard
¼ teaspoon pepper
Collard greens (optional)

In a large mixing bowl stir together black-eyed peas, tomatoes, corn, green onion, and jalapeño pepper. Cover and chill for several hours.

For dressing, in a screw-top jar combine salad oil, red wine vinegar, lemon juice, thyme, mustard, and pepper. Cover and shake well. Chill dressing for several hours.

Just before serving, shake dressing well; pour dressing over the vegetable mixture. Toss gently to coat. If desired, garnish with collard greens. Makes 6 servings.

Nutrition information per serving: 236 calories, 7 g protein, 24 g carbohydrate, 13 g total fat (2 g saturated), 0 mg cholesterol, 368 mg sodium, 182 mg potassium

Louisiana

OKRA MIX

Black slaves carried okra seeds from West Africa to the American South. The vegetable took root in southern soil and in the southern diet, appearing in vegetable casseroles like this one. These mixtures were never bland. Pepper sauce was used to turn up the heat.

1 10-ounce package frozen cut okra
1 8-ounce can stewed tomatoes
1 8¾-ounce can whole kernel corn, drained
½ cup finely chopped onion
¼ teaspoon garlic powder
⅛ teaspoon pepper
Dash bottled hot pepper sauce

In a medium saucepan combine okra, tomatoes, corn, onion, garlic powder, pepper, and hot pepper sauce. Bring to boiling. Reduce heat; cover and simmer for 6 to 8 minutes or till tender. Makes 4 to 6 servings.

Nutrition information per serving: 83 calories, 3 g protein, 19 g carbohydrate, 1 g total fat (0 g saturated), 0 mg cholesterol, 288 m sodium, 279 mg potassium

Virginia

BEATEN BISCUITS

Beaten biscuits were a true test of the fabled southern hospitality. If the biscuits were for family, it was acceptable to stop working the dough after 300 whacks with an ax handle. However, biscuits for company demanded twice as many.

2   cups all-purpose flour
1   teaspoon sugar
½   teaspoon salt
⅛   teaspoon baking powder
¼   cup shortening *or* lard
⅓   cup ice water
⅓   cup cold milk

In a medium mixing bowl stir together flour, sugar, salt, and baking powder. Using a pastry blender or two knives, cut in shortening or lard till mixture resembles coarse crumbs. Make a well in the center of the dry ingredients. Add ice water and milk all at once. Using a fork, stir just till moistened. If necessary, stir in enough additional ice water to make dough cling together. (Dough will be very stiff.)

Turn dough out onto a lightly floured surface. Using the flat side of a wooden spoon or a metal meat mallet, beat dough vigorously for 15 minutes, folding dough over and giving it a quarter turn frequently. Dip spoon or mallet into flour as necessary to prevent sticking.

Lightly roll or pat dough to ⅜-inch thickness. Cut dough with a floured 2-inch biscuit cutter, dipping the cutter into flour between cuts. Place biscuits 1 inch apart on an ungreased baking sheet. Using the tines of a fork, prick biscuits several times. Bake in a 400° oven about 20 minutes or till light brown. Serve warm. Makes 24 biscuits.

Nutrition information per serving: 59 calories, 1 g protein, 8 g carbohydrate, 2 g total fat (1 g saturated), 0 mg cholesterol, 48 mg sodium, 16 mg potassium

Virginia

PEACH CHUTNEY

Condiments have appeared on southern tables since colonial days. Their piquancy woke up dull winter meals. Pickles and preserves were put up from a cornucopia of fruits, nuts, and vegetables.

½   cup chopped onion
1   to 2 teaspoons grated
    gingerroot
2   cloves garlic, minced
1   tablespoon cooking oil
⅓   cup sugar
2   teaspoons cornstarch
¼   cup balsamic vinegar *or*
    red wine vinegar
1   tablespoon lemon juice
¼   teaspoon dry mustard
¼   teaspoon ground allspice
    Dash ground cloves

1½   cups chopped, peeled
     peaches
½   cup dried tart red cherries
     or raisins
⅓   cup toasted chopped
     almonds (optional)

In a medium saucepan cook onion, gingerroot, and garlic in hot oil till tender but not brown.

Stir together the sugar and cornstarch. Stir into saucepan. Stir in vinegar, lemon juice, mustard, allspice, and cloves till well blended. Stir in the peaches and cherries. Cook and stir till slightly thickened and heated through. If desired, stir in almonds. Serve warm as a meat or fish accompaniment. Makes about 2 cups.

Nutrition information per tablespoon: 24 calories, 0 g protein, 5 g carbohydrate, 0 g total fat (0 g saturated), 0 mg cholesterol, 1 mg sodium, 23 mg potassium

South Carolina

SPOON BREAD

A well-known 1847 Carolina recipe for soufflélike spoon bread from The Carolina Housewife, *by Sara Rutledge, described it this way: "It has the appearance when cooked, of a baked batter pudding, and when rich, and well mixed, it has almost the delicacy of a baked custard." A serving spoon was required tableware for this dish.*

4   slices bacon
1   cup water
½   cup yellow cornmeal
1   cup shredded cheddar
    cheese (4 ounces)
1   8¾-ounce can cream-style
    corn
2   tablespoons margarine *or*
    butter
¼   teaspoon onion powder
    Dash garlic powder
¾   cup milk
3   egg yolks
1   teaspoon baking powder
3   egg whites

Cook bacon till crisp; drain and crumble. Set bacon aside. In a medium saucepan combine water and cornmeal; bring to boiling. Reduce heat; cook and stir till very thick, about 1 minute. Remove from heat. Stir in cheese, corn, margarine, onion powder, and garlic powder. Stir till cheese melts and mixture is smooth. Stir in milk.

In a small mixing bowl beat egg yolks and baking powder till well blended. Stir into cornmeal mixture along with bacon.

In a medium mixing bowl beat egg whites till stiff peaks form. Fold beaten egg whites into cornmeal mixture. Pour into a lightly greased 1½-quart casserole. Bake in a 325° oven for 50 to 60 minutes or till a knife inserted near the center comes out clean. Serve immediately. Makes 6 servings.

Nutrition information per serving: 227 calories, 11 g protein, 12 g carbohydrate, 15 g total fat (6 g saturated), 132 mg cholesterol, 431 mg sodium, 178 mg potassium

North Carolina

LEMONY MORAVIAN SUGAR BREAD

The Moravians, a religious sect from Bohemia, established settlements in the mid-1800s in Pennsylvania, Georgia, and North Carolina. They were famous bakers and served this flat, sweet bread during the Christmas holidays and at their religious love feasts, a ritualized sharing of food and drink.

1	cup Sourdough Starter (see recipe, page 187)
3½	cups all-purpose flour
1	package active dry yeast
½	cup sugar
½	cup milk
¼	cup margarine *or* butter
½	teaspoon salt
2	slightly beaten eggs
2	tablespoons lemon juice
2	teaspoons finely shredded lemon peel
¾	cup packed brown sugar
⅓	cup margarine *or* butter
1	teaspoon ground cinnamon

Bring the Sourdough Starter to room temperature. In a large mixing bowl stir together *1½ cups* of the flour and the yeast.

In a small saucepan heat and stir sugar, milk, the ¼ cup margarine or butter, and salt till warm (120° to 130°) and margarine almost melts. Add to the flour mixture. Add Sourdough Starter, eggs, and lemon juice. Beat with an electric mixer on low speed for 30 seconds, scraping the sides of the bowl constantly. Beat on high speed about 2 minutes. Using a spoon, stir in lemon peel and remaining flour.

Lightly grease a 13x9x2-inch baking pan. Transfer dough to the prepared baking pan and pat dough evenly into the pan with your floured hands. Cover and let rise in a warm place till nearly double (about 60 minutes).

In a small saucepan combine brown sugar, the ⅓ cup margarine or butter, and cinnamon. Heat and stir till melted and smooth. Poke holes in dough with the handle of a wooden spoon. Pour brown sugar mixture over dough. Bake in a 375° oven for 20 to 25 minutes or till done. Serve warm. Serves 12.

Nutrition information per serving: 339 calories, 7 g protein, 55 g carbohydrate, 10 g total fat (2 g saturated), 36 mg cholesterol, 184 mg sodium, 123 mg potassium

Louisiana

FRIED OKRA

A number of influences are at work in this recipe: the cornmeal is definitely New World, but okra is African, as is the generous dose of pepper in the batter.

1	pound fresh okra (about 45 small to medium)
½	cup all-purpose flour
½	cup yellow cornmeal
½	teaspoon salt
¼	teaspoon ground red pepper

¼ teaspoon ground black pepper
1 egg
2 tablespoons milk
Cooking oil for deep-fat frying

Wash okra; trim ends. Slice okra into bite-size pieces; set aside. In a medium bowl combine flour, cornmeal, salt, red pepper, and black pepper; mix well.

In a shallow bowl beat together egg and milk. Dip okra into milk mixture, then into cornmeal mixture; coat well. Fry about *one-third* of the okra at a time in deep, hot fat (365°) for 3 to 4 minutes or till tender. Remove with a slotted spoon. Drain on paper towels. Keep warm in a 300° oven while frying remaining okra. Makes 6 servings.

Nutrition information per serving:
208 calories, 4 g protein, 16 g carbohydrate, 15 g total fat (2 g saturated), 36 mg cholesterol, 195 mg sodium, 267 mg potassium

Mississippi

CANDIED SWEET POTATOES WITH APPLES

In his 1952 novel, Invisible Man, *Ralph Ellison evokes memories of favorite sweet potato dishes: "Yes, and we'd loved them candied, or baked in a cobbler, deep-fat fried in a packet of dough, or roasted with pork and glazed with the well-browned fat. . . ."*

3 medium sweet potatoes (about 1 pound)
1 large cooking apple
⅓ cup packed brown sugar
1 tablespoon water
1 tablespoon margarine *or* butter
Dash ground cloves
¼ cup chopped pecans *or* walnuts, toasted

Wash and peel sweet potatoes. Cut off woody portions and ends. Cut potatoes diagonally into ½-inch-thick slices. Place a steamer basket in a saucepan. Add water to just below the bottom of the steamer basket. Bring to boiling. Add potato slices. Cover and reduce heat. Steam for 10 to 15 minutes or till just tender; cool.

Meanwhile, core the unpeeled apple and cut into 12 wedges. In a greased, two-quart casserole combine potato slices and apple wedges.

In a small saucepan bring the brown sugar, water, margarine or butter, and cloves to boiling. Drizzle the mixture evenly over potatoes and apples.

Bake, uncovered, in a 350° oven for 30 to 35 minutes or till potatoes and apples are glazed, stirring twice. Sprinkle potatoes and apples with toasted pecans or walnuts. Makes 4 servings.

Nutrition information per serving:
255 calories, 2 g protein, 47 g carbohydrate, 8 g total fat (1 g saturated), 0 mg cholesterol, 48 mg sodium, 448 mg potassium

Arkansas

CORN BREAD

In the South cornmeal is white, and yellow meal is dismissed as inferior. One nineteenth-century woman complained that in the corn bread she encountered on her travels outside the south, yellow corn was used and the meal was too fine, which made clammy bread!

1¼ cups cornmeal
¾ cup all-purpose flour
1 tablespoon baking powder
¼ teaspoon baking soda
¼ teaspoon salt
2 eggs
1 cup buttermilk *or* sour milk
¼ cup honey *or* maple-flavored syrup
2 tablespoons margarine *or* butter, melted, *or* cooking oil

In a mixing bowl stir together cornmeal, flour, baking powder, baking soda, and salt.

In another bowl beat together eggs, buttermilk, honey or syrup, and melted margarine or butter or cooking oil. Add to cornmeal mixture and stir just till combined. *Do not overbeat.*

Pour into a greased 9x9x2-inch baking pan. Bake in a 425° oven about 20 minutes or till golden brown. Makes 9 servings.

Nutrition information per serving: 187 calories, 5 g protein, 32 g carbohydrate, 4 g total fat (1 g saturated), 48 mg cholesterol, 256 mg sodium, 101 mg potassium

Alabama

SALLY LUNN

Did an English baker, Sally Lunn, sell these rich, briochelike tea cakes in the streets of eighteenth-century Bath? Or is the name a mispronunciation of the French soleil lune, meaning "sun and moon"? No one knows for sure. The recipe is probably French, but it was the English who brought it with them to America. It has always been a particular favorite in the South.

3 cups all-purpose flour
1 package active dry yeast
1 cup milk
3 tablespoons sugar
3 tablespoons margarine *or* butter
½ teaspoon salt
2 eggs

In a bowl stir together *1½ cups* of the flour and the yeast; set aside. In a medium saucepan heat and stir the milk, sugar, margarine or butter, and salt just till warm (120° to 130°) and margarine almost melts. Add to the flour mixture. Then add eggs. Beat with an electric mixer on low to medium speed for 30 seconds, scraping sides of bowl. Beat on high speed for 3 minutes.

Using a spoon, stir in enough of the remaining flour to make a stiff batter. Cover; let rise in a warm place till double (about 1 hour).

Stir down batter; spoon into a well-greased Turk's head mold or

7-cup tube mold. Cover; let rise in a warm place till nearly double (about 45 minutes). Bake in a 375° oven about 40 minutes or till bread sounds hollow when tapped. Remove from pan. Serve warm or cool. Makes 1 loaf (24 servings).

Nutrition information per serving: *88 calories, 3 g protein, 14 g carbohydrate, 2 g total fat (0 g saturated), 18 mg cholesterol, 67 mg sodium, 39 mg potassium*

South Carolina

BLONDIES

These butterscotch bar cookies are an example of the South's partiality for brown sugar in baked goods. Short'nin' bread, a Scottish shortbread made with brown sugar rather than white, is another.

2	cups packed brown sugar
⅔	cup margarine *or* butter
2	eggs
2	teaspoons vanilla
2	cups all-purpose flour
1	teaspoon baking powder
¼	teaspoon baking soda
1	cup semisweet chocolate pieces
1	cup chopped nuts

Heat sugar and margarine, stirring till sugar dissolves. Cool slightly. Stir in eggs, one at a time, and vanilla. Stir in flour, baking powder, and soda. Spread in a greased 13x9x2-inch baking pan. Sprinkle with chocolate and nuts. Bake in a 350° oven 25 to 30 minutes or till done. Cut while warm. Makes 36.

Nutrition information per bar: *134 calories, 2 g protein, 17 g carbohydrate, 7 g total fat (2 g saturated), 12 mg cholesterol, 51 mg sodium, 71 mg potassium*

Louisiana

BANANAS FOSTER

Created in the 1950s at Brennan's in New Orleans, the dish was originally part of the breakfast menu. It was named after Richard Foster, a Brennan's regular.

⅓	cup butter
⅓	cup brown sugar
3	ripe bananas, bias-sliced (2 cups)
¼	teaspoon ground cinnamon
2	tablespoons crème de cocoa *or* banana liqueur
¼	cup rum
	Rich vanilla ice cream (about 2 cups)

In a skillet melt butter; stir in brown sugar till melted. Add bananas; cook and gently stir over medium heat about 2 minutes or till heated through. Sprinkle with cinnamon. Stir in crème de cocoa or banana liqueur.

In a small saucepan, heat rum till it almost simmers. Carefully ignite rum and pour over bananas, coating evenly. Serve immediately with ice cream. Makes 4 servings.

Nutrition information per serving: *490 calories, 4 g protein, 50 g carbohydrate, 28 g total fat (17 g saturated), 86 mg cholesterol, 50 mg sodium, 465 mg potassium*

South Carolina

LORD BALTIMORE CAKE

This recipe is a variation of one of the South's most famous desserts. Writer Owen Wister was so taken with an elaborate cake created by a Charleston, South Carolina, woman that he popularized it in his 1906 novel, Lady Baltimore.

2¼ cups all-purpose flour
1¼ cups sugar
1 tablespoon baking powder
½ teaspoon salt
¾ cup margarine *or* butter
¾ cup milk
1 tablespoon rum
½ teaspoon lemon extract
8 egg yolks
  Fluffy Frosting
  Lord Baltimore Filling

Grease and lightly flour two 9x1½-inch round baking pans; set aside. In a large mixing bowl combine flour, sugar, baking powder, and salt. Add margarine or butter, milk, rum, and lemon extract. Beat with an electric mixer on low speed till combined. Beat on high speed for 2 minutes. Add egg yolks and beat 1 minute more or till combined. Pour into prepared pans.

Bake in a 350° oven for 25 to 30 minutes or till a toothpick inserted near the center comes out clean. Cool 10 minutes on wire racks. Remove from pans; cool.

Meanwhile, prepare Fluffy Frosting and Lord Baltimore Filling. Spread filling between cake layers. Frost the top and sides of the cake with the remaining frosting. Makes 12 servings.

Fluffy Frosting: In a medium saucepan combine 1½ cups packed *brown sugar,* ⅓ cup *water,* and ¼ teaspoon *cream of tartar.* Cook and stir till bubbly and sugar dissolves.

In a large mixing bowl combine 2 *egg whites* and 1 teaspoon *vanilla.* Add hot sugar mixture very slowly to egg white mixture, beating constantly with an electric mixer on high speed about 7 minutes or till stiff peaks form (tips stand up).

Lord Baltimore Filling: Combine *1 cup* of the *Fluffy Frosting,* ½ cup crumbled *soft macaroons,* ½ cup chopped *pecans,* and 12 *candied cherries,* chopped (about ¼ cup).

Nutrition information per serving: 496 calories, 6 g protein, 69 g carbohydrate, 22 g total fat (3 g saturated), 143 mg cholesterol, 319 mg sodium, 189 mg potassium

Florida

KEY LIME PIE

This pie was perhaps created to showcase sweetened condensed milk, a new product developed by Gail Borden in 1858, as much as to feature the extra tart Key lime of south Florida.

3 eggs
1 14½-ounce can (1¼ cups) sweetened condensed milk
½ to ¾ teaspoon finely shredded Key lime peel *or* 1½ teaspoons finely shredded Persian lime peel

⅓ cup lime juice (8 to 10 Key limes *or* 2 to 3 Persian limes)
½ cup water
Few drops green food coloring (optional)
Pastry for Single-Crust Pie (see recipe, page 30)
½ teaspoon vanilla
¼ teaspoon cream of tartar
⅓ cup sugar

Separate egg yolks from whites; set whites aside for meringue. In a bowl beat yolks well with a fork or whisk. Gradually stir in sweetened condensed milk and lime peel. Add lime juice, water, and, if desired, food coloring; mix well. (Mixture will thicken.) Spoon into pastry shell. Bake in a 325° oven for 30 minutes. Remove from oven. Increase oven temperature to 350°.

Meanwhile, for meringue, in a mixing bowl combine egg whites, vanilla, and cream of tartar. Beat with an electric mixer on medium speed about 1 minute or till soft peaks form (tips curl). Gradually add sugar, 1 tablespoon at a time, beating on high speed about 4 minutes more or till mixture forms stiff, glossy peaks and sugar dissolves. Immediately spread meringue over hot pie filling; seal to edge of pastry. Bake in a 350° oven 15 minutes; cool 1 hour. Chill to store. Serves 8.

Nutrition information per serving: *351 calories, 8 g protein, 49 g carbohydrate, 14 g total fat (5 g saturated), 97 mg cholesterol, 218 mg sodium, 221 mg potassium*

Tennessee

LEMON CHESS PIE

Chess is another example of a word that likely evolved from one that sounded similar, in this case cheese (as in cheesecake). The heritage of the pie is British, the inclusion of lemon particularly southern. Basically, it is a lemon custard pie.

Pastry for Single-Crust Pie (see recipe, page 30)
4 slightly beaten eggs
1½ cups sugar
¼ cup margarine *or* butter, melted
2 teaspoons finely shredded lemon peel
2 tablespoons lemon juice
1 tablespoon cornmeal
1½ teaspoons vanilla
½ cup light raisins

Line pastry-lined 9-inch pie plate with a double thickness of foil. Bake in a 450° oven 5 minutes; remove foil. Bake 5 minutes more.

For filling, in a mixing bowl stir together the eggs, sugar, margarine or butter, lemon peel, lemon juice, cornmeal, and vanilla. Mix well. Stir in raisins. Place the prepared pastry shell on the oven rack. Pour filling into the pastry shell.

To prevent overbrowning, cover edge of pie with foil. Reduce oven temperature to 350° and bake for 20 minutes. Remove foil. Bake for 20 to 25 minutes more or till a knife inserted near the center comes out clean. Cool pie on a wire rack. Cover and chill to store. Serves 8.

Nutrition information per serving: *457 calories, 6 g protein, 64 g carbohydrate, 21 g total fat (5 g saturated), 107 mg cholesterol, 274 mg sodium, 111 mg potassium*

Louisiana

RAISIN BREAD PUDDING WITH WHISKEY SAUCE

Another New Orleans classic, bread pudding most likely developed as a way to recycle what was left of yesterday's loaf. The result is truly sublime, as is the rich sauce that blankets every serving. It's an indulgence well worth the calories.

3	cups French bread cubes
⅔	cup sugar
¼	cup margarine *or* butter
2	eggs
1	cup whipping cream
3	tablespoons raisins
2	teaspoons vanilla
¾	cup sugar
2	teaspoons cornstarch
	Dash cinnamon *or* nutmeg
¾	cup whipping cream
1	to 2 tablespoons bourbon whiskey

Arrange bread cubes in a single layer in a 2-quart square baking dish or 10-inch round baking dish.

Beat the ⅔ cup sugar and margarine or butter till creamy. Add eggs; beat till fluffy. Stir in the 1 cup whipping cream, raisins, and vanilla. Pour over bread cubes.

Place baking dish in a larger baking pan on the oven rack. Pour boiling water into larger pan around dish to a depth of 1 inch. Bake in a 325° oven for 40 to 50 minutes or till a knife inserted near the center comes out clean. Remove dish from hot water. Cool slightly.

Meanwhile, for sauce, in a small saucepan combine the remaining sugar, cornstarch, and cinnamon. Stir in the remaining whipping cream. Cook and stir over medium heat till thickened and bubbly. Cook and stir for 1 minute more. Remove from heat; stir in bourbon.

Serve warm bread pudding with the whiskey sauce. Store any remaining sauce in a covered container in refrigerator. Reheat over low heat, stirring occasionally. Makes 6 servings.

Nutrition information per serving: *605 calories, 6 g protein, 67 g carbohydrate, 36 g total fat (18 g saturated), 166 mg cholesterol, 256 mg sodium, 123 mg potassium*

South Carolina

TRIPLE PEANUT BARS

"Goodness how delicious, eating goober peas." The old Southern ditty is really about peanuts, not peas. Goober is derived from the African nguba. *Southerners enjoy peanuts raw, baked, roasted, and boiled, and in peanut butter, peanut soup, peanut gravy, and peanut brittle.*

¾	cup peanut butter
¼	cup cooking oil
1½	cups all-purpose flour
½	cup packed brown sugar
½	cup sugar
2	eggs
¾	cup milk
1	teaspoon vanilla
½	teaspoon baking powder
¼	teaspoon baking soda
⅔	cup chopped peanuts
1½	cups semisweet chocolate pieces
	Peanut Butter Icing

In a bowl beat peanut butter and oil with an electric mixer on low to medium speed about 30 seconds or till combined. Add about *half* of the flour, the brown sugar, sugar, eggs, about *half* of the milk, the vanilla, baking powder, and baking soda. Beat till combined. Stir in remaining flour and milk. Stir in peanuts.

Spread batter in a greased 15x10x1-inch baking pan. Bake in a 350° oven about 20 minutes or till a toothpick inserted near the center comes out clean. Place pan on a wire rack. Sprinkle with chocolate pieces; let stand 5 minutes. Spread chocolate over the surface. Cool. Drizzle with Peanut Butter Icing. Cut into bars. Makes 48 bars.

Peanut Butter Icing: Beat together ¾ cup sifted *powdered sugar*, ¼ cup *creamy peanut butter*, and enough *milk* (2 to 3 tablespoons) to make icing of drizzling consistency.

Nutrition information per bar: 118 calories, 3 g protein, 13 g carbohydrate, 7 g total fat (2 g saturated), 9 mg cholesterol, 58 mg sodium, 90 mg potassium

Louisiana

PRALINES

New Orleans satisfies its sweet tooth with pralines, a confection made from caramel and nuts. Like many dishes linked with this city, its origins are French. It was named after a seventeenth-century French aristocrat, Cesar du Plessis-Pralin.

1½	**cups sugar**
1½	**cups packed brown sugar**
1	**cup half-and-half *or* light cream**
3	**tablespoons margarine *or* butter**
2	**cups pecan halves**

Butter the sides of a heavy 2-quart saucepan. In the saucepan combine sugar, brown sugar, and half-and-half. Cook over medium-high heat to boiling, stirring constantly with a wooden spoon to dissolve sugars. (This should take 6 to 8 minutes.) Avoid splashing the mixture on sides of the pan.

Carefully clip a candy thermometer to pan. Cook over medium-low heat, stirring occasionally, till thermometer registers 234° (soft-ball stage). Mixture should boil at a moderate, steady rate over entire surface. Reaching soft-ball stage should take 18 to 20 minutes.

Remove pan from heat. Add margarine but *do not stir*. Cool, without stirring, to 150°. (This should take about 30 minutes.) Remove thermometer, then stir in pecans. Beat vigorously with a wooden spoon till candy is just beginning to thicken but is still glossy. This should take about 2 to 3 minutes.

Drop about *2 tablespoons* candy from a large serving spoon onto baking sheets lined with waxed paper, forming 3-inch pralines. If candy becomes too stiff to drop, stir in a few drops of hot water. Store in a tightly covered container. Makes 15 large pralines.

Nutrition information per praline: 269 calories, 2 g protein, 37 g carbohydrate, 14 g total fat (2 g saturated), 6 mg cholesterol, 32 mg sodium, 129 mg potassium

Mississippi

SWEET POTATO PIE WITH HAZELNUT STREUSEL TOPPING

The American version of sweet potato pie may have English roots, but more likely it was the creation of black slaves. They prepared sweet potatoes in dozens of ways, a legacy of African cooking, which used similar tubers.

1	pound sweet potatoes
¼	cup margarine *or* butter
	Cornmeal Pastry
½	cup packed brown sugar
1	tablespoon finely shredded orange peel
1	teaspoon ground cinnamon
½	teaspoon ground nutmeg
½	teaspoon ground ginger
3	slightly beaten eggs
1	cup half-and-half *or* light cream
	Hazelnut Streusel Topping

Peel sweet potatoes. Cut off woody portions and ends. Cut into quarters. Cook, covered, in enough boiling salted water to cover for 25 to 35 minutes or till tender; drain and mash. (You should have 1½ cups.) Cut up margarine; add to hot potatoes, stirring till melted.

Meanwhile, prepare Cornmeal Pastry. Roll dough into a 12-inch circle; ease into a 9-inch pie plate. Trim pastry to ½ inch beyond edge of plate. Fold under extra pastry; crimp edge high. *Do not prick pastry.*

For filling, add brown sugar, orange peel, cinnamon, nutmeg, and ginger to potatoes. Stir in eggs and half-and-half. Place pastry shell on the oven rack; pour in filling. Cover edge of pie with foil. Bake in a 375° oven 30 minutes. Remove foil. Sprinkle with Hazelnut Streusel Topping. Bake 20 to 25 minutes more or till knife inserted near center comes out clean, cool. Serves 8.

Cornmeal Pastry: Mix ¾ cup *all-purpose flour*, ½ cup *yellow cornmeal*, 1 tablespoon *sugar*, and ¼ teaspoon *salt*. Cut in ⅓ cup *shortening or lard* till pieces are the size of small peas. Sprinkle 3 to 5 tablespoons cold *water*, 1 tablespoon at a time, over mixture, tossing with a fork after each addition till all is moistened. Form into a ball.

Hazelnut Streusel Topping: Mix ¼ cup *all-purpose flour*, ¼ cup packed *brown sugar*, ⅛ teaspoon ground *cinnamon*, and ⅛ teaspoon ground *nutmeg*. Cut in 2 tablespoons *margarine or butter* till mixture resembles coarse crumbs. Stir in ¼ cup chopped, toasted *hazelnuts (filberts) or almonds*.

Nutrition information per serving: 456 calories, 7 g protein, 52 g carbohydrate, 25 g total fat (6 g saturated), 91 mg cholesterol, 214 mg sodium, 341 mg potassium

South Carolina

HUGUENOT APPLE-PECAN TORTE

Close to half of the Europeans who settled in South Carolina in the seventeenth century were French Huguenots fleeing Catholic persecution. The food of Charleston and all of South Carolina reflects their influence.

2   tablespoons all-purpose flour
1   teaspoon baking powder
1   teaspoon finely shredded lemon peel
4   eggs
¾   cup sugar
1   teaspoon vanilla
2½ cups pecans
1   cup water
1   tablespoon lemon juice
2   cups sliced, peeled apple
1   cup whipping cream
2   tablespoons sugar
    Toasted pecan halves (optional)

Stir together flour, baking powder, and lemon peel; set aside.

In a blender container or food processor bowl place eggs, sugar, and vanilla. Cover and blend or process till smooth. Add the 2½ cups pecans. Blend or process about 1 minute or till nearly smooth. Add flour mixture; blend or process just till combined. Spread the batter evenly into 2 greased and floured 8x1½-inch round baking pans. Bake in a 350° oven for 20 to 25 minutes or till lightly browned. Cool on wire racks for 10 minutes. Remove from pans; cool thoroughly on racks.

Meanwhile, in a skillet heat water and lemon juice to boiling. Add apple slices. Reduce heat. Cover; simmer 2 to 3 minutes or just till tender. Drain apple slices.

In a medium bowl beat whipping cream and sugar till soft peaks form. Place a torte layer on a cake plate. Spread about *half* of the whipped cream evenly over layer. Arrange apple slices in a single layer on whipped cream, using as many as needed to cover surface and reserving remaining for top. Top with second torte layer. Spread remaining whipped cream on top of second torte layer. Arrange remaining apple slices and, if desired, pecan halves on top. Chill 1 to 2 hours. Makes 12 servings.

Nutrition information per serving: *331 calories, 5 g protein, 24 g carbohydrate, 26 g total fat (6 g saturated), 98 mg cholesterol, 55 mg sodium, 136 mg potassium*

Georgia

SOUTHERN PECAN PIE

Depending on which part of the South the recipe came from, a pecan pie might be made with corn syrup or molasses or brown sugar, or even sweet potatoes.

1¼	cups all-purpose flour
¼	teaspoon salt
⅓	cup shortening
¼	cup finely chopped pecans
3	to 4 tablespoons cold water
3	eggs
1	cup corn syrup
⅔	cup sugar
⅓	cup margarine *or* butter, melted
1	tablespoon all-purpose flour
2	tablespoons bourbon whiskey
1	teaspoon vanilla
1½	cups pecan halves
	Whipped cream

For pastry, in a bowl stir together the 1¼ cups flour and salt. Cut in shortening till pieces are the size of small peas. Stir in finely chopped pecans. Sprinkle *1 tablespoon* of the water over part of the mixture; gently toss with a fork. Push to side of bowl. Repeat till all is moistened. Form dough into a ball.

On a lightly floured surface, flatten dough with your hands. Roll dough from center to edges, forming a circle about 12 inches in diameter. Wrap pastry around a rolling pin. Unroll pastry onto a 9-inch pie plate. Ease pastry into pie plate, being careful not to stretch pastry. Trim pastry to ½ inch beyond edge of pie plate; fold under extra pastry. Make a fluted edge. *Do not prick pastry.*

For filling, in a mixing bowl beat eggs lightly with a rotary beater till combined. Stir in corn syrup, sugar, margarine, the 1 tablespoon flour, the bourbon, and vanilla. Mix well. Stir in the pecan halves.

Place pastry-lined pie plate on the oven rack. Pour the filling into the pastry-lined pie plate. Cover edge of pie with foil. Bake in a 350° oven for 25 minutes. Remove foil; bake for 20 to 25 minutes more or till a knife inserted near the center comes out clean. Cool.

Serve with whipped cream. Cover and chill to store. Makes 8 servings.

Nutrition information per serving: *608 calories, 7 g protein, 69 g carbohydrate, 36 g total fat (5 g saturated), 80 mg cholesterol, 204 mg sodium, 130 mg potassium*

Louisiana

CAFÉ BRÛLOT

Brûlot *means "burnt brandy" in French. Special fireproof* brûlot *bowls were important tableware in fine New Orleans homes during the 1800s. For a dramatic effect, the lights were dimmed before the mixture was flamed and the coffee added to it.*

3　inches stick cinnamon, broken
6　whole cloves
4　sugar cubes
1　3x¼-inch strip orange peel, membrane removed
1　3x¼-inch strip lemon peel, membrane removed
½　cup brandy
2　cups hot, double-strength coffee

In the blazer pan of a chafing dish combine cinnamon, cloves, sugar cubes, orange peel, and lemon peel.

In a small saucepan heat brandy till it almost simmers. Remove from heat and ignite. Pour over mixture in blazer pan. Place blazer pan over chafing dish burner. Spoon brandy over sugar till cubes melt. Stir in coffee. Makes 4 (4-ounce) servings.

Nutrition information per serving: 87 calories, 0 g protein, 6 g carbohydrate, 0 g total fat (0 g saturated), 0 mg cholesterol, 5 mg sodium, 133 mg potassium

Kentucky

MINT JULEP

On eighteenth-century plantations, juleps were sipped in the morning before breakfast. They were thought to have medicinal properties. According to Kentucky tradition, a proper julep can be mixed only in a silver goblet.

1　cup water
½　cup sugar
1　cup fresh mint sprigs
9　ounces bourbon whiskey *or* rum
6　cups crushed ice
　Fresh mint (optional)

In a small saucepan combine water and sugar; bring to boiling. Add the 1 cup mint. Reduce heat; cover and simmer 10 minutes. Remove from heat; cool. Cover and chill mint mixture several hours or overnight. Strain syrup; discard mint leaves.

For *each* drink, place about *1 cup* crushed ice in a mug. Pour *1½ ounces* bourbon or rum and *3 tablespoons* mint syrup over ice. If desired, garnish with fresh mint. Serves 6.

Nutrition information per serving: 174 calories, 0 g protein, 17 g carbohydrate, 0 g total fat (0 g saturated), 0 mg cholesterol, 6 mg sodium, 56 mg potassium

Georgia

PEACH PIE

When the first settlers arrived in the Piedmont area of Georgia, peach trees were already flourishing. They were planted from seed by Native Americans who quickly took to the fruit after it was brought to America by the Spanish in the sixteenth century.

½   to ¾ cup sugar
3   tablespoons all-purpose
    flour
½   teaspoon ground cinnamon
    Dash ground nutmeg
6   cups thinly sliced, peeled
    peaches *or* frozen,
    unsweetened peach
    slices
    Pastry for Double-Crust
    Pie (see recipe,
    page 213)
1   teaspoon sugar
    Dash ground cinnamon
    Milk

In a large mixing bowl stir together the ½ to ¾ cup sugar, the flour, the ½ teaspoon cinnamon, and nutmeg. Add fresh or frozen peaches. Gently toss till the peaches are coated. If using frozen peaches, let stand for 15 to 30 minutes or till peaches are partially thawed but still icy.

Prepare and roll out the pastry as directed. Line a 9-inch pie plate with *half* of the pastry. Stir peach mixture, then transfer to the pastry-lined pie plate. Trim the bottom pastry to the edge of the pie plate.

Cut slits in the top crust. Place top crust on filling. Seal and crimp edge. In a small bowl stir together the 1 teaspoon sugar and the dash cinnamon. Brush top crust with milk and sprinkle with sugar-cinnamon mixture.

To prevent overbrowning, cover edge of pie with foil. Bake in a 375° oven for 25 minutes for fresh peaches (50 minutes for frozen peaches). Remove foil. Bake for 20 to 25 minutes more for fresh peaches (20 to 30 minutes more for frozen peaches) or till top is golden. Cool pie on a wire rack. Makes 8 servings.

Nutrition information per serving: 382 calories, 4 g protein, 53 g carbohydrate, 18 g total fat (4 g saturated), 0 mg cholesterol, 134 mg sodium, 289 mg potassium

Louisiana

BEIGNETS

The New Orleans version of a doughnut and cup of joe is the sugar-dusted, deep-fried beignet (French for fritter) and strong, chicory-laced Creole coffee. Together they've been a French Quarter tradition for generations of Big Easy residents and visitors.

2¾   to 3¼ cups all-purpose
     flour
1   package active dry yeast
½   teaspoon ground nutmeg
     (optional)
1   cup milk
¼   cup sugar
2   tablespoons shortening
½   teaspoon salt
1   egg

Shortening *or* cooking oil
for deep-fat frying
Powdered sugar

In a bowl stir together *1¼ cups* of the flour, yeast, and, if desired, nutmeg. In a saucepan heat milk, sugar, the 2 tablespoons shortening, and salt just till warm (120° to 130°) and the shortening is almost melted, stirring constantly.

Add the heated mixture to the flour mixture. Add egg. Beat with an electric mixer on low speed for 30 seconds, scraping sides of bowl. Beat for 3 minutes on high speed. Using a wooden spoon, stir in enough of the remaining flour to make a soft dough. Place dough in a greased bowl; turn once to grease the surface. Cover bowl and refrigerate the dough overnight or till well chilled.

Turn the dough out onto a lightly floured surface. Cover and let rest for 10 minutes. Roll into an 18x12-inch rectangle. Cut into thirty-six 3x2-inch rectangles. Cover and let rest for 30 minutes (dough will not be doubled).

In a large, deep saucepan or deep-fat fryer heat 2 inches of shortening or cooking oil to 375°. Fry 2 or 3 of the dough rectangles at a time about 1 minute or till golden, turning once. Drain on paper towels. Sift powdered sugar atop. Makes 36 beignets.

Nutrition information per beignet:
101 calories, 1 g protein, 11 g carbohydrate, 6 g total fat (1 g saturated), 6 mg cholesterol, 5 mg sodium, 25 mg potassium

Louisiana

CAFÉ AU LAIT

Creole coffee, from New Orleans, gets its distinctive bitter flavor from the addition of chicory to the grind. Adding milk or cream softens its bite. Chicory was first used as an extender for coffee during the hard times of the Civil War. Now it's used because locals demand it.

1 cup ground coffee with chicory
3 cups water
3 cups half-and-half, light cream, *or* milk

Using coffee with chicory and water, prepare coffee in a coffee maker according to manufacturer's directions.

Meanwhile, heat the half-and-half, light cream, or milk over low heat. Beat with a rotary beater till foamy. Transfer cream to a warmed serving container.

Stir coffee. Pour coffee and cream in equal amounts into serving cups. Makes twelve 4-ounce servings.

Nutrition information per serving: 81 calories, 2 g protein, 3 g carbohydrate, 7 g total fat (4 g saturated), 22 mg cholesterol, 27 mg sodium, 139 mg potassium

Alabama

CAPPUCCINO EGGNOG

Along with hoppin John and collard greens, eggnog is part of Christmas and New Year's celebrations in the South. It is closely related to syllabub, a recipe that appears in many early southern cookbooks, except that it uses hard liquor, while the latter requires wine.

6   beaten eggs
2   cups milk
⅓   cup sugar
1   tablespoon instant espresso powder *or* 4 teaspoons instant coffee crystals
¼   cup light rum *or* milk
1   teaspoon vanilla
1   cup whipping cream
2   tablespoons sugar
3   tablespoons finely shredded orange peel
10   long cinnamon sticks

In a large, heavy saucepan mix eggs, milk, the ⅓ cup sugar, and espresso or coffee. Cook and stir over medium heat about 8 minutes or till mixture coats a metal spoon. Remove from heat. Cool quickly by placing pan in a sink or bowl of *ice*

water and stirring for 1 to 2 minutes. Stir in rum or milk and vanilla. Cover surface with plastic wrap. Chill 4 to 24 hours.

At serving time, in a medium mixing bowl beat whipping cream and the 2 tablespoons sugar with an electric mixer on medium speed till soft peaks form. Transfer chilled egg mixture to a punch bowl. Fold in whipped cream mixture. Serve at once. Sprinkle each serving with shredded orange peel and serve with cinnamon sticks. Makes ten 4-ounce servings.

Nutrition information per serving: 203 calories, 6 g protein, 13 g carbohydrate, 13 g total fat (7 g saturated), 164 mg cholesterol, 71 mg sodium, 110 mg potassium

lavors from the Midwest

WISCONSIN CHEDDAR-BACON PUFFS

An abundance of milk led to Wisconsin's first cottage-industry cheese factory. In 1841, Mrs. Anne Pickett began manufacturing cheese at her home using milk from a neighbor's cows. A few decades later, another Wisconsin cheesemaker, John Smith, was successful enough to market his product outside of the state.

⅓   **cup margarine *or* butter**
1   **cup all-purpose flour**
4   **eggs**
½   **cup shredded sharp cheddar cheese (2 ounces)**
4   **slices bacon, crisp-cooked, drained, and crumbled**
2   **tablespoons grated Parmesan cheese**

In a medium saucepan combine margarine and 1 cup *water.* Bring to boiling, stirring till margarine melts. Add flour all at once, stirring vigorously. Cook and stir till mixture forms a ball that doesn't separate. Remove from heat; cool 10 minutes.

Add eggs, one at a time, beating after each addition about 1 minute or till smooth. Beat in cheddar cheese and crumbled bacon.

On a well-greased extra-large baking sheet drop dough by well-rounded tablespoons into 2 rings of 10 mounds per ring with the mounds spaced about ½ inch apart. Sprinkle rings with Parmesan cheese. Bake in a 400° oven about 30 minutes or till golden brown and puffed. Remove from baking sheet; cool slightly. Serve warm. Serves 20.

Nutrition information per serving: 86 calories, 3 g protein, 5 g carbohydrate, 6 g total fat (2 g saturated), 47 mg cholesterol, 87 mg sodium, 18 mg potassium

Michigan

CHERRY-SWISS CHEESE SPREAD

French colonists from Normandy planted cherry trees in the Great Lakes area of the Midwest. They carried pits with them from France to ensure a ready supply of this well-loved fruit. Michigan's first cherry orchards were the work of a Presbyterian minister, Peter Dougherty, in 1852. Today, the state is the nation's leading producer of tart cherries.

3 cups shredded Swiss
    cheese
¼ cup margarine *or* butter
½ cup dried tart red cherries
½ cup mayonnaise *or* salad
    dressing
2 teaspoons Dijon-style
    mustard
½ cup finely chopped green
    onion

Bring cheese and margarine to room temperature. Meanwhile, pour boiling water over cherries to cover; let stand 10 minutes. Drain well; pat with paper towels; set aside. In a food processor bowl, process cheese, margarine, mayonnaise, and mustard till combined. Stir in cherries and onion. Serve in a bowl or on a serving plate with crackers. Makes 12 to 16 servings.

Nutrition information per serving: 226 calories, 9 g protein, 6 g carbohydrate, 19 g total fat (7 g saturated), 31 mg cholesterol, 184 mg sodium, 49 mg potassium

Wisconsin

BEEF POT ROAST

Pot roast was the first recipe in the meat chapter of the 1903 Settlement Cookbook, written by Mrs. Simon Kander. It was a favorite of the Germans who settled in Wisconsin and all over the Midwest.

1 1½- to 2-pound beef chuck
    pot roast
1 teaspoon lemon-pepper
    seasoning *or* ½ teaspoon
    cracked black pepper
1 tablespoon cooking oil
½ cup water
¼ cup tomato juice
¼ cup dry white wine,
    beef broth, *or* water
1 teaspoon instant beef
    bouillon granules
½ teaspoon dried thyme,
    crushed
4 medium carrots, cut into
    1½-inch pieces
2 medium potatoes, peeled
    and quartered
1 medium onion, cut into
    wedges
⅓ cup cold water
3 tablespoons all-purpose
    flour

Trim separable fat from roast. Rub 1 side with lemon-pepper seasoning. In a Dutch oven brown roast on all sides in hot oil. Drain off fat.

Combine the ½ cup water; tomato juice; wine, beef broth, or water; bouillon granules; and thyme. Pour around roast in Dutch oven. Bring to boiling; reduce heat. Cover and simmer 1 hour. (Or, bake, covered, in a 325° oven 1 hour.)

Add carrots, potatoes, and onion to meat. Cover; simmer or bake 45 to 60 minutes more or till tender, adding additional water, if necessary. Use a slotted spoon to remove meat and vegetables; keep warm.

For gravy, pour pan juices into a large measuring cup. Skim off fat; discard. If necessary, add water to pan juices to equal 1¼ cups. Return liquid to Dutch oven. Combine cold water and flour. Stir into juices in Dutch oven. Cook and stir till thickened and bubbly. Cook and stir 1 minute more. Serve with meat and vegetables. Serves 4 to 6.

Nutrition information per serving: 432 calories, 34 g protein, 28 g carbohydrate, 19 g total fat (7 g saturated), 105 mg cholesterol, 587 mg sodium, 796 mg potassium

Illinois

WINE-AND-HERB-MARINATED RIB EYE ROAST

Chicago has been a center for the meat industry in the United States since before the Civil War. At first its stockyards were a rest stop for cattle destined for slaughter in the East. With the development of refrigerated rail-cars, cattle was processed in Chicago slaughterhouses and then shipped by rail to retail markets.

1	4-pound beef rib eye roast
¾	cup dry red wine
¼	cup lemon juice
2	tablespoons olive oil *or* cooking oil
1	tablespoon coarsely ground black pepper
1	tablespoon snipped fresh rosemary *or* 1 teaspoon dried rosemary, crushed
1	tablespoon snipped fresh marjoram *or* 1 teaspoon dried marjoram, crushed
1	tablespoon Worcestershire sauce
1	tablespoon Dijon-style mustard
¼	teaspoon garlic salt

Place roast in a plastic bag set in a deep bowl. For marinade, in a mixing bowl combine wine, lemon juice, olive oil or cooking oil, pepper, rosemary, marjoram, Worcestershire sauce, mustard, and garlic salt. Pour marinade over roast. Seal bag. Marinate in the refrigerator for 6 to 24 hours, turning bag occasionally.

Remove roast from bag, reserving marinade. Place roast, fat side up, on a rack in a shallow roasting pan. Insert a meat thermometer. Roast in a 350° oven for 1¼ to 2 hours for rare (140°), 1¼ to 2¼ hours for medium (160°), or 1½ to 2½ hours for well-done (170°), brushing with marinade occasionally. (Do not brush with marinade during the last 5 minutes of roasting.) Cover with foil and let stand 15 minutes before carving. Makes 8 to 10 servings.

Nutrition information per serving: 441 calories, 44 g protein, 2 g carbohydrate, 26 g total fat (9 g saturated), 128 mg cholesterol, 247 mg sodium, 665 mg potassium

Iowa

CHICKEN-FRIED STEAK WITH GRAVY

In some areas of the Midwest, chicken was such a favorite that it was considered food for company. Perhaps this dish came about as way to satisfy appetites that would rather be eating a piece of crumb-coated, gravy-smothered hen than a tough slice of meat.

1	pound beef top round steak, cut ½ inch thick
¾	cup fine dry bread crumbs
1½	teaspoons snipped fresh basil *or* oregano *or* ½ teaspoon dried basil *or* oregano, crushed
½	teaspoon salt
¼	teaspoon pepper
1	beaten egg
1	tablespoon milk
2	tablespoons cooking oil
1	small onion, sliced and separated into rings
2	tablespoons all-purpose flour
1⅓	cups milk

Cut steak into 4 serving-size pieces. Trim fat. Place meat pieces between 2 pieces of plastic wrap. Pound meat with a meat mallet to ¼-inch thickness.

In a dish or on a piece of waxed paper combine bread crumbs, basil or oregano, salt, and pepper. In another shallow dish stir together egg and the 1 tablespoon milk. Dip meat pieces in egg mixture, then coat with bread crumb mixture.

In a 12-inch skillet brown meat pieces in hot oil over medium heat about 3 minutes on each side. Reduce heat to low. Cover and cook for 45 to 60 minutes more or till tender. Transfer meat pieces to a platter. Cover to keep warm.

For gravy, cook onion in pan drippings till tender but not brown. (Add more oil, if necessary.) Stir in flour. Add the 1⅓ cups milk all at once. Cook and stir till thickened and bubbly. Cook and stir for 1 minute more. Season to taste with salt and pepper. Serve gravy with meat. Makes 4 servings.

Nutrition information per serving: 363 calories, 32 g protein, 22 g carbohydrate, 16 g total fat (4 g saturated), 118 mg cholesterol, 539 mg sodium, 538 mg potassium

Oklahoma

BEER-MARINATED PEPPERED T-BONES

The Oklahoma Territory was the last area of the plains to be opened to homesteaders. The date? High noon, April 22, 1889. Oklahoma has always had ties to both the Midwest and the Southwest, a split that is reflected in the slightly spicy flavor of its down-home cooking.

1	cup chopped onion
½	of a 12-ounce can (¾ cup) beer
¾	cup chili sauce
¼	cup parsley
3	tablespoons Dijon-style mustard
1	tablespoon Worcestershire sauce

2 teaspoons brown sugar
½ teaspoon paprika
½ teaspoon ground black pepper
3 beef T-bone steaks, cut 1 inch thick (about 1 pound each), *or* 6 beef top loin steaks, cut 1 inch thick (about 1¾ pounds total)
1 to 1½ teaspoons cracked black pepper
Fresh herbs (optional)

In a large glass baking dish combine onion, beer, chili sauce, parsley, mustard, Worcestershire sauce, brown sugar, paprika, and the ½ teaspoon pepper. Place steaks in marinade. Cover and refrigerate 4 to 6 hours or overnight, turning steaks over occasionally.

Remove steaks from marinade; discard marinade. Sprinkle both sides of steaks with the cracked black pepper.

Grill steaks on an uncovered grill directly over *medium-hot* coals for 5 minutes. Turn and grill to desired doneness, allowing 3 to 7 minutes more for rare or 7 to 10 minutes more for medium. If desired, garnish with fresh herbs. Serves 6.

Nutrition information per serving:
231 calories, 27 g protein, 7 g carbohydrate, 10 g total fat (4 g saturated), 73 mg cholesterol, 390 mg sodium, 486 mg potassium

Kansas

BIEROCKS

Like Cornish pasties, German Bierocks (also called Runzas) are hand-held dinner pies. They were popular in wheat-growing areas of the Midwest.

1 16-ounce package hot roll mix
1 pound ground beef
1 cup finely chopped onion
3 cups shredded cabbage
Milk

Make roll mix according to package directions for basic recipe through kneading step. Cover; let dough rest.

Meanwhile, for filling, cook beef and onion till meat is brown. Drain fat. Stir in the cabbage and ¼ cup *water.* Cook for 5 minutes or till cabbage is tender; drain well. Stir in ¼ teaspoon *salt* and ¼ to ½ teaspoon *pepper.*

Divide dough into 6 pieces. Roll each piece to a 7x5-inch rectangle. Spoon filling lengthwise down center of rectangles. Bring long edges of dough together over filling; pinch edges and ends to seal. Place bundles, seam sides down, on a greased baking sheet. Let stand in a warm place 20 minutes; brush with milk. Bake in a 350° oven for 25 to 30 minutes or till golden. Serves 6.

Nutrition information per serving:
438 calories, 25 g protein, 60 g carbohydrate, 10 g total fat (4 g saturated), 56 mg cholesterol, 663 mg sodium, 445 mg potassium

Michigan

CORNISH BEEF PASTIES

Cornishmen came to the United States to work in the iron and copper mines in Michigan's Upper Peninsula. Their lunch in the new country was the same as it was in the old: this meat-and-potato turnover, which they carried to the mines in a cotton pouch called a crib bag.

3 cups all-purpose flour
1 cup shortening
7 to 8 tablespoons cold water
1½ cups chopped peeled potatoes
1 pound beef round steak, cut in ¼-inch cubes
¾ cup peeled turnip cut in ¼-inch cubes
½ cup finely chopped onion
½ cup catsup (optional)

Combine flour and 1½ teaspoons *salt.* Cut in the shortening till the mixture resembles coarse crumbs. Gradually add the 7 to 8 table-spoons cold water, *1 tablespoon at a time,* tossing with a fork till all is moistened. Form dough into a ball. If desired, cover and chill the dough 1 hour.

Meanwhile, for filling, combine potato, beef, turnip, onion, 1½ tea-spoons *salt,* and ¼ teaspoon *pepper.* Set aside. Divide dough into 6 equal pieces. Roll each piece into a 9-inch circle. Place about *1 cup* fill-ing on *half* of *each* circle; fold other half of dough over filling. Seal edge; cut slits in top for steam to escape. Place on an ungreased bak-ing sheet. If desired, brush with milk. Bake in a 400° oven about 45 minutes or till golden. If desired, mix catsup and ¼ cup *water;* heat through. Serve with pasties. Makes 6 servings.

Nutrition information per serving: *824 calories, 29 g protein, 73 g carbohydrate, 46 g total fat (12 g saturated), 47 mg cho-lesterol, 1,126 mg sodium, 632 mg potassium*

Minnesota

CREAM OF CHICKEN AND WILD RICE SOUP

Wild rice is rich in nutrients and was a dietary staple of the Native Americans, who would collect it by hand from the waterways of the Great Lakes region. The wild crop is still gathered that way. A recent innovation, begun in Minnesota in the mid-1960s, is machine-harvested cultivated wild rice

2 14½-ounce cans chicken broth (3½ cups)
1 cup sliced carrots
½ cup sliced celery
⅓ cup wild rice
⅓ cup sliced leek *or* green onion
½ teaspoon dried thyme, crushed
2 tablespoons margarine *or* butter
3 tablespoons all-purpose flour

1 cup half-and-half *or* milk
1½ cups chopped cooked chicken
2 tablespoons dry sherry

In a saucepan mix broth, carrots, celery, *uncooked* rice, leek, thyme, and ¼ teaspoon *pepper.* Bring to boiling; reduce heat. Cover; simmer 50 minutes or till rice is tender. Meanwhile, melt margarine. Stir in flour, then stir in half-and-half. Cook and stir till bubbly. Cook and stir 1 minute more. Slowly add half-and-half mixture to rice mixture, stirring constantly. Stir in chicken and sherry; heat through. Serves 4.

Nutrition information per serving: *342 calories, 25 g protein, 23 g carbohydrate, 16 g total fat (6 g saturated), 67 mg cholesterol, 809 mg sodium, 585 mg potassium*

Minnesota

SWEDISH MEATBALLS

The great Swedish immigration to America began in the 1850s. Minnesota was the destination of the majority of the immigrants. Most became farmers, while others found jobs as railroaders and carpenters, or in similar trades requiring skilled labor.

1½ cups soft bread crumbs
⅔ cup half-and-half, light cream, *or* milk
1 slightly beaten egg
½ cup finely chopped onion
¼ cup finely snipped parsley

½ teaspoon salt
⅛ teaspoon ground ginger
⅛ teaspoon ground nutmeg
¾ pound lean ground beef
½ pound ground veal
¼ pound ground pork
2 tablespoons margarine *or* butter
2 tablespoons all-purpose flour
⅔ cup half-and-half, light cream, *or* milk
1¼ cups water
1 teaspoon instant beef bouillon granules
½ teaspoon instant coffee crystals

In a mixing bowl soak the bread crumbs in ⅔ cup half-and-half for 5 minutes. Add egg, onion, parsley, salt, ginger, and nutmeg. Add ground meats; mix well. Shape into 1- to 1¼-inch-thick meatballs.

In an ungreased shallow baking pan bake meatballs in a 350° oven 15 to 20 minutes or till no longer pink. Drain well on paper towels.

Meanwhile, melt margarine or butter in a large skillet. Stir in flour. Stir in the remaining half-and-half, the water, bouillon granules, and coffee crystals. Cook and stir till thickened and bubbly. Add meatballs to skillet and heat through, about 1 minute. Makes 8 servings.

Nutrition information per serving: *270 calories, 21 g protein, 9 g carbohydrate, 16 g total fat (7 g saturated), 110 mg cholesterol, 399 mg sodium, 324 mg potassium*

Ohio

PORK TENDERLOIN SANDWICHES

Although cattle drives are more famous, hogs were taken to market the same way, by foot. Before the Civil War, hog drovers moved their large herds hundreds of miles at a time to eastern markets from Ohio, the center of the pork industry at the time. It was slow going, averaging five to eight miles a day.

¾   **pound pork tenderloin**
¼   **cup all-purpose flour**
¼   **teaspoon onion powder *or* garlic powder**
¼   **teaspoon pepper**
1   **beaten egg**
1   **tablespoon milk *or* water**
1   **cup finely crushed rich round crackers (about 24) *or* ¾ cup fine dry bread crumbs**
1   **tablespoon cooking oil**
4   **hamburger buns *or* kaiser rolls, split and toasted**
    Mustard, catsup, onion slices, dill pickle slices, *and/or* roasted red sweet peppers (optional)

Cut pork crosswise into 4 slices. With a meat mallet, pound each pork slice between plastic wrap to ¼-inch thickness.

In a shallow bowl combine flour, onion or garlic powder, and pepper. In another shallow bowl combine egg and milk or water. In a third bowl place crushed crackers or bread crumbs. Dip each pork slice into the flour mixture, coating well, then into the egg mixture, and then into the crumbs to coat.

In a large skillet cook 2 pork slices in hot oil over medium heat for 6 to 8 minutes or till pork is no longer pink, turning once. Remove from skillet; keep warm. Repeat with remaining slices, adding more oil, if necessary.

Place on buns. If desired, serve with mustard, catsup, onion, pickle, and/or peppers. Serves 4.

Nutrition information per serving: 405 calories, 26 g protein, 40 g carbohydrate, 15 g total fat (4 g saturated), 114 mg cholesterol, 477 mg sodium, 460 mg potassium

Missouri

HAMBURGERS

Despite attempts to dress it up with fancy buns and special sauces, the hamburger has always been food for the masses. It became popular at the St. Louis Exposition of 1904 and probably was named after the German city of Hamburg.

1   **pound ground beef, ground pork, *or* ground turkey**
2   **tablespoons catsup**
1   **teaspoon prepared mustard**
1   **teaspoon Worcestershire sauce**
½   **teaspoon onion salt *or* garlic salt**
¼   **teaspoon pepper**
4   **slices American, Swiss, cheddar, *or* brick cheese (optional)**
4   **hamburger buns, split and toasted**
    Catsup, mustard, *and/or* pickle slices (optional)

In a mixing bowl stir together the ground beef, pork, or turkey; catsup; mustard; Worcestershire sauce; onion salt or garlic salt; and pepper.

Shape the meat mixture into four ½- or ¾-inch-thick patties. Place patties on the unheated rack of a broiler pan. Broil 3 to 4 inches from the heat till no pink remains, turning once. Allow 10 to 12 minutes for ½-inch-thick patties or 15 to 18 minutes for ¾-inch-thick patties.

If desired, top burgers with a slice of cheese. Broil just till cheese melts. Place burgers on toasted buns. If desired, serve with catsup, mustard, and/or pickle slices. Makes 4 servings.

Nutrition information per serving: 351 calories, 23 g protein, 25 g carbohydrate, 17 g total fat (6 g saturated), 68 mg cholesterol, 652 mg sodium, 338 mg potassium

Ohio

CINCINNATI CHILI

Texas "chili heads" probably wouldn't eat it, but Cincinnatians love chili their way, or actually three-way, four-way, or five-way. Three-way means chili, spaghetti, and grated yellow cheese. Four-way is three-way plus beans or onions. With five-way, you get it all: chili, spaghetti, cheese, beans, and onions.

2	pounds ground beef
3	large onions, chopped (3 cups)
3	cloves garlic, minced
1	15-ounce can tomato sauce
1	cup beef broth
2	tablespoons chili powder
2	tablespoons semisweet chocolate pieces
2	tablespoons vinegar
2	tablespoons honey
1	tablespoon pumpkin pie spice
1	teaspoon ground cumin
½	teaspoon ground cardamom
¼	teaspoon ground cloves
16	ounces fettuccine, broken into 4-inch lengths
2	15½-ounce cans kidney beans
3	cups shredded American cheese (12 ounces)

In a 4½-quart Dutch oven cook beef, *2 cups* of the onions, and garlic till beef is brown and onion is tender. Drain fat. Stir in remaining ingredients *except* fettuccine, kidney beans, cheese, and remaining onion. Bring to boiling; reduce heat. Cover and simmer over low heat for 1 hour. Skim off fat.

Cook fettuccine; drain. Keep warm. In a 2-quart saucepan heat kidney beans; drain. Keep warm. To serve, divide fettuccine among 8 plates. Make an indentation in center of each fettuccine portion. Top with meat sauce, beans, remaining onions, and cheese. Makes 8 servings.

Nutrition information per serving: 768 calories, 49 g protein, 77 g carbohydrate, 30 g total fat (14 g saturated), 136 mg cholesterol, 1,123 mg sodium, 1,151 mg potassium

Missouri

KC BARBECUED RIBS

Kansas City barbecue boosters aren't shy about promoting their own. Natives of this Missouri city, including writer Calvin Trillin, insist that the smoky, wood-infused barbecue of their hometown is the best.

1   cup water
1   cup catsup
3   tablespoons vinegar
1   tablespoon sugar
1   tablespoon Worcestershire
    sauce
1   teaspoon celery seed
¼   teaspoon bottled hot
    pepper sauce
4   pounds pork loin back ribs
    or meaty spareribs
    (2 strips)

For barbecue sauce, in a saucepan combine water, catsup, vinegar, sugar, Worcestershire sauce, celery seed, and bottled hot pepper sauce. Heat to boiling; reduce heat. Simmer, uncovered, for 30 minutes, stirring occasionally.

Sprinkle ribs with salt and pepper. Lace ribs, accordion style, onto a spit rod, securing with holding forks. Test balance. Arrange *medium-hot* coals around a drip pan; test for *medium* heat where meat will be.

Attach spit, turn on the motor, and lower grill hood. Let ribs rotate over drip pan for 1¼ to 1½ hours or till well-done, brushing ribs with sauce the last 15 minutes of cooking. To serve, remove the meat from the spit. Servings 4..

Indirect grilling: Prepare sauce and ribs as directed. In a covered grill arrange *medium-hot* coals around a drip pan. Test for *medium* heat above the drip pan. Place ribs, fat side up, on the grill rack over the drip pan but not over the coals. Lower grill hood. Grill ribs for 1¼ to 1½ hours or till well-done, brushing often with sauce the last 15 minutes of cooking.

Nutrition information per serving: 498 calories, 49 g protein, 21 g carbohydrate, 24 g total fat (8 g saturated), 134 mg cholesterol, 849 mg sodium, 1,066 mg potassium

Michigan

HAM BALLS WITH CURRANT GLAZE

Red currants grew across northern Europe and were a favorite of the Dutch and the Scandinavians, who would use the fruit in sauces, soups, jellies, and desserts. When they immigrated to the Midwest, these groups cultivated the berry.

2   beaten eggs
¾   cup finely crushed
    graham crackers
    (11 or 12 squares)
½   cup chopped onion
¼   cup milk
1   tablespoon Dijon-style
    mustard
¼   teaspoon pepper
1   pound ground fully cooked
    ham
8   ounces ground pork
    Currant Glaze
    Kumquats (optional)

In a large mixing bowl combine eggs, crushed crackers, onion, milk, mustard, and pepper. Add ground ham and ground pork; mix well. Shape into 12 balls, using about ⅓ *cup* mixture for each ball. Place ham balls in a lightly greased 2-quart rectangular baking dish.

Bake ham balls, uncovered, in a 350° oven about 45 minutes or till juices run clear. Remove balls from baking dish; spoon Currant Glaze over ham balls. If desired garnish with kumquats. Makes 6 servings.

Currant Glaze: In a small saucepan combine ½ cup *currant jelly*, 1 tablespoon *prepared horseradish*, 1 teaspoon finely shredded *orange peel*, and 1 tablespoon *orange juice*. Cook and stir till jelly melts and mixture is smooth.

Nutrition information per serving:
356 calories, 30 g protein, 31 g carbohydrate, 12 g total fat (4 g saturated), 141 mg cholesterol, 1,227 mg sodium, 428 mg potassium

Minnesota

SPINACH-TOPPED PIKE WITH CHEESE SAUCE

Along the upper reaches of the Midwest, hardy fishermen bait their lines and go for pike during the cold winter. The white-fleshed fish lives in lakes and streams in the northern United States and Canada. The Shakers of northern Ohio would fish for pike in the waters of Lake Erie.

6   fresh *or* frozen northern pike *or* whitefish fillets (about 1½ pounds)
2   tablespoons margarine *or* butter
2   tablespoons all-purpose flour
1¼ cups milk
1   cup shredded cheddar cheese (4 ounces)
1   10-ounce package frozen, chopped spinach, thawed and well drained
1   beaten egg
1   cup corn-bread stuffing mix
¼   cup grated Parmesan cheese *or* Romano cheese
¼   cup dairy sour cream
4   slices bacon, crisp-cooked, drained, and crumbled

Thaw fish, if frozen. For sauce, in a saucepan melt margarine. Stir in flour. Add milk all at once. Cook and stir till bubbly. Cook and stir 1 minute more. Add cheddar cheese; stir till cheese melts. Set aside.

For stuffing, mix spinach, egg, stuffing mix, Parmesan cheese, sour cream, and crumbled bacon. Stir ⅓ *cup* of the sauce into the stuffing.

Place fillets lengthwise in a 3-quart rectangular baking dish. Spoon *one-sixth* of the stuffing over each fillet in dish. Bake, covered, in a 350° oven for 25 to 30 minutes or till fish flakes easily with a fork.

To serve, reheat sauce and serve over each fillet and stuffing. Pass remaining sauce. Makes 6 servings.

Nutrition information per serving:
555 calories, 53 g protein, 23 g carbohydrate, 28 g total fat (13 g saturated), 172 mg cholesterol, 790 mg sodium, 862 mg potassium

Iowa

SAUSAGE-AND-APPLE-STUFFED IOWA CHOPS

After the Civil War, the introduction of refrigerated railroad cars allowed the center of the pork industry to shift from the Ohio Valley (Cincinnati was once known as Porkopolis) to a handful of states farther to the west. Iowa is now the country's top pork producer.

4 pork loin rib chops,
     cut 1¼ inches thick
     (about 2 pounds total)
½ pound bulk pork sausage
1 cup chopped onion
1 cup corn-bread stuffing
     mix
⅔ cup shredded apple
2 teaspoons snipped fresh
     thyme *or* ½ teaspoon
     dried thyme, crushed
¼ teaspoon pepper
⅓ cup apple cider *or* apple
     juice
⅓ cup apple jelly
1 tablespoon lemon juice
     Apple wedges (optional)

Trim fat from chops. Cut a pocket in each chop by cutting a slit the length of the fat side almost to the bone. Set chops aside.

For stuffing, in a large skillet cook sausage and onion till sausage is brown and onion is tender; drain well. Stir in stuffing mix, shredded apple, thyme, and pepper. Drizzle with *2 tablespoons* of the apple cider to moisten, tossing lightly.

Spoon about *2 tablespoons* of the stuffing into each pork chop pocket. Secure pockets with wooden

toothpicks. Stir remaining apple cider into remaining stuffing.

Place stuffed pork chops on a rack in a shallow roasting pan. Place remaining stuffing in a greased 1-quart casserole. Cover and refrigerate till ready to bake.

For glaze, in a small saucepan, combine apple jelly and lemon juice. Cook and stir till jelly melts; brush chops with some of the glaze.

Bake chops, uncovered, in a 375° oven for 20 minutes. Brush again with glaze. Place covered casserole of stuffing in oven beside pork chops. Bake about 20 minutes more or till no pink remains in chops and stuffing is heated through. If desired, garnish with apple wedges. Makes 4 servings.

Nutrition information per serving: *569 calories, 45 g protein, 48 g carbohydrate, 23 g total fat (8 g saturated), 118 mg cholesterol, 998 mg sodium, 735 mg potassium*

Illinois

BIGOS

A majority of the Polish immigrants who arrived in the United States after 1900 chose city life over rural and became factory workers. Chicago's Polish population rivals that of Warsaw. This hunter's stew is an old-world recipe originally prepared with bear or other game.

6 slices bacon, cut in 1-inch
     pieces
1 large onion, chopped (1
     cup)
8 ounces boneless beef,
     cut in 1-inch cubes
8 ounces boneless pork,
     cut in 1-inch cubes

8 ounces fully cooked Polish
sausage, sliced
2 cups sliced fresh mush-
rooms
2 cups beef broth
½ cup dry white wine
1 teaspoon paprika
1 bay leaf
2 16-ounce cans sauerkraut,
drained and snipped

Cook bacon and onion till bacon is cooked and onion is tender. Drain, reserving *2 tablespoons* drippings. Set aside. Brown beef and pork cubes in reserved drippings; drain.

Stir in bacon-onion mixture, sausage, mushrooms, broth, wine, paprika, and bay leaf. Simmer till meat is tender, about 1½ to 2 hours. Stir in sauerkraut. Heat through. Remove bay leaf. Makes 6 servings.

Nutrition information per serving: 272 calories, 20 g protein, 7 g carbohydrate, 17 g total fat (6 g saturated), 68 mg cholesterol, 943 mg sodium, 545 mg potassium

Iowa

CHICKEN WITH MAYTAG BLUE CHEESE SAUCE

Across the top of the stationery of the Maytag Dairy Farms in Newton, Iowa, is written "Famous Blue Cheese." For over fifty years, the small dairy, located about an hour from Des Moines and owned by the family that developed the Maytag washing machine, has been producing a quality product from its herd of prize Holsteins.

4 medium skinless, boneless,
chicken breast halves
(12 ounces total)
1 tablespoon olive oil *or*
cooking oil
⅓ cup finely chopped green
onion
1 clove garlic, minced
2 tablespoons margarine *or*
butter
3 tablespoons all-purpose
flour
¼ teaspoon pepper
¾ cup chicken broth
½ cup whipping cream
1½ teaspoons white wine
Worcestershire sauce
1 beaten egg yolk
¼ cup crumbled Maytag blue
cheese *or* other blue
cheese

In a large skillet cook chicken in hot oil over medium heat for 8 to 10 minutes or till chicken is tender and no pink remains, turning often to brown evenly.

Meanwhile, in a medium saucepan cook green onion and garlic in margarine or butter till tender. Stir in flour and pepper. Add chicken broth, whipping cream, and white wine Worcestershire sauce all at once. Cook and stir over medium heat till thickened and bubbly. Reduce heat. Gradually stir about *half* of the hot mixture into the beaten egg yolk. Transfer entire egg mixture to saucepan. Bring to a gentle boil. Cook and stir 2 minutes more. Stir in blue cheese. Serve sauce over chicken. Serves 4.

Nutrition information per serving: 372 calories, 25 g protein, 7 g carbohydrate, 27 g total fat (11 g saturated), 155 mg cholesterol, 395 mg sodium, 298 mg potassium

Wisconsin

SAUSAGE AND KRAUT

The Germans are master-wurst makers. They also know how to ferment sliced cabbage in a caraway-seasoned brine to make a crunchy sauerkraut accompaniment. Sauerkraut is so popular in the Midwest that one regional cookbook offers a recipe for a sauerkraut sandwich: kraut, mustard dressing, and radishes!

4	fully cooked smoked bratwurst, knockwurst, *or* Polish sausage (about 12 ounces total)
6	cups shredded cabbage
1	cup water
½	cup chopped onion
½	cup shredded carrot
1	teaspoon caraway seed
¼	teaspoon pepper
⅛	teaspoon salt
4	slices process Swiss cheese, torn (4 ounces)

Make slits in bratwurst at 1-inch intervals, cutting to, but not through, opposite side. Set aside.

In a 12-inch skillet combine cabbage, water, onion, carrot, caraway seed, pepper, and salt. Arrange bratwurst atop cabbage mixture. Bring to boiling; reduce heat. Cover and simmer for 10 to 15 minutes or till cabbage is tender and bratwurst in heated through.

Remove bratwurst from skillet; keep warm. Drain cabbage mixture. Add Swiss cheese to cabbage. Stir over low heat till cheese is melted. Serve cabbage with bratwurst. Makes 4 servings.

Nutrition information per serving: 344 calories, 17 g protein, 11 g carbohydrate, 26 g total fat (12 g saturated), 63 mg cholesterol, 1,164 mg sodium, 540 mg potassium

Wisconsin

BRATS AND BEER

Milwaukee, on the Wisconsin side of Lake Michigan, attracted a large number of Germans immigrating to this country after 1830. It's not surprising that a brewery opened in that city early in the next decade. Bottled beer is a Milwaukee invention of the 1870s. Beer and bratwurst are the usual fare at local events wherever Germans have settled.

4	fresh bratwursts (about 12 ounces total)
1	12-ounce can beer
10	whole black peppercorns
1	large onion, sliced and separated into rings
1	tablespoon margarine *or* butter
1½	teaspoons caraway seed
2	tablespoons white wine vinegar
1	teaspoon Worcestershire sauce
4	frankfurter buns, split and toasted Coarse-grain brown mustard

Use a fork to prick several holes in the skin of each bratwurst. In a saucepan combine bratwursts, beer, and peppercorns. Bring to boiling; reduce heat. Cover; simmer about 20 minutes or till bratwursts are no longer pink. Drain.

Meanwhile, in a small skillet cook onion in hot margarine till tender but not brown. Add caraway seed and cook 5 minutes more. Stir in the vinegar and the Worcestershire sauce.

Grill bratwursts on an uncovered grill directly over *medium-hot* coals for 7 to 8 minutes or till skins are golden, turning frequently. Serve bratwursts on buns with mustard. Spoon onion mixture over brat-wursts. Makes 4 servings.

Nutrition information per serving:
362 calories, 12 g protein, 28 g carbohydrate, 20 g total fat (6 g saturated), 34 mg cholesterol, 585 mg sodium, 273 mg potassium

South Dakota

PHEASANT MARSALA

Pheasant was not one of the wild game birds available to the pioneers. It was introduced at the turn of the century. The ring-necked pheasant continues to be a favorite of Midwest hunters.

2	to 2½ pounds cut-up pheasant *or* broiler-fryer chicken
2	tablespoons cooking oil
2	tablespoons margarine *or* butter

3	cups sliced fresh mushrooms
1	cup small onion wedges
2	garlic cloves, minced
½	cup chicken broth
¼	cup marsala wine
½	teaspoon finely shredded orange peel
¼	teaspoon juniper berries
1	8-ounce carton dairy sour cream
2	tablespoons all-purpose flour

Rinse pheasant breasts and remove skin. In a large skillet, heat oil and margarine or butter. Brown pheasant in hot oil mixture till golden. Place in a 2-quart rectangular baking dish or a 2-quart casserole. Sprinkle with salt and pepper. Add mushrooms, onion, and garlic to skillet. Cook till onion is tender. Stir in broth, wine, orange peel, and juniper berries. Pour over breasts. Cover; bake in a 325° oven for 45 to 60 minutes or till meat is tender.

Using a slotted spoon, transfer meat and vegetables to a serving platter; keep warm.

Pour juices into a saucepan. Stir together sour cream and flour. Add to juices; cook and stir till bubbly. Cook and stir 1 minute more. Pour some sour cream sauce over meat and vegetables; pass remaining sauce when serving. Serves 4.

Nutrition information per serving:
595 calories, 60 g protein, 12 g carbohydrate, 32 g total fat (12 g saturated), 156 mg cholesterol, 388 mg sodium, 944 mg potassium

Wisconsin

WISCONSIN BEER-CHEESE CHOWDER

This recipe is a showcase for Wisconsin fine foods. The state is one of the nation's largest cheese producers, manufacturing about one-third of the entire domestic supply, while Milwaukee is famous for its beer and sausage.

1½	cups small broccoli flowerets
¾	cup shredded carrot
¾	cup chicken broth *or* water
¼	cup chopped onion
¼	cup margarine *or* butter
¼	cup all-purpose flour
½	teaspoon dry mustard
¼	teaspoon pepper
2	cups milk
1	3-ounce package cream cheese, cut into cubes and softened
8	ounces fully cooked Polish sausage, cut into thin slices
1½	cups shredded sharp cheddar cheese *or* American cheese (6 ounces)
¾	cup beer

In a medium saucepan combine broccoli, carrot, chicken broth or water, and onion. Bring to boiling. Reduce heat and simmer, covered, for 8 to 10 minutes or till tender. *Do not drain;* set aside.

Meanwhile, in a large saucepan melt margarine or butter. Stir in flour, dry mustard, and pepper. Add milk all at once. Cook and stir till thickened and bubbly. Cook and stir 1 minute more. In a mixing bowl stir about ½ *cup* of the hot milk mixture into the cream cheese; stir till well combined. Stir cream cheese mixture into remaining milk mixture in saucepan. Stir sausage, cheddar or American cheese, and beer into thickened mixture. Cook and stir over low heat till cheese melts and sausage is heated through. Stir in *undrained* vegetables; heat through. Ladle into soup bowls. Makes 4 servings.

Nutrition information per serving: 669 calories, 28 g protein, 21 g carbohydrate, 52 g total fat (23 g saturated), 117 mg cholesterol, 1,142 mg sodium, 648 mg potassium

Michigan

TURKEY WITH CREAMY MOREL SAUCE

In the spring, mushroom hunters throughout the Midwest thrill to the chase: it's time to stalk that most special fungus, the wild morel. Michigan is particularly well known for this woodland delicacy.

4	turkey breast steaks *or* 4 medium skinless, boneless, chicken breast halves (12 ounces total)
3	tablespoons all-purpose flour
¼	teaspoon salt
¼	teaspoon lemon-pepper seasoning
3	tablespoons margarine *or* butter

2   ounces fresh morels *or*
    ½ ounce dried morels,
    rehydrated*
2   tablespoons sliced green
    onion
1   clove garlic, minced
1¼ cups half-and-half, light
    cream, *or* milk
1   tablespoon all-purpose
    flour
1   tablespoon dry sherry
    Fresh herbs (optional)

Rinse turkey; pat dry. Combine the 3 tablespoons flour, salt, and lemon-pepper seasoning; coat turkey with flour mixture.

In a large skillet cook turkey in *2 tablespoons* of the margarine or butter over medium heat for 8 to 10 minutes or till tender and no pink remains, turning once. Transfer turkey to individual plates; cover to keep warm.

Cut any large morels into bite-size strips. For sauce, in the same skillet cook morels, green onion, and garlic in the remaining margarine or butter for 3 to 4 minutes or till tender.

Combine half-and-half and the 1 tablespoon flour; add to vegetables in skillet. Cook and stir till thickened and bubbly; add sherry. Cook and stir for 1 minute more. Season to taste with salt and pepper.

Spoon some of the sauce over turkey; pass remainder when serving. If desired, garnish with fresh herbs. Makes 4 servings.

*Note: To rehydrate dried morels, cover them with warm water. Let stand for 30 to 45 minutes; drain. You should have ¾ cup.

Nutrition information per serving:
301 calories, 23 g protein, 11 g carbohydrate, 18 g total fat (7 g saturated), 83 mg cholesterol, 324 mg sodium, 353 mg potassium

Minnesota

NORWEGIAN FRUIT SOUP

Of all the Scandinavians to settle in the United States, the Norwegians were firstcomers, beginning in earnest in the 1840s and reaching a total of three-quarters of a million by World War I. Cold fruit soups are a Scandinavian specialty.

1   8-ounce package mixed
     dried fruit
3½   cups water
¼   cup packed brown sugar
4   teaspoons quick-cooking
     tapioca
¼   teaspoon ground nutmeg
1   16-ounce can pitted light
     sweet cherries
¼   cup orange liqueur *or*
     cream sherry

Pit prunes (from mixed dried fruit), if necessary, and cut fruit into bite-size pieces. In a large saucepan stir together the water, brown sugar, quick-cooking tapioca, and nutmeg. Let stand for 5 minutes. Stir in dried fruit. Bring to boiling. Reduce heat and simmer, covered, for 8 to 10 minutes or till fruit is tender. Mixture should be slightly thickened and tapioca should be clear.

Stir in *undrained* cherries and orange liqueur or sherry. Heat through. Serve warm or chilled in bowls. Makes 8 servings.

Nutrition information per serving:
164 calories, 1 g protein, 38 g carbohydrate, 1 g total fat (1 g saturated), 1 mg cholesterol, 16 mg sodium, 326 mg potassium

Illinois

CHICAGO-STYLE DEEP-DISH SPINACH PIZZA

When Chicagoans Ike Sewell and Ric Riccardo decided to open Pizzeria Uno in 1943, they concluded that the traditional thin-crusted pizza so popular in the East just wouldn't make it in the Windy City. They developed a substantial two-crust version that became wildly successful and widely imitated.

¾ pound bulk Italian sausage
1 cup chopped onion
1 8-ounce can pizza sauce
1 4-ounce can sliced mushrooms, drained
1 3-ounce package sliced pepperoni
2 tablespoons snipped fresh basil *or* 2 teaspoons dried basil, crushed
1 tablespoon snipped fresh oregano *or* 1 teaspoon dried oregano, crushed
¼ teaspoon crushed red pepper
1 16-ounce loaf frozen whole wheat bread dough *or* white bread dough, thawed
1½ cups shredded mozzarella cheese (6 ounces)

1 10-ounce package frozen chopped spinach, thawed and well drained
1 slightly beaten egg
1 tablespoon margarine *or* butter, melted
2 tablespoons grated Parmesan cheese *or* Romano cheese

For meat filling, in a large skillet cook Italian sausage and onion till meat is brown and onion is tender. Drain fat. Pat with paper towels to remove additional fat. Stir in pizza sauce, mushrooms, pepperoni, basil, oregano, and red pepper.

For crust, on a lightly floured surface roll *two-thirds* of the bread dough into a 12-inch circle. (If necessary, let dough rest once or twice during rolling.) Carefully place the circle in a greased 9-inch spring-form pan, pressing the dough 1½-inches up the sides. Sprinkle bottom of the dough with *½ cup* of the mozzarella cheese. Spoon meat filling over cheese.

Pat spinach dry with paper towels. Mix spinach, egg, and remaining mozzarella cheese. Spread spinach mixture over meat filling.

Roll remaining dough into a 10-inch circle on a lightly floured surface.

Cut circle into 10 to 12 wedges. Arrange wedges atop spinach mixture, slightly overlapping edges and sealing ends to bottom crust along edge of pan. Brush top with melted margarine or butter and sprinkle with Parmesan or Romano cheese.

Bake in a 375° oven for 40 to 45 minutes or till filling is hot and bread is done. If necessary, cover with foil the last 10 minutes of baking to prevent overbrowning. Cool on a wire rack for 10 minutes. Remove sides of springform pan. Cut into wedges. Makes 8 servings.

Nutrition information per serving: 392 calories, 22 g protein, 32 g carbohydrate, 20 g total fat (17 g saturated), 71 mg cholesterol, 1,078 mg sodium, 293 mg potassium

Nebraska

PORK ROAST WITH APPLES AND MUSHROOMS

Pork was the meat most available to plains homesteaders. It appeared on the table with unfailing regularity, as well as in the household's soap and shortening (in the form of lard). One Nebraska cook even made her fruitcake with chopped pork, probably in an attempt to create something new with the same tiresome ingredients.

2   tablespoons snipped fresh
    thyme *or* 2 teaspoons
    dried thyme, crushed
½   teaspoon salt
¼   teaspoon pepper
1   3 to 4-pound boneless
    pork loin roast
    (double loin, tied)
⅓   cup apple cider *or* apple
    juice
2   cups whipping cream
1   cup chicken broth
¼   cup dry sherry
2   tablespoons margarine *or*
    butter
3   or 4 small cooking apples,
    peeled, cored, and cut
    into wedges
2   cups sliced fresh mush-
    rooms

Combine thyme, salt, and pepper; rub pork roast with thyme mixture. Place roast on a rack in a shallow roasting pan. Insert meat thermometer. Roast in a 325° oven for 1½ to 2½ hours or till meat thermometer registers 160°. Transfer meat to a platter; keep warm.

For sauce, skim fat from pan juices. Place roasting pan over medium heat; add apple cider or apple juice, stirring to scrape up any browned bits. Pour into a large saucepan. Stir in whipping cream, chicken broth, and dry sherry. Bring to boiling. Cook over medium-high heat about 20 minutes or till reduced to 1½ cups, stirring occasionally.

Meanwhile, in a large skillet melt the margarine or butter; add apple wedges and cook and stir till golden. Remove apple wedges from skillet with slotted spoon, reserving drippings; keep warm.

In the same skillet; add mushrooms to reserved drippings and cook till tender. Stir into thickened cream mixture.

To serve, place slices of pork roast and apples wedges on individual plates. Spoon sauce over meat. Makes 12 to 14 servings.

Nutrition information per serving: 344 calories, 26 g protein, 6 g carbohydrate, 25 g total fat (13 g saturated), 122 mg cholesterol, 225 mg sodium, 489 mg potassium

Minnesota

SWEDISH LIMPA BREAD

In Swedish, limpa means "loaf of bread," usually one made with rye flour. To Swedes in this country, it is specifically a type of free-form rye bread flavored with grated orange peel.

3¼   to 3¾ cups all-purpose
       flour
2   packages active dry yeast
2   teaspoons caraway seed
½   teaspoon fennel seed
       (optional)
2   cups milk
½   cup packed brown sugar
2   tablespoons molasses
2   tablespoons margarine *or*
       butter
1   teaspoon salt
2   tablespoons grated orange
       peel
2½   cups rye flour

In a large mixing bowl combine *2½ cups* of the all-purpose flour, the yeast, caraway seed, and, if desired, fennel seed.

In a saucepan combine the milk, brown sugar, molasses, margarine or butter, and salt; heat just till warm (120° to130°), stirring con-stantly. Add to dry mixture in mixing bowl; add orange peel. Beat with an electric mixer on low speed for 30 seconds, scraping sides of bowl. Beat 3 minutes at high speed. Use a wooden spoon to stir in as much of the rye flour as you can.

Turn dough out onto a floured surface. Knead in enough of the remaining all-purpose flour to make a moderately stiff dough that is smooth and elastic (6 to 8 minutes). Shape the dough into a ball. Place dough in a greased bowl; turn once to grease surface. Cover and let rise in a warm place till double (about 1 hour).

Punch dough down; divide in half. Cover and let rest 10 minutes. Shape into 2 round loaves; place loaves on a greased baking sheet. Cover and let rise in a warm place till nearly double (about 30 minutes). Bake in a 375° oven about 35 minutes. Remove from pans; cool on a wire rack. Makes 2 loaves (32 servings).

Nutrition information per serving:
102 calories, 3 g protein, 20 g carbohydrate, 1 g total fat (0 g saturated), 1 mg cholesterol, 82 mg sodium, 102 mg potassium

Kansas

KANSAS WHOLE WHEAT-HONEY BREAD

One problem in opening up the prairie was that wheat did not grow well there. Then in the early 1870s, members of the German religious sect called Mennonites immigrated to Kansas. Each family brought along carefully selected seed wheat which had come originally from Turkey. This hard winter wheat, known as Turkey red, thrived where other varieties failed.

3 to 3½ cups all-purpose flour
1 package active dry yeast
1½ cups water
⅓ cup honey
3 tablespoons shortening, margarine, *or* butter
1 teaspoon salt
2 cups whole wheat flour
1 slightly beaten egg white
1 tablespoon water
2 tablespoons roasted sunflower nuts *or* chopped toasted pine nuts

In a large mixing bowl combine *2 cups* of the all-purpose flour and the yeast; set aside. In a medium saucepan heat and stir water, honey, shortening, and salt just till warm (120° to 130°) and shortening almost melts. Add to flour mixture. Beat with an electric mixer on low speed for 30 seconds, scraping bowl constantly. Beat on high speed for 3 minutes. Using a wooden spoon, stir in the whole wheat flour and as much of the remaining all-purpose flour as you can.

Turn out onto a lightly floured surface. Knead in enough remaining all-purpose flour to make a moderately stiff dough that is smooth and elastic (6 to 8 minutes total). Shape dough into a ball. Place dough in a lightly greased bowl; turn once to grease surface. Cover and let rise in a warm place till double (1 to 1½ hours).

Punch dough down. Turn out onto a lightly floured surface. Divide dough into 4 equal portions. Cover and let rest 10 minutes.

Roll each portion into an evenly thick 14-inch-long rope. Loosely twist 2 ropes together; press ends together to seal. Repeat with remaining 2 ropes. Place bread twists on a greased baking sheet. Cover; let rise in a warm place till nearly double (30 to 35 minutes).

Mix egg white and water; brush tops of loaves. Sprinkle loaves with sunflower nuts or pine nuts. Bake in a 375° oven about 35 minutes or till bread sounds hollow when tapped. If necessary, cover loosely with foil the last 10 to 15 minutes to prevent overbrowning. Cool. Makes 2 loaves (32 servings).

Nutrition information per serving: 94 calories, 3 g protein, 17 g carbohydrate, 2 g total fat (0 g saturated), 0 mg cholesterol, 69 mg sodium, 54 mg potassium

Illinois

PIEROGIS

*Polish-Americans maintain strong
cultural ties to the old country,
especially when it comes to food. Pierogis
are a Christmas tradition. These little
cheese-filled pouches are an important
part of the Festival of the Star, a dinner
to commemorate the birth of Christ.*

1	beaten egg yolk
½	cup water
¼	teaspoon salt
1½	cups all-purpose flour
¾	cup cream-style cottage cheese, drained
1	slightly beaten egg white
1	tablespoon sugar
⅛	teaspoon salt
1	cup chopped onion
3	tablespoons margarine *or* butter

In a bowl combine the egg yolk,
water, and salt. Stir in flour to
make a stiff dough. On floured surface knead till smooth. Divide
dough in half. Roll *half* the dough
to less than ⅛ inch thick. Cut into
twenty-eight 3-inch circles.

For filling, combine cottage
cheese, egg white, sugar, and salt.
To make pierogi, place *1 teaspoon*
cottage cheese filling on half of
each circle. Fold dough over the
filling to form a half-circle; seal
edge with the tines of a fork. Set
aside. Repeat with remaining
dough and filling.

Cook onion in margarine or butter over low heat about 20 minutes
or till very tender. Keep warm.

Meanwhile, in a large kettle
bring 12 cups *salted water* to boiling.
Add 10 to 12 pierogis; cook 8 to 10
minutes. Drain on paper towels.

Transfer to a serving dish; keep
warm. Repeat till all are cooked.
Serve pierogis topped with cooked
onions. Makes 7 servings.

Nutrition information per serving:
*149 calories, 7 g protein, 25 g carbohydrate,
2 g total fat (1 g saturated), 34 mg cholesterol, 221 mg sodium, 93 mg potassium*

Ohio

BLACK WALNUT AND DATE PUDDING CAKE

*Cakewalks were social events that
afforded isolated homesteaders
the opportunity to show off their baking
skills. For a fee, a participant was
allowed to walk to music around a
circle of numbers marked on the floor.
When the music stopped, a number
would be called. Whoever was standing
on that number won a cake donated by
one of the guests.*

1¼	cups all-purpose flour
⅓	cup packed brown sugar
¾	teaspoon baking soda
½	teaspoon baking powder
⅛	teaspoon ground nutmeg
	Dash ground cloves
1	cup pitted whole dates, snipped
3	tablespoons margarine *or* butter, cut up
1	cup boiling water
1	teaspoon vanilla
½	cup chopped black walnuts
1½	cups boiling water
1	cup packed brown sugar
	Whipped cream (optional)

Combine the flour, the ⅓ cup brown sugar, the baking soda, baking powder, nutmeg, cloves, and ¼ teaspoon *salt.* Set aside.

Combine dates and margarine. Add the 1 cup boiling water. Stir till margarine melts. Stir in vanilla. Stir date mixture and black walnuts into the flour mixture just till smooth. Spread in an ungreased 2-quart square baking dish.

Stir together the 1½ cups boiling water and the 1 cup brown sugar. Pour evenly over batter in pan. Bake in a 350° oven about 45 minutes or till cake tests done. Serve cake warm. If desired, serve with whipped cream. Makes 9 servings.

Nutrition information per *servings:* *275 calories, 4 g protein, 50 g carbohydrate, 8 g total fat (1 g saturated), 0 mg cholesterol, 187 mg sodium, 260 mg potassium*

North Dakota

HOT GERMAN POTATO AND PEA SALAD

Potato salad made an appearance at just about every church supper and family reunion in the Midwest. If the salad was German style, the potatoes were tossed while still warm in a vinegar-based dressing.

4	medium potatoes (about 1¼ pounds)
4	slices bacon
½	cup chopped onion
1	tablespoon all-purpose flour
1	tablespoon sugar
¾	teaspoon salt
½	teaspoon celery seed
⅛	teaspoon pepper
⅔	cup water
¼	cup balsamic vinegar *or* white wine vinegar
1	cup frozen peas
¼	cup snipped fresh basil, oregano, *or* parsley

In a covered saucepan cook potatoes in boiling salted water for 20 to 25 minutes or till potatoes are just tender; drain well. Cool slightly. Peel and slice potatoes. Set potatoes aside while preparing dressing.

For dressing, in a large skillet cook bacon till crisp. Drain bacon on paper towels, reserving *2 tablespoons* drippings in skillet. Crumble bacon and set aside. Cook onion in reserved drippings till tender.

Stir in flour, sugar, salt, celery seed, and pepper. Stir in water and vinegar. Cook and stir till thickened and bubbly. Stir in potatoes, bacon, and peas. Cook for 2 to 3 minutes more or till heated through, stirring gently. Fold in basil, oregano, or parsley. Transfer to a serving bowl. Serve warm. Makes 4 servings.

Nutrition information per *serving:* *276 calories, 7 g protein, 39 g carbohydrate, 10 g total fat (4 g saturated), 13 mg cholesterol, 591 mg sodium, 659 mg potassium*

Wisconsin

APPLE STRUDEL

According to the famous Settlement Cookbook *of 1903 by Mrs. Simon Kander, a proper strudel dough must be worked "until it is as large as the table and as thin as paper." Frozen phyllo dough lends modern convenience to an otherwise lengthy task.*

½   cup packed brown sugar
¾   teaspoon ground cinnamon
½   teaspoon finely shredded
        orange peel
3   cups thinly sliced, peeled
        tart apples *or* pears
⅓   cup raisins
10   to 12 sheets frozen phyllo
        dough, thawed
⅓   cup margarine *or* butter,
        melted
2   tablespoons margarine *or*
        butter, melted
2   tablespoons finely crushed
        vanilla wafers
        (optional)
2   cups whipped cream

For filling, in a bowl stir together brown sugar, cinnamon, and orange peel. Add apples or pears and raisins, then gently toss till coated. Set filling aside. Lightly grease a 15x10x1-inch baking pan; set aside.

Cover a large surface with a cloth; flour cloth. Stack 2 sheets of phyllo on the floured cloth. *(Do not brush margarine or butter between sheets.)* Arrange another stack of 2 sheets on the cloth, overlapping the stacks 2 inches. Add 3 or 4 more stacks, forming a rectangle about 40x20 inches (stagger stacks so all seams are not down the middle). Trim to a 40x20-inch rectangle. Brush with the *⅓ cup* melted margarine or butter

Beginning 4 inches from a short side of dough, spoon the filling in a 4-inch-wide band across dough. Using the cloth underneath dough as a guide, gently lift the 4-inch piece of dough and lay it over the filling. Slowly and evenly lift the cloth and roll the dough and filling, jelly-roll style, into a tight roll. If necessary, cut excess dough from ends to within 1 inch of filling. Fold ends under to seal.

Carefully transfer strudel roll to the prepared baking pan. Curve ends together to form an 8-inch ring. Brush top of strudel with the 2 tablespoons melted margarine. If desired, sprinkle with vanilla wafer crumbs. Bake in a 350° oven for 35 to 40 minutes or till golden. Carefully remove from pan; cool.

Serve whipped cream with strudel. Makes 12 to 16 servings.

Nutrition information per serving: 272 calories, 3 g protein, 27 g carbohydrate, 18 g total fat (6 g saturated), 45 mg cholesterol, 95 mg sodium, 126 mg potassium

Ohio

WALNUT POTICA

The Slovenes are a central European group from the area that was known until recently as northwestern Yugoslavia. This rich nut roll is a Slovenian favorite.

2	to 2½ cups all-purpose flour
1	package active dry yeast
⅓	cup milk
¼	cup margarine *or* butter
2	tablespoons sugar
2	eggs
3	cups ground walnuts
¾	cup sugar
¼	cup margarine *or* butter,
¼	cup honey
1	slightly beaten egg
3	tablespoons milk
½	teaspoon vanilla

In a bowl combine *1 cup* of the flour and the yeast; set aside. In a saucepan heat the ⅓ cup milk, ¼ cup margarine, the 2 tablespoons sugar, and ½ teaspoon *salt* just till warm (120° to 130°) and margarine almost melts. Add to flour mixture. Then add 2 eggs. Beat with an electric mixer on low to medium speed for 30 seconds, scraping bowl. Beat on high speed for 3 minutes. Using a wooden spoon, stir in as much of the remaining flour as you can.

On a lightly floured surface, knead in enough of the remaining flour to make a moderately soft dough that is smooth and elastic (3 to 5 minutes total). Shape into a ball. Place dough in a greased bowl, turning once to grease surface. Cover and let rise in a warm place till double (1 to 1¼ hours).

Meanwhile, for filling, mix walnuts, the ¾ cup sugar, ¼ cup margarine, honey, remaining egg and milk, and the vanilla. Set aside.

Punch dough down. Cover and let rest 10 minutes. Meanwhile, lightly grease two 7½x3½x2- or 8x4x2-inch loaf pans. Cover with a floured cloth. On the cloth, roll dough into a 15-inch square. Cover and let rest 10 minutes. Then roll dough into a 30x20-inch rectangle.

To assemble, cut dough lengthwise in half to form two 30x10-inch sheets. Spread filling evenly over surface of both dough rectangles, keeping to within 1 inch of the edges. Using the cloth as a guide, roll each rectangle up jelly-roll style, starting from a short side. Pinch seams and ends to seal. Place loaves, seam sides down, in the prepared loaf pans. Cover and let rise till nearly double (45 to 60 minutes).

Bake in a 325° oven 45 to 50 minutes or till golden brown. If necessary, cover with foil the last 15 minutes of baking to prevent overbrowning. Remove from pans; cool. Makes 2 loaves (32 servings).

Nutrition information per serving: *165 calories, 3 g protein, 16 g carbohydrate, 10 g total fat (1 g saturated), 20 mg cholesterol, 67 mg sodium, 78 mg potassium*

Missouri

FRESH TOMATO SCALLOP WITH HORSERADISH SAUCE

Missouri was populated with immigrants from Europe and also with New Englanders and southerners who wanted to move west. Mary Randolph's 1824 cookbook, The Virginia Housewife, *included a recipe for "scolloped" tomatoes that is very similar to ones that appear in Missouri collections.*

3 large tomatoes
3 tablespoons fine dry bread crumbs
2 tablespoons finely chopped toasted pecans
1 tablespoon grated Parmesan cheese *or* Romano cheese
1 tablespoon snipped fresh marjoram, basil, *or* rosemary *or* ½ teaspoon dried marjoram, basil, *or* rosemary, crushed
1 tablespoon snipped fresh chives
1 tablespoon margarine *or* butter, melted
⅛ teaspoon pepper
   Dash garlic salt
   Horseradish Sauce

Cut each tomato crosswise into 4 slices. Arrange tomato slices in a 2-quart square baking dish, overlapping as necessary.

For topping, combine bread crumbs, pecans, Parmesan cheese, herb, chives, melted margarine, pepper, and garlic salt. Sprinkle topping over tomato slices.

Bake in a 375° oven for 10 to 15 minutes or till hot. Serve with Horseradish Sauce. Serves 4.

Horseradish Sauce: Beat ⅓ cup *whipping cream* till soft peaks form. Fold in 1 to 2 tablespoons *prepared horseradish.* (*Or,* stir 1 to 2 tablespoons *prepared horseradish* into one 8-ounce container *dairy sour cream.*)

Nutrition information per serving: *172 calories, 3 g protein, 11 g carbohydrate, 14 g total fat (5 g saturated), 28 mg cholesterol, 142 mg sodium, 336 mg potassium*

Minnesota

FRUITY WILD RICE PILAF

French and English explorers called the wild water grass enjoyed by Native Americans by a number of names: wild oats, fool's oats, Indian rice, and wild rice.

½ cup chopped onion
½ cup chopped celery
2 tablespoons margarine *or* butter
1½ cups water
¾ cup wild rice, rinsed
1½ teaspoons instant chicken bouillon granules
1 small apple, cored and chopped (1 cup)
2 tablespoons chopped toasted almonds *or* pecans
½ teaspoon finely shredded lemon *or* orange peel

Cook the onion and celery in hot margarine or butter till the vegetables are tender but not brown.

Stir in the water, wild rice, and chicken bouillon granules. Bring to boiling; reduce heat. Cover and simmer for 45 to 50 minutes or till the rice is tender and the liquid is absorbed. Remove from heat.

Gently fold in the apple, almonds or pecans, and lemon or orange peel. Makes 4 to 6 servings.

Nutrition information per serving: 191 calories, 5 g protein, 27 g carbohydrate, 8 g total fat (1 g saturated), 0 mg cholesterol, 402 mg sodium, 224 mg potassium

Indiana

CORN ON THE COB

Corn was one of the first crops planted on the frontier, and it was the food most likely on hand when everything else was gone. As a service to its readers, one Nebraska farm paper of 1862 came up with thirty-three different uses for this vegetable.

4   medium ears of fresh corn
¼   cup butter
1½ teaspoons snipped fresh
    savory *or* thyme *or*
    ½ teaspoon dried
    savory *or* thyme,
    crushed
½   teaspoon finely shredded
    lime peel

Remove husks from corn; scrub with a stiff brush to remove silks. Rinse corn. Cook, uncovered, in enough boiling water to cover for 5 to 7 minutes or till tender.

Meanwhile, mix butter, savory or thyme, and lime peel. Serve with hot corn. Makes 4 servings.

Nutrition information per serving: 183 calories, 3 g protein, 19 g carbohydrate, 12 g total fat (7 g saturated), 31 mg cholesterol, 129 mg sodium, 197 mg potassium

Minnesota

WILD RICE MUFFINS

The Ojibwas (also called Chippewas) of Minnesota still gather the wild grass that they call manomin (good berry) the traditional way: from canoes that they pole through the rice beds that form in local lakes.

1¾ cups all-purpose flour
½   cup shredded cheddar
    cheese (2 ounces)
2   tablespoons sugar
2   teaspoons baking powder
1   beaten egg
1   cup cooked wild rice
¾   cup milk
¼   cup cooking oil

Mix flour, cheese, sugar, baking powder, and ¼ teaspoon *salt*. Make a well in center of dry ingredients.

In another bowl mix egg, cooked rice, milk, and oil; add all at once to dry ingredients. Stir just till moistened (batter should be lumpy).

Lightly grease muffin cups or line them with paper bake cups; fill each cup ⅔ full. Bake in a 400° oven about 20 minutes or till golden. Remove muffins from pans and serve warm. Makes 10 to 12 muffins.

Nutrition information per muffin: 194 calories, 6 g protein, 24 g carbohydrate, 8 g total fat (2 g saturated), 29 mg cholesterol, 168 mg sodium, 74 mg potassium

Missouri

BLACK WALNUT-WILD RASPBERRY BREAD

Black walnuts appear in many old-time midwestern recipes. They are a favorite not only in the Midwest, but in the South and the eastern heartland of Pennsylvania Dutch country.

3	cups all-purpose flour
1	cup sugar
1	tablespoon baking powder
2	teaspoons finely shredded orange peel
¼	teaspoon baking soda
1	beaten egg
1	cup milk
⅔	cup orange juice
¼	cup cooking oil
1	cup fresh *or* frozen wild raspberries *or* raspberries
¾	cup chopped black walnuts
½	cup sifted powdered sugar
2	to 3 teaspoons orange juice

Combine flour, sugar, baking powder, orange peel, baking soda, and ½ teaspoon *salt*. Combine egg, milk, the ⅔ cup orange juice, and oil. Add to flour mixture, stirring just till combined. Stir in raspberries and walnuts.

Pour batter into a greased 9x5x3-inch loaf pan, two 7½x3½x2-inch loaf pans, or six 4½x2½x1½-inch loaf pans. Bake in a 350° oven about 1¼ hours for the 9x5x3-inch loaf (40 to 45 minutes for the 7½x3½x2-inch loaves and 30 to 35 minutes for the 4½x2½x1½-inch loaves)or till a toothpick inserted near the center comes out clean.

Cool in pan(s) for 10 minutes; remove from pan(s). Combine powdered sugar and enough of the 2 to 3 teaspoons orange juice to make an icing of drizzling consistency. Drizzle over warm bread.

Cool bread thoroughly; wrap and store overnight before serving. Makes 1 large loaf, 2 small loaves, or 6 mini loaves (18 servings).

Nutrition information per serving: *207 calories, 4 g protein, 33 g carbohydrate, 7 g total fat (1 g saturated), 13 mg cholesterol, 135 mg sodium, 101 mg potassium*

Nebraska

WHOLE WHEAT-RHUBARB PUDDING CAKE

Early settlers were starved for fresh fruits and vegetables. Planting a garden and orchard was among the first tasks of the homesteaders. Rhubarb thrived on the plains. As it appeared in early spring, it was a symbol of the fresh bounty to come after a long winter of eating dried and preserved foods.

5	cups sliced rhubarb
¼	cup sugar
1¼	cups all-purpose flour
1	cup sugar
½	cup whole wheat flour
½	cup chopped pecans
1¼	teaspoons baking powder
½	teaspoon ground cinnamon
⅛	teaspoon ground nutmeg

¾ cup milk
¼ cup margarine *or* butter, melted
1¼ cups sugar
1 tablespoon cornstarch
Whipped cream (optional)

In a 3-quart rectangular baking dish mix rhubarb and ¼ cup sugar.

Mix the all-purpose flour, the 1 cup sugar, the whole wheat flour, pecans, baking powder, cinnamon, nutmeg and ¼ teaspoon *salt*. Stir in milk and melted margarine. Spread batter evenly over rhubarb.

Mix 1¼ cups sugar and cornstarch. Add 1¼ cups *boiling water;* stir till sugar dissolves. Slowly pour over batter. Bake in a 375° oven about 45 minutes or till top tests done. If necessary, cover the last 10 minutes to prevent overbrowning. Serve warm. If desired, serve with whipped cream. Serves 8 to 10.

Nutrition information per serving: 445 calories, 5 g protein, 86 g carbohydrate, 11 g fat (2 g saturated), 2 mg cholesterol, 195 mg sodium, 313 mg potassium

Minnesota

KRINGLE

Most of the Norwegians who settled in the United States before the Civil War moved to the newly opened territories of the upper Mississippi Valley. Later on, many more homesteaded in the Dakotas, Utah, and Washington.

3 cups all-purpose flour
2½ teaspoons baking powder
1 teaspoon baking soda
¼ teaspoon ground nutmeg *or* cardamom
½ cup butter
1 cup sugar
1 egg
1 teaspoon vanilla
¾ cup buttermilk

Combine flour, baking powder, soda, and nutmeg or cardamom. In a mixing bowl beat butter till softened. Add sugar and beat till fluffy. Add egg and vanilla and beat well. Alternately add flour mixture and buttermilk, beating till well mixed. Chill about 4 hours or overnight.

Divide dough in half. On a floured surface, roll each half into a 10x5-inch rectangle. With a sharp knife, cut each rectangle into twenty 5x½-inch strips. Roll each strip into a 10-inch-long rope. Shape each rope into a loop, crossing 1½ inches from ends. Twist rope at crossing point. Lift loop over to touch ends and seal, forming a pretzel shape. Place cookies on an ungreased cookie sheet.

Bake in a 425° oven about 5 minutes or till cookie bottoms are lightly brown (tops will be pale). Remove from cookie sheet and cool on a wire rack. Makes 40 cookies.

Nutrition information per cookie: 78 calories, 1 g protein, 12 g carbohydrate, 3 g total fat (1 g saturated), 12 mg cholesterol, 57 mg sodium, 18 mg potassium

Iowa

WHOOPIE PIES

These sandwich cookies are real farmhouse treats: a pair of chocolate wafers filled with rich vanilla buttercream and iced with chocolate butter frosting.

½   cup shortening
2   cups all-purpose flour
1¼   cups buttermilk *or* sour milk
1   cup sugar
⅔   cup unsweetened cocoa powder
1   egg
1   teaspoon baking soda
1   teaspoon vanilla
¾   cup milk
¼   cup all-purpose flour
¾   cup margarine *or* butter
2   cups sifted powdered sugar
1   teaspoon vanilla
     Chocolate Butter Frosting

For cookies, beat shortening with an electric mixer on medium to high speed for 30 seconds. Add about *1 cup* of the flour, *half* the buttermilk, sugar, cocoa, egg, baking soda, 1 teaspoon vanilla, and ⅛ teaspoon *salt*. Beat till thoroughly combined. Beat in remaining 1 cup flour and remaining buttermilk. Drop by rounded tablespoons 2 inches apart onto ungreased cookie sheets. Bake in a 350° oven for 8 to 10 minutes or till the edges are firm; cool on a wire rack.

For filling, in a saucepan combine milk and the ¼ cup flour. Cook and stir till thickened and bubbly. Cook and stir 2 minutes more. Remove from heat; cool.

In a mixing bowl beat margarine or butter with an electric mixer on medium to high speed for 30 seconds. Add powdered sugar; beat till fluffy. Add 1 teaspoon vanilla. Beat cooled milk mixture, 1 large spoonful at a time, into margarine mixture. Beat on high for 1 minute or till filling is smooth and fluffy. Spread about *2 tablespoons* filling on the flat side of *half* the cooled cookies. Top with the remaining cookies, flat side down. Frost cookies with Chocolate Butter Frosting. Store in the refrigerator. Makes 14 filled cookies.

Chocolate Butter Frosting: Beat together ¼ cup *unsweetened cocoa powder* and 3 tablespoons *butter or margarine.* Gradually beat in 1 cup sifted *powdered sugar.* Slowly beat in 2 tablespoons *milk* and ½ teaspoon *vanilla.* Gradually beat in another 1 cup sifted *powdered sugar.* Beat in additional *milk,* if needed, to reach spreading consistency.

Nutrition information per serving: *421 calories, 5 g protein, 56 g carbohydrate, 21 g total fat (6 g saturated), 24 mg cholesterol, 222 mg sodium, 171 mg potassium*

Wisconsin

CREAM-AND-LINGONBERRY-FILLED PASTRY CONES

Swedes immigrating to the Midwest didn't have to forgo at least one of their favorite foods. The lingonberries that grew wild in Scandinavia also flourished in the bogs of northern Wisconsin and Minnesota.

2 egg whites
¼ cup butter
½ cup sugar
½ cup all-purpose flour
2 cups Sweetened Whipped Cream
1 14½-ounce can lingonberries, drained, *or* 1 cup fresh raspberries

In a medium mixing bowl let egg whites stand at room temperature for 30 minutes. Meanwhile, generously grease a cookie sheet. (Repeat greasing the cookie sheet for each batch.) Set the cookie sheet aside.

In a small saucepan heat butter over low heat *just till melted.* Set aside to cool.

Beat egg whites with an electric mixer on medium to high speed till soft peaks form (tips curl). Gradually add the sugar, 1 tablespoon at a time, beating on medium to high speed till stiff peaks form (tips stand straight). Fold about *half* of the flour into the egg white

mixture. Gently stir in the butter. Fold in the remaining flour till thoroughly combined.

Drop batter from a *heaping tablespoon* about 3 inches apart on the prepared cookie sheet. (Bake only 3 cookies at a time.) Using a knife or narrow metal spatula, spread batter into 4-inch circles. Bake in a 375° oven for 5 to 6 minutes or till edges of cookies begin to brown.

Immediately remove cookies from cookie sheet, one at a time. Roll each cookie, bottom side in, around a metal cone. *Or,* to form cookie cups, place each cookie over an inverted glass, then gently fold edges down to form ruffles or pleats. (If cookies harden before you can shape them, reheat them in the oven about 1 minute or till softened.) When cookie is firm, slide cookie off cone or remove from glass and cool on a wire rack.

Just before serving, spoon the Sweetened Whipped Cream into a decorating bag fitted with a medium star or round tip (about a ¼-inch opening). Pipe some of the whipped cream into each cookie cone or cup. Sprinkle with lingonberries or raspberries. Makes 14 cones.

Sweetened Whipped Cream: Chill a mixing bowl and the beaters of an electric mixer in the refrigerator. In the chilled bowl combine 1 cup *whipping cream,* 2 tablespoons *powdered sugar,* and ½ teaspoon *vanilla.* Beat mixture with the chilled beaters on low speed till soft peaks form.

Nutrition information per cone: 142 calories, 1 g protein, 13 g carbohydrate, 10 g total fat (6 g saturated), 32 mg cholesterol, 47 mg sodium, 38 mg potassium

Ohio

BLACKBERRY JAM CAKE WITH LEMON-BUTTERCREAM FROSTING

Some of the berries that grew wild around early frontier homesteads were made into jellies and jams. They were usually served with bread, but sometimes they were used as cake filling for the fresh flavor they would impart.

3	cups all-purpose flour
2	cups sugar
1	tablespoon baking powder
1	teaspoon finely shredded lemon peel
1½	cups milk
½	cup margarine *or* butter, softened
1½	teaspoons vanilla
2	eggs
¾	cup seedless blackberry *or* raspberry jam
	Lemon-Buttercream Frosting
	Lemon peel (optional)

In a medium mixing bowl combine flour, sugar, baking powder, and lemon peel. Add milk, margarine or butter, and vanilla. Beat with an electric mixer on low speed till combined. Beat on medium to high speed for 2 minutes. Add eggs and beat 2 minutes more. Pour into 2 greased and floured 9x1½-inch round baking pans.

Bake in a 375° oven for 25 to 30 minutes or till a wooden toothpick inserted near the center comes out clean. Cool on wire racks for 10 minutes. Remove from pans. Cool thoroughly on racks.

Split cakes in half horizontally to form 4 layers. Place 1 cake layer on a serving plate. Spread with ¼ cup of the jam. Top with a second cake layer and spread with another ¼ cup of the jam. Top with a third cake layer and spread with the remaining jam. Top with remaining cake layer. Frost top and sides of cake with Lemon-Buttercream Frosting. If desired, garnish with long, thin pieces of lemon peel. Lightly cover and refrigerate to store. Makes 12 servings.

Lemon-Buttercream Frosting: In a small heavy saucepan combine ⅔ cup *sugar,* 2 tablespoons *water,* and 2 tablespoons *lemon juice.* Bring to boiling. Remove from heat. Gradually stir about *half* of the sugar mixture into 4 slightly beaten *egg yolks.* Transfer all of the egg yolk mixture to saucepan. Bring to a gentle boil; reduce heat. Cook and stir for 2 minutes. Remove from heat. Stir in 1 teaspoon *vanilla.* Cover surface and cool to room temperature.

In a large mixing bowl beat 1 cup softened *butter* and ½ teaspoon finely shredded *lemon peel* with an electric mixer on medium to high speed till fluffy. Add cooled sugar mixture, beating till combined. If necessary, chill till easy to spread.

Nutrition information per serving:
592 calories, 7 g protein, 84 g carbohydrate,
26 g total fat (12 g saturated), 150 mg cholesterol, 332 mg sodium, 117 mg potassium

FINNISH SPICE CAKE

Mining families from Finland populated
the northern sections of Michigan and
Wisconsin. Like the Cornish who
arrived in the 1850s some fifty years
earlier, the Finns brought their food
customs with them. They even had their
own version of a pasty, the famous
savory turnover most commonly linked
with Cornwall, England.

3   tablespoons ground
    almonds
1¼ cups all-purpose flour
1½ teaspoons ground car-
    damom
1   teaspoon ground cinnamon
1   teaspoon baking powder
½   teaspoon baking soda
¼   teaspoon ground cloves
⅛   teaspoon salt
2   eggs
1   cup packed brown sugar
1   teaspoon vanilla
½   cup margarine or butter,
    melted
¾   cup dairy sour cream
⅔   cup chopped raisins or
    currants
½   cup sifted powdered sugar
1   tablespoon brown sugar

1   to 2 tablespoons whipping
    cream or milk
2   tablespoons toasted sliced
    almonds

Generously grease an 8-inch fluted
tube pan. Sprinkle the pan with
ground almonds; set aside. In a
bowl stir together the flour, cardamom, cinnamon, baking powder,
baking soda, cloves, and salt; set
mixture aside.

In a large bowl beat the eggs,
the 1 cup brown sugar, and the
vanilla on medium-high speed for 4
minutes or till thick. Pour in melted
margarine or butter; mix well.
Alternately add flour mixture and
sour cream, beating on low speed
after each addition just till combined. Stir in raisins or currants.
Pour into prepared pan. Bake in a
350° oven for 45 to 55 minutes or
till a wooden toothpick inserted in
the center of cake comes out clean.
Cool in pan on a wire rack for 10
minutes. Remove from pan; cool.
Combine powdered sugar and the
1 tablespoon brown sugar. Stir in
enough cream or milk to reach
drizzling consistency. Drizzle over
cooled cake; garnish with sliced
almonds. Makes 12 servings.

Nutrition information per serving:
275 calories, 4 g protein, 36 g carbohydrate,
14 g total fat (4 g saturated), 44 mg cholesterol, 173 mg sodium, 179 mg potassium

Minnesota

DANISH PEPPERNUTS

Despite its name, this rich Danish cookie doesn't use pepper, unlike the similar German Pfeffernusse, which does. It is seasoned with cardamom, a very traditional Scandinavian spice.

¾   cup sugar
⅔   cup dark corn syrup
¼   cup milk
¼   cup shortening
1   teaspoon anise extract
½   teaspoon baking powder
½   teaspoon vanilla
¼   teaspoon salt
¼   teaspoon ground cinnamon
¼   teaspoon ground cardamom
¼   teaspoon ground cloves
3½ cups all-purpose flour
    Sifted powdered sugar

In a large saucepan combine sugar, corn syrup, milk, and shortening. Bring to boiling. Remove from heat and cool about 15 minutes. Stir in anise extract, baking powder, vanilla, salt, cinnamon, cardamom, and cloves. Stir in the flour till well mixed. Cover and chill about 2 hours or till easy to handle.

Divide dough into 24 equal portions. On a surface dusted lightly with sifted powdered sugar, roll each portion of the dough into a ¼-inch-thick rope. Cut into pieces about ⅜ inch long. Place 1 inch apart on a greased cookie sheet.

Bake in a 375° oven about 10 minutes or till lightly browned on bottom. Immediately remove and cool on paper towels. Makes 8 cups of cookies.

Nutrition information per ¼-cup serving: 100 calories, 1 g protein, 20 g carbohydrate, 2 g total fat (0 g saturated), 0 mg cholesterol, 33 mg sodium, 20 mg potassium

Nebraska

PINK RHUBARB PUNCH

The rhubarb plant was as hardy and versatile as the pioneers who depended on it. Not only was it used as a pie filling, but it was cooked down for jams, or boiled until very soft and then strained to make a refreshing syrupy beverage.

6   cups fresh rhubarb, cut in ½-inch pieces, *or* 6 cups frozen unsweetened, sliced rhubarb (24 ounces)
3   cups water
1   cup sugar
1   6-ounce can frozen pink lemonade concentrate
¼   cup lemon juice
1   1-liter bottle lemon-lime carbonated beverage, chilled
    Fresh mint leaves *and/or* lemon slices (optional)

In a large saucepan, combine the rhubarb and water. Bring to boiling; reduce heat. Cover and simmer for 5 minutes. Remove from heat; cool slightly. Strain rhubarb mixture, pressing to remove all juices. Discard pulp. Add sugar, lemonade concentrate, and lemon juice to rhubarb juice, stirring to dissolve sugar. Cover and chill.

To serve, combine rhubarb mixture with chilled lemon-lime beverage in a punch bowl or large pitcher. Serve with crushed ice. If desired, garnish with fresh mint and/or lemon slices. Makes ten 8-ounce servings.

Nutrition information per serving: 168 calories, 1 g protein, 42 g carbohydrate, 1 g total fat (0 g saturated), 0 mg cholesterol, 7 mg sodium, 238 mg potassium

FINNISH VIIPURI TWIST

This Finnish Christmas pastry looks like a huge pretzel. The two loops created by its shape are traditionally filled with all sorts of cookies.

5¾   to 6¼ cups all-purpose
       flour
2   packages active dry yeast
½   teaspoon ground
       cardamom
½   teaspoon ground nutmeg
2   cups milk
¾   cup sugar
¼   cup margarine *or* butter
1   teaspoon salt
2   eggs
1   tablespoon water

In a bowl combine *2½ cups* of flour, the yeast, and spices. Set aside.

In a saucepan heat and stir milk, sugar, margarine, and salt just till warm (120° to 130°) and margarine is almost melted. Add to flour mixture; add *one* egg. Beat

with an electric mixer on low speed 30 seconds, scraping bowl constantly. Beat on high speed for 3 minutes. Using a wooden spoon, stir in as much of the remaining flour as you can.

Turn dough out onto a lightly floured surface. Knead in enough of the remaining flour to make a moderately soft dough that is smooth and elastic (3 to 5 minutes). Place in a lightly greased bowl; turn once to grease surface. Cover and let rise in a warm place till double (about 1 hour). Punch dough down. Turn dough out onto a lightly floured surface. Divide dough into 3 equal portions. Cover; let rest 10 minutes.

Shape each portion into a 42 inch-long rope. Form 1 dough rope into a circle, leaving both ends extended 6 inches at the bottom of the circle. Holding ends of dough rope toward center of circle, twist together. Pull rope ends to top of circle and tuck ends under, forming a pretzel-shaped roll. Place on a greased baking sheet. Repeat with remaining dough ropes.

Cover dough and let rise till nearly double (about 30 minutes). Brush dough with a mixture of the remaining egg and the water. Bake in a 375° oven about 20 minutes or till bread tests done. Makes 3 loaves (36 servings).

Nutrition information per serving: 112 calories, 3 g protein, 20 g carbohydrate, 2 g total fat (0 g saturated), 13 mg cholesterol, 81 mg sodium, 51 mg potassium

Illinois

SWEDISH TORTE

The town of Bishop Hill was founded in 1840 by Eric Janson, a Swede who sought an austere way of life, free from the corruption of the church in Sweden. As time passed, the restrictions were eased, and the tables at Bishop Hill eventually reflected the bounty of the surrounding Illinois farmland.

4   egg whites
1⅓ cups all-purpose flour
⅔   cup sugar
2   teaspoons baking powder
⅔   cup milk
¼   cup butter *or* margarine
1   egg
½   teaspoon finely shredded
      lemon peel
¼   teaspoon almond extract
¼   teaspoon cream of tartar
      Dash salt
1   cup sugar
¼   cup sliced almonds
⅓   cup sugar
1   tablespoon all-purpose
      flour
1   tablespoon cornstarch
      Dash salt

¾   cup milk
1   slightly beaten egg yolk
1   tablespoon butter *or*
      margarine
1   teaspoon vanilla
2   cups whipped cream
      (optional)

Place egg whites in a large mixing bowl; set aside. For cake layer, in a bowl combine the 1⅓ cups flour, the ⅔ cup sugar, and baking powder. Add the ⅔ cup milk, the ¼ cup butter or margarine, egg, lemon peel, and almond extract. Beat with an electric mixer on low speed till combined. Beat on medium speed 1 minute. Divide batter between two greased and floured 8x1½-inch round baking pans. The batter will be in a thin layer. Set aside.

For meringue layer, add cream of tartar and dash salt to the egg whites. Beat with an electric mixer on medium speed till soft peaks form (tips curl). Add the 1 cup sugar, 1 tablespoon at a time, beating on high speed till very stiff peaks form (tips stand straight) and sugar is almost dissolved. Divide meringue mixture between the two cake pans, spreading evenly over the cake batter. Sprinkle sliced almonds on top of meringue.

Bake in a 350° oven for 25 to 35 minutes or till golden brown. Cool in pans on a wire rack for 10 minutes. Carefully remove from pans and cool completely on wire rack, meringue side up. (Meringues will puff while baking but will sink again while cooling.)

For filling, in a saucepan combine the ⅓ cup sugar, the 1 tablespoon flour, cornstarch, and dash salt. Stir in the ¾ cup milk. Cook and stir till thickened and bubbly. Reduce heat; cook and stir 2 minutes more. Stir about *½ cup* of the hot mixture into the beaten egg yolk; transfer entire mixture to saucepan. Cook and stir 2 minutes more, but *do not boil.* Remove from heat. Stir in the 1 tablespoon butter and vanilla. Cover surface with plastic wrap; cool completely.

To assemble, place a torte layer on a cake plate, meringue side up. Spread custard filling evenly over meringue. Top with second layer, meringue side up. Cover and chill for 2 to 6 hours. If desired, serve with whipped cream. Makes 8 to 10 servings.

Nutrition information per serving:
404 calories, 7 g protein, 70 g carbohydrate, 11 g total fat (6 g saturated), 76 mg cholesterol, 248 mg sodium, 143 mg potassium

Flavors from the Southwest

Arizona

VEGETABLE-TOPPED CHEESE QUESADILLA

In the Southwest, a quesadilla is a turnover. At its simplest, it's a quick snack made with a corn or flour tortilla topped with cheese, then folded and browned. Another approach, like that for an empanada, uses a masa (corn) dough to completely enclose the filling. Once assembled, it is either deep-fried or baked.

    4   7-inch flour tortillas
        (see recipe, page 156,
        or use purchased)
    1   cup shredded Monterey
        Jack cheese with
        peppers (4 ounces)
    1   cup shredded sharp
        cheddar cheese
        (4 ounces)
    2   tablespoons snipped
        cilantro
    ½   cup shredded jicama
    ¼   cup chopped tomato
    ¼   cup chopped green onion
    ¼   cup dairy sour cream
    2   tablespoons chopped ripe
        olives

On a large baking sheet place *two* of the tortillas. Combine Monterey Jack cheese, cheddar cheese, and cilantro. Sprinkle *half* of the cheese mixture evenly on each tortilla. Top with second tortilla, pressing

slightly. Bake in a 400° oven for 10 to 15 minutes or till cheese starts to melt. Transfer to a wire rack.

In a small bowl stir together the jicama, tomato, and green onion. Spread sour cream on top of hot quesadillas. Top with jicama mixture; sprinkle with olives. Cut each quesadilla into 6 wedges and serve warm. Makes 6 appetizer servings.

Nutrition information per serving: *245 calories, 12 g protein, 14 g carbohydrate, 16 g total fat (9 g saturated), 41 mg cholesterol, 346 mg sodium, 130 mg potassium*

New Mexico

CHORIZO CON QUESO DIP

Early southwestern cooks learned how to make cheese and sausage from Spanish colonists, who brought the basic ingredients—cows and pigs—with them.

    ½   pound chorizo *or* bulk
        pork sausage
    ½   cup chopped onion
    2   cups chopped fresh
        mushrooms

½ cup tomato juice
2 cups shredded Monterey Jack cheese (8 ounces)
2 cups shredded American cheese (8 ounces)
2 tablespoons chopped jalapeño pepper
Tortilla chips *or* corn chips

In a large skillet cook chorizo and onion till no pink remains and onion is tender. Drain well. Add mushrooms; cook till tender. Stir in tomato juice, cheeses, and jalapeño pepper. Cook and stir just till cheese is melted and mixture is blended. Serve hot with chips. Makes 12 to 14 appetizer servings.

Nutrition information per serving: 213 calories, 13 g protein, 2 g carbohydrate, 17 g total fat (9 g saturated), 47 mg cholesterol, 604 mg sodium, 180 mg potassium

GUACAMOLE

Guacamole is a combination of two Aztec words: ahuacatl, *meaning "avocado," and* molli, *"mixture." While it is sometimes used as a sauce in Mexican cooking, in the Southwest it is served as an* antojito *(appetizer), as a salad with lettuce, and as a garnish for tacos, burritos, and tostadas.*

2 medium avocados, seeded, peeled, and cut up
1 medium tomato, peeled, seeded, and coarsely chopped

½ of a small onion, cut up
1 tablespoon chopped serrano pepper *or* jalapeño pepper
1 tablespoon snipped cilantro *or* parsley
1 tablespoon lemon juice *or* lime juice
¼ teaspoon salt
Chopped tomato (optional)
Chopped onion (optional)

In a blender container or food processor bowl combine the avocados, tomato, onion, serrano or jalapeño pepper, cilantro or parsley, lemon or lime juice, and salt.

Cover and blend or process till well combined, stopping machine occasionally to scrape down sides. Transfer mixture to a serving bowl. Cover and chill up to 4 hours. If desired, garnish with additional chopped tomato and onion. Use as a dip for chips or as a topping for main dishes. Makes about 1¾ cups.

Nutrition information per tablespoon: 24 calories, 0 g protein, 1 g carbohydrate, 2 g total fat (0 g saturated), 0 mg cholesterol, 21 mg sodium, 93 mg potassium

New Mexico

PINE NUT-CHEESE BITES

In September, the pine trees indigenous to the southwestern Rocky Mountains drop their cones, releasing the rich flavorful nuts known as piñons.

4   ounces process Swiss cheese, shredded
¼   cup margarine *or* butter
¼   teaspoon dry mustard
⅛   teaspoon pepper
½   cup all-purpose flour
2   tablespoons pine nuts

Bring cheese and margarine to room temperature. In a mixing bowl combine cheese, margarine, mustard, and pepper. Beat with an electric mixer till combined. Add flour to cheese mixture. Beat on low speed till well blended. Transfer to a lightly floured surface and knead about 30 seconds.

Using *1 teaspoon* for each, form into ¾-inch balls; place on baking sheet. Flatten slightly with bottom of a glass that has been dipped in flour. Sprinkle a few pine nuts on top of each flattened ball; press nuts into dough with the glass.

Bake in a 400° oven for 6 to 8 minutes or till set and edges start to turn golden. Cool on a wire rack. Makes about 48 appetizers.

Nutrition information per appetizer:
25 calories, 1 g protein, 1 g carbohydrate, 2 g total fat (1 g saturated), 2 mg cholesterol, 14 mg sodium, 8 mg potassium

Texas

SHRIMP WITH CILANTRO-LIME COCKTAIL SAUCE

Limes, brought to the New World by Spanish conquistadores, add a fresh citrus note to seafood dishes. Perhaps the best known is seviche, a cold salad that uses citric acid to "cook" raw fish. Cilantro, which looks like flat-leaf parsley, appears in Mexican-American cooking as a flavoring and garnish, and in table condiments like this sauce.

¾   cup catsup
2   tablespoons snipped fresh cilantro
1   tablespoon lime juice
1   tablespoon prepared horseradish
   Several dashes bottled hot pepper sauce
1   pound fresh *or* frozen peeled, large shrimp, cooked, deveined, and chilled
   Cracked ice
   Lime wedges *or* lime slices

For sauce, in a small mixing bowl combine catsup, cilantro, lime juice, horseradish, and hot pepper sauce. Cover and store in the refrigerator for at least 3 hours.

Serve shrimp on a bed of cracked ice. Garnish with lime wedges and serve with sauce. Makes 4 appetizer servings.

Nutrition information per serving:
134 calories, 19 g protein, 13 g carbohydrate, 1 g total fat (0 g saturated), 166 mg cholesterol, 738 mg sodium, 393 mg potassium

Texas

TEXAS-STYLE BEEF BRISKET WITH FIVE-ALARM SAUCE

While the Spanish contributed the main ingredient to Texas barbecue, beef cattle, and gave it a name, barbacoa, *Native Americans developed the technique of roasting over a pit filled with coals. Typically, the meat gets a double dousing with sauce, one as it cooks (the mop), the other when it's served (the sop).*

4   to 6 cups mesquite wood chips
1   2- to 3-pound fresh beef brisket
2   teaspoons seasoned salt
1   teaspoon paprika
1   teaspoon pepper
    Brushing Sauce
    Five-Alarm Sauce

At least 1 hour before grilling, soak wood chips in enough water to cover. Trim excess fat from the beef. In a small mixing bowl stir together the seasoned salt, paprika, and pepper; rub onto brisket. Drain the wood chips.

In a covered grill arrange *medium-slow* coals around a drip pan. Pour 1 inch of water into the drip pan. Sprinkle some of the wood chips onto the coals. Test for *slow* heat above the pan. Place brisket, fat side up, on the grill rack over the drip pan but not over the coals. Lower the grill hood. Grill for 2 to 2½ hours or till meat is very tender. Every 30 minutes or as needed, brush meat with Brushing Sauce, and add more coals, drained wood chips, and water.

For serving, thinly slice the meat across the grain; arrange on plates. Top with some of the Five-Alarm Sauce; pass remaining sauce. Makes 12 servings.

Brushing Sauce: In a small bowl stir together ¼ cup *dry red wine,* 4 teaspoons *Worcestershire sauce,* 1 tablespoon *cooking oil,* 1 tablespoon *red wine vinegar or cider vinegar,* 1 clove minced *garlic,* ½ teaspoon crushed *coriander seed,* ½ teaspoon *hot-style mustard,* and a dash ground *red pepper.* Makes ⅔ cup.

Five-Alarm Sauce: In a small saucepan stir together 1 cup *catsup;* ¾ cup peeled, seeded, and chopped *tomato;* ½ cup chopped *green pepper;* 2 tablespoons chopped *onion;* 2 tablespoons *brown sugar;* 1 to 2 tablespoons *steak sauce;* 1 to 2 tablespoons *Worcestershire sauce;* ½ teaspoon *garlic powder;* ¼ teaspoon ground *nutmeg;* ¼ teaspoon ground *cinnamon;* ¼ teaspoon ground *cloves;* ⅛ teaspoon ground *ginger;* and ⅛ teaspoon *pepper.* Bring to boiling; reduce heat. Cover; simmer about 5 minutes or till green pepper is crisp-tender. Serve warm or at room temperature. Makes about 2½ cups.

Nutrition information per serving: 188 calories, 17 g protein, 10 g carbohydrate, 9 g total fat (3 g saturated), 53 mg cholesterol, 547 mg sodium, 345 mg potassium

New Mexico

GREEN CHILI CHEESE SPREAD

In rural New Mexico, cheesemaking is still done at home. Sometimes cheese is prepared with cow's milk, sometimes with milk from the family's goats. Chile verde con queso, *"green chili with cheese," is a popular combination.*

½ of an 8-ounce package cream cheese
¼ cup dairy sour cream
2   tablespoons margarine *or* butter
1   4-ounce can chopped green chilies, drained
1   tablespoon finely chopped serrano pepper *or* jalapeño pepper
1   tablespoon snipped fresh cilantro *or* parsley
1   tablespoon finely chopped onion
1   teaspoon snipped fresh oregano *or* ¼ teaspoon dried oregano, crushed
¼ teaspoon seasoned salt
    Snipped fresh cilantro (optional)

Allow cream cheese, sour cream, and margarine to stand at room temperature for 30 minutes. Beat with an electric mixer till combined. Stir in chilies, serrano pepper, cilantro, onion, oregano, and seasoned salt. Cover and chill for 4 to 24 hours. If desired, sprinkle with additional cilantro. Serve with crackers, toasted tortilla wedges, corn chips, or raw vegetables. Makes 10 to 12 appetizer servings.

Nutrition information per serving: 76 calories, 1 g protein, 1 g carbohydrate, 7 g total fat (4 g saturated), 15 mg cholesterol, 232 mg sodium, 48 mg potassium

Texas

PICADILLO

Savory meat dishes sweetened with spices and dried fruits are a legacy from Spain. This is a favorite filling for tortillas, tacos, and empanadas. Its name is Spanish for hash, *probably because it looks like a jumble of chopped-up ingredients.*

1   pound lean ground beef
½ cup chopped onion
2   cloves garlic, minced
2   medium tomatoes
1   medium apple
⅓ cup raisins
2   tablespoons thinly sliced, pimiento-stuffed olives
1   tablespoon chopped, pickled jalapeño pepper
1   tablespoon vinegar
1   teaspoon sugar
½ teaspoon salt
½ teaspoon ground cinnamon
½ teaspoon ground cumin
⅛ teaspoon ground cloves
¼ cup toasted slivered almonds

In a large skillet cook ground beef, onion, and garlic till meat is brown and onion is tender. Drain off fat.

Meanwhile, peel and chop tomatoes. Peel, core, and chop apple. Stir tomatoes, apple, raisins, olives, jalapeño pepper, vinegar, sugar, salt, cinnamon, cumin, and cloves into the beef mixture. Cook, covered, over low heat for 20 minutes. Stir in the toasted almonds. Cook, uncovered, for 2 minutes more. Serve it with large corn chips or tortilla chips or in taco shells or flour tortillas. Makes about 3 cups.

Nutrition information per tablespoon: 25 calories, 2 g protein, 2 g carbohydrate, 1 g total fat (0 g saturated), 5 mg cholesterol, 16 mg sodium, 62 mg potassium

Arizona

EMPANADITAS

Like their cousins, the savory Cornish pasties of the Midwest and the fried fruit pies so relished in the South, these southwestern turnovers are beloved regional treats. At Christmas, they are filled with dried fruits preserved from the fall harvest.

1   **cup chopped cooked beef *or* pork**
¼   **cup chopped green chilies**
2   **tablespoons raisins**
1   **tablespoon finely chopped onion**
1   **teaspoon garlic salt**
⅛   **teaspoon cumin**
⅛   **teaspoon ground red pepper**

Pastry for Double-Crust Pie (see recipe, page 213)
Milk
Salsa (optional)
Dairy sour cream (optional)

For filling, in a mixing bowl combine the meat, chilies, raisins, onion, garlic salt, cumin, and red pepper. Set aside.

Divide pastry in half. On a lightly floured surface, roll half of the pastry into a circle about 12 inches in diameter. With a 3½-inch round cutter, cut the pastry into ten circles, rerolling the scraps as necessary.

Place a scant *1 tablespoon* filling on each circle. Moisten edges with water; fold each circle of dough in half, pressing edges with a fork to seal. Prick once or twice with fork to allow steam to escape.

Place on a baking sheet. Repeat with remaining dough and filling. Brush with milk. Bake in a 400° oven about 15 minutes or till golden. Serve warm. If desired, top with salsa and sour cream. Makes about 20 empanaditas.

Nutrition information per empanadita: 122 calories, 3 g protein, 10 g carbohydrate, 7 g total fat (2 g saturated), 5 mg cholesterol, 163 mg sodium, 53 mg potassium

New Mexico

SWORDFISH AND SALSA VERDE

In New Mexico, salsa verde — "green sauce" — gets its color from chilies picked before they ripen to a rich, deep red. The addition of tart, lemony tomatillos, or husk tomatoes, is a Mexican touch.

5   or 6 fresh tomatillos
      (6 ounces), husks
      removed and finely
      chopped, *or* one
      13-ounce can tomatillos,
      drained, rinsed, and
      finely chopped
2   tablespoons finely chopped
      onion
2   serrano peppers *or*
      jalapeño peppers,
      seeded and finely
      chopped
1   tablespoon snipped fresh
      cilantro *or* parsley
1   teaspoon finely shredded
      lime peel *or* grapefruit
      peel
½   teaspoon sugar
¼   teaspoon salt
¼   teaspoon ground cumin
¼   teaspoon pepper
4   swordfish steaks *or* tuna
      steaks, ¾ to 1 inch thick
      (1¼ pounds total)
1   tablespoon lime juice *or*
      grapefruit juice
½   of an avocado, seeded,
      peeled, and chopped

      Tomato slices (optional)
      Lime wedges (optional)
      Fresh tomatillos (optional)
      Fresh cilantro *or* green
         onion tops (optional)

For salsa verde, in a mixing bowl stir together tomatillos, onion, serrano or jalapeño peppers, cilantro or parsley, lime or grapefruit peel, and sugar; set aside. (To make ahead, cover and chill for up to 2 days.)

Combine salt, cumin, and pepper. Place fish in a 3-quart rectangular baking dish. Brush fish with lime juice. Sprinkle with cumin mixture. Stir avocado into salsa verde. Spoon salsa verde atop fish.

Bake fish, uncovered, in a 450° oven till fish flakes easily when tested with a fork, allowing 5 to 7 minutes per ½-inch thickness of fish. If desired, garnish with tomato slices, lime wedges, tomatillos, and cilantro. Makes 4 servings.

Nutrition information per serving: 221 calories, 29 g protein, 6 g carbohydrate, 10 g total fat (2 g saturated), 53 mg cholesterol, 260 mg sodium, 678 mg potassium

Arizona

CHICKEN ENCHILADAS

In Spanish, enchilada *means "spiced with chili," a requisite step in preparing this casserole. Sometimes the tortillas are dipped in a chili sauce; sometimes they're covered with it. In New Mexico, tortillas made with blue corn are preferred for enchiladas (and just about everything else), but tortillas made of yellow or white cornmeal will do.*

¼ cup chopped pecans
¼ cup chopped onion
1 tablespoon margarine *or* butter
1 3-ounce package cream cheese, softened
1 tablespoon milk
¼ teaspoon ground cumin
2 cups chopped cooked chicken
6 8-inch flour tortillas (see recipe, page 156, *or* use purchased)
1 10¾-ounce can condensed cream of chicken soup
1 8-ounce carton dairy sour cream
1 cup milk
5 or 6 chopped pickled jalapeño peppers, rinsed, seeded, and chopped
1 cup shredded cheddar cheese *and/or* Monterey Jack Cheese (4 ounces)
2 tablespoons chopped pecans

In a medium skillet cook the ¼ cup pecans and onion in margarine or butter till onion is tender and pecans are lightly toasted. Remove from heat.

In a bowl combine the softened cream cheese, the 1 tablespoon milk, and cumin. Add nut mixture and chicken. Stir together till well combined.

Spoon about ⅓ *cup* chicken mixture onto each tortilla near one edge; roll up. Place filled tortillas, seam side down, in a greased 2-quart square baking dish.

In a bowl combine soup, sour cream, the 1 cup milk, and the pickled jalapeño peppers. Pour the soup mixture evenly over the tortillas in the baking dish. Cover with foil; bake in a 350° oven about 45 minutes or till heated through.

Remove foil. Sprinkle enchiladas with cheese and the 2 tablespoons pecans. Bake for 4 to 5 minutes more or till cheese is melted. Makes 6 servings.

Nutrition information per serving: 541 calories, 28 g protein, 30 g carbohydrate, 35 g total fat (15 g saturated), 99 mg cholesterol, 924 mg sodium, 405 mg potassium

New Mexico

CHORIZO-STUFFED CHAYOTE

The mild flavor of chayote (it tastes something like a cucumber) makes it a good foil for spicy foods like chorizo. The Aztecs named it chayotli *in their Nahuatl language. The Southwest isn't alone in pairing the two foods. Louisiana Cajuns call chayote* mirliton, *and chorizo,* chaurice.

3   medium chayote squash (about 8 ounces each)
4   ounces chorizo
1   12-ounce can whole kernel corn with red and green sweet peppers, drained
½   cup salsa
1   tablespoon snipped fresh cilantro *or* parsley
¾   cup shredded Monterey Jack cheese *or* mild cheddar cheese (3 ounces)

Cut chayotes in half lengthwise. Cook in boiling water about 15 minutes or till tender. *Do not overcook.* Drain and cool chayotes. Scoop out the flesh and seeds, leaving a shell about ⅛ to ¼ inch thick. Discard seeds; set shells aside. Chop flesh; set aside.

In a skillet cook chorizo till no pink remains; drain well. Stir in corn, salsa, cilantro, and chopped chayote. Fill the chayote halves with meat mixture. Place in a 2-quart rectangular baking dish.

Cover; bake in a 375° oven for 25 to 30 minutes or till heated through. Sprinkle with cheese. Bake for 2 minutes more to melt cheese. Makes 6 side-dish servings.

Nutrition information per serving: 194 calories, 9 g protein, 18 g carbohydrate, 10 g total fat (5 g saturated), 25 mg cholesterol, 580 mg sodium, 367 mg potassium

Texas

PORK TENDERLOIN IN CORN BREAD

This dish is an emapanada gone uptown, or perhaps a southwestern version of beef Wellington. It is a fine example of how new dishes evolve out of traditional recipes and ingredients.

1¼   cups all-purpose flour
¼   cup cornmeal
1   teaspoon sugar
¾   teaspoon baking powder
¼   cup cooking oil
1   beaten egg
3   tablespoons water
2   to 3 tablespoons snipped fresh cilantro *or* parsley
1   teaspoon chili powder
1   12 to 14-ounce pork tenderloin
¾   cup salsa *or* picante sauce

Mix the flour, cornmeal, sugar, baking powder, and ¼ teaspoon *salt.* Combine oil, egg, and water. Stir liquid mixture into dry mixture till well blended, forming a ball.

On a lightly floured piece of waxed paper, roll or pat the dough into an 8-inch square. Combine the cilantro, chili powder, ¼ teaspoon *salt* and ¼ teaspoon *pepper*. Rub cilantro mixture on surface of pork, coating evenly. Place tenderloin across center of dough, folding under narrow end of tenderloin to make an even thickness. With aid of the waxed paper, roll dough around tenderloin. Seal edge and ends. Place seam side down on a lightly greased baking sheet. Bake in a 425° oven 20 minutes. Cover loosely with foil; bake 15 to 20 minutes more or till a meat thermometer inserted in center of meat registers 155° to 160°. Serve with salsa. If desired, garnish with lemon leaves. Serves 4.

Nutrition information per serving:
434 calories, 25 g protein, 42 g carbohydrate, 19 g total fat (3 g saturated), 104 mg cholesterol, 674 mg sodium, 509 mg potassium

Arizona

CHILI RELLENOS CASSEROLE

When fresh chilies are available in the Southwest, cooks prefer them over canned for this classic stuffed-pepper dish, even though they require extra effort. As a subtle clue to guests that they are getting the real McCoy, the stems are left on. Canned peppers come stemmed, peeled, and seeded—no additional prep required.

2 large poblano peppers *or* green sweet peppers (8 ounces)
1 cup shredded Monterey Jack cheese with jalapeño peppers (4 ounces)
3 beaten eggs
¼ cup milk
⅓ cup all-purpose flour
½ teaspoon baking powder
¼ teaspoon ground red pepper
⅛ teaspoon salt
¾ cup shredded cheddar cheese (3 ounces)
1 cup picante sauce
¼ cup dairy sour cream

Halve or quarter the peppers and remove seeds and veins. Remove stems, if desired. Immerse peppers into boiling water for 3 minutes; drain. Invert peppers on paper towels to drain well. Place the peppers in a well-greased 1½-quart casserole. Top with shredded Monterey Jack cheese.

In a medium mixing bowl combine eggs and milk. Add flour, baking powder, red pepper, and salt. Beat till smooth. Pour egg mixture over peppers. Bake, uncovered, in a 450° oven for 15 minutes or till set. Sprinkle with the shredded cheddar cheese. Let stand about 5 minutes or till cheese melts. Serve with picante sauce and sour cream. Makes 4 servings.

Nutrition information per serving:
352 calories, 20 g protein, 17 g carbohydrate, 24 g total fat (13 g saturated), 215 mg cholesterol, 891 mg sodium, 382 mg potassium

Texas

TURKEY AND CHORIZO MOLE

Turkey and chocolate were enjoyed by Aztec nobility, so it's not surprising that both appear in a dish supposedly invented in honor of an archbishop's visit to a Mexican convent. Chocolate traveled north in the packs of Spanish traders, but southwestern Native Americans already knew about turkey, which they valued for its feathers.

4 ounces chorizo *or* bulk pork sausage, crumbled *or* sliced (optional)
1 tablespoon cooking oil (optional)
¾ cup whole almonds
1 small onion, chopped (¼ cup)
1 6-inch flour tortilla, torn, *or* 1 slice dry bread, torn
1 clove garlic, minced
¼ teaspoon ground cinnamon
⅛ teaspoon ground cloves
1 10-ounce can tomatoes with green chili peppers
¾ cup chicken broth
1 square (1 ounce) unsweetened chocolate, chopped

6 turkey breast tenderloin steaks (1 to 1½ pounds total)
½ cup shredded Monterey Jack cheese (2 ounces)
Red sweet pepper strips (optional)
Fresh herbs (optional)

If using sausage, in a 12-inch skillet cook chorizo or bulk pork sausage till brown. Remove with a slotted spoon, reserving *1 tablespoon* drippings in skillet; set sausage aside. If not using sausage, heat cooking oil in skillet.

Add the almonds, onion, tortilla or bread, garlic, cinnamon, and cloves to the skillet. Cook, uncovered, over medium heat, stirring frequently, about 5 minutes.

In a blender container or food processor bowl place almond mixture, *undrained* tomatoes, broth, chocolate, and ⅛ teaspoon *salt*. Cover and blend or process till nearly smooth.

Pour tomato mixture into the skillet. Bring to boiling; reduce heat. Add cooked sausage (if using) and turkey steaks. Return to boiling; reduce heat. Cover; simmer 15 to 20 minutes or till turkey is no longer pink, stirring once or twice.

To serve, transfer sauce and turkey to dinner plates. Sprinkle with cheese. If desired, garnish with red sweet pepper strips and fresh herbs. Makes 6 servings.

Nutrition information per serving:
271 calories, 25 g protein, 10 g carbohydrate, 16 g total fat (4 g saturated), 56 mg cholesterol, 390 mg sodium, 438 mg potassium

Texas

FLAUTAS

Another of the seemingly endless variations of the basic filled tortilla, these are poetically named "little flutes" because of their tubular shape. They are stuffed and rolled like enchiladas, and finished by frying like chimichangas. The inclusion of cinnamon and cloves hints at their Spanish heritage.

12 ounces lean ground beef *or* pork
¼ cup chopped fresh poblano pepper *or* Anaheim pepper
½ cup chopped onion
2 garlic cloves, minced
1 tablespoon snipped fresh oregano *or* 1 teaspoon dried oregano, crushed
½ teaspoon ground cumin
¼ teaspoon salt
Dash ground cinnamon
Dash ground cloves
8 8-inch flour tortillas (see recipe, page 156, *or* use purchased)
Cooking oil for frying
Shredded lettuce
Salsa

Dairy sour cream
1 ripe avocado, seeded, peeled and sliced

For filling, in a medium skillet cook meat, pepper, onion, and garlic till no pink remains. Drain fat. Stir in oregano, cumin, salt, cinnamon, and cloves. Cover; cook over low heat for 3 minutes to blend flavors, stirring occasionally. Remove from heat; set aside. Meanwhile, stack tortillas and wrap tightly in foil. Heat in a 350° oven for 10 minutes to soften.

For each flauta, spoon about *2 tablespoons* of the meat filling lengthwise down the center of tortilla. Roll up lightly; secure with a wooden toothpick.

In a large skillet heat about ½ inch of oil over medium-high heat till a small piece of tortilla or bread sizzles when dropped into oil. Fry 3 or 4 flautas at a time, about 3 minutes or till crisp and golden, turning once. Use tongs to lift flautas from oil; tip carefully to allow fat to drain out of each end.

Drain on paper towels. Keep warm in a 300° oven while frying remaining flautas. To serve, remove toothpicks. Serve on shredded lettuce with salsa, sour cream, and avocado slices. Serves 4.

Nutrition information per serving: 929 calories, 27 g protein, 47 g carbohydrate, 72 g total fat (12 g saturated), 56 mg cholesterol, 718 mg sodium, 683 mg potassium

Arizona

CHIMICHANGAS

*These fried burritos are considered
border food, a unique culinary
subcategory that developed in the
southernmost areas of Arizona, Texas,
and New Mexico. Oversize flour
tortillas are typically Arizona-Mex.*

4 dried tomato halves
    (not oil-packed)
12 ounces boneless beef round
    or chuck, cut into
    ½-inch cubes
½ cup chopped onion
2 garlic cloves, minced
1 tablespoon cooking oil
¾ cup beef broth
1 tablespoon finely chopped
    jalapeño pepper
1 teaspoon dried oregano,
    crushed
½ teaspoon salt
¼ teaspoon ground cumin
¼ teaspoon pepper
1 medium potato, peeled and
    cut in ½-inch cubes
    (1 cup)
8 10-inch flour tortillas
    (see recipe, page 156,
    or use purchased)
    Cooking oil for frying
1 cup shredded cheddar
    cheese *or* Monterey
    Jack cheese (4 ounces)
    (optional)
    Avocado Salsa
    (see recipe, page 161)
    or purchased salsa
    (optional)

In a small bowl, cover dried tomato halves with hot water. Let stand for 10 minutes or till softened; drain. Snip and set aside.

For filling, in a large saucepan brown meat, onion, and garlic in hot oil. Drain well. Add tomato, broth, jalapeño pepper, oregano, salt, cumin, and pepper. Bring to boiling. Reduce heat. Cover and simmer for 30 minutes. Stir in potatoes; simmer about 30 minutes or till meat and potatoes are tender. If necessary, add additional broth during cooking. Mixture should be slightly moist but not soupy.

Meanwhile, stack tortillas and wrap tightly in foil. Heat in a 350° oven for 10 minutes to soften. Spoon about ¼ cup filling in center of each tortilla. Fold one edge over filling just till filling is covered. Fold in the 2 opposite sides, then the remaining side.

In a deep skillet or saucepan heat about ½ inch of oil till a small piece of tortilla or bread sizzles when dropped into oil. Place the chimichangas seam side down in oil. Fry 2 or 3 at a time about 1 minute on each side or till crisp and golden. Drain on paper towels.

Keep warm in a 300° oven while frying remaining Chimichangas. If desired, serve with cheese and salsa. Makes 4 servings.

Nutrition information per serving:
1,005 calories, 37 g protein, 76 g carbohydrate, 62 g total fat (14 g saturated), 74 mg cholesterol, 1,376 mg sodium, 764 mg potassium

New Mexico

BLACK BEAN AND CHAYOTE BURRITOS

Beans and squash, along with corn, were the three staple foods of southwestern Native Americans. The chayote, or vegetable pear, is in the squash family, but wasn't used by the Indians until it was introduced from Mexico. Burrito means "little donkey."

4 medium skinless, boneless chicken breast halves (12 ounces total)
1 cup chicken broth *or* water
1 bay leaf
½ teaspoon ground cumin
8 10-inch flour tortillas (see recipe, page 156, *or* use purchased)
½ cup chopped onion
1 tablespoon cooking oil
1 15-ounce can black beans *or* pinto beans, rinsed and drained
1 or 2 jalapeño peppers *or* serrano peppers, seeded and finely chopped, *or* one 4-ounce can diced green chilies, drained
1 ripe medium chayote squash, thinly sliced, *or* 2 oranges, peeled and sectioned
1 cup shredded Monterey Jack cheese *or* mozzarella cheese (4 ounces)
¼ cup snipped fresh cilantro *or* parsley
1 cup salsa (optional)

In a medium skillet place chicken breasts, chicken broth or water, bay leaf, and cumin. Bring to boiling; reduce heat. Simmer, covered, for 15 to 20 minutes or till chicken is tender and no longer pink. Drain, reserving broth. Let chicken stand till cool. Use a fork to pull chicken apart into long, thin shreds. Set aside. Remove bay leaf from broth.

Stack tortillas and wrap tightly in foil. Heat in a 350° oven for 10 minutes to soften.

Meanwhile, in a large skillet cook the chopped onion in hot oil till tender but not brown. Carefully add beans; jalapeño, serrano, or green chilies; and ¼ cup of the reserved broth. With a wooden spoon or potato masher, mash beans in skillet (mixture should be thick). Remove from heat.

Spread *2 to 3 tablespoons* of the bean mixture down the middle of each tortilla. Top each with some of the shredded chicken, chayote or orange, cheese, and cilantro or parsley. Fold the sides of each tortilla over the filling, overlapping the sides and forming a cone shape. Fasten each burrito with a wooden toothpick.

Arrange the burritos on a baking sheet. Cover lightly with foil. Bake in a 350° oven for 15 to 20 minutes or till the burritos are heated through. If desired, serve with salsa and garnish with cherry tomatoes and thyme sprigs. Makes 4 to 6 servings.

Nutrition information per serving: 723 calories, 44 g protein, 82 g carbohydrate, 23 g total fat (8 g saturated), 80 mg cholesterol, 909 mg sodium, 775 mg potassium

Arizona

TACO SALAD

Salads are not a traditional course in Mexican cooking. This contemporary southwestern buffet favorite is an Anglo invention that incorporates all the components of a tortilla-based main dish: meat, beans, vegetables, salsa, and fried tortillas.

1   pound ground beef *or* ground raw turkey
3   cloves garlic, minced
1   16-ounce can dark red kidney beans
1   8-ounce jar taco sauce
1   tablespoon chili powder
2   cups chopped tomatoes
2   cups shredded cheddar cheese (8 ounces)
1   cup chopped green pepper
½   cup sliced pitted ripe olives
¼   cup sliced green onion
    Lettuce leaves
1   medium avocado, seeded, peeled, and sliced (optional)
    Lime wedges (optional)
    Dairy sour cream (optional)
    Salsa *or* taco sauce (optional)

For meat mixture, in a large skillet cook beef or turkey and garlic till meat is no longer pink. Drain off fat. Stir in *undrained* kidney beans, taco sauce, and chili powder. Bring to boiling; reduce heat. Cover and simmer for 10 minutes.

Meanwhile, in a large mixing bowl combine tomatoes, cheddar cheese, green pepper, olives, and green onion; add hot meat mixture.

Toss lightly to mix. Line 6 salad plates with lettuce leaves. Divide salad mixture among plates. If desired, garnish with avocado slices and, lime wedges, and serve with sour cream and salsa or additional taco sauce. Serves 6.

Nutrition information per serving: *407 calories, 30 g protein, 22 g carbohydrate, 23 g total fat (12 g saturated), 87 mg cholesterol, 800 mg sodium, 737 mg potassium*

Texas

TEXAS CHILI

According to Frank Tolbert, who immortalized Texas chili in A Bowl of Red, the authentic, original recipe included beef, hot peppers, oregano, cumin, and garlic—no beans. Beans are now considered acceptable, but "chili heads" are a contentious bunch. Their current controversy: beans in the chili or served alongside?

1½   pounds boneless beef top round steak
1   tablespoon cooking oil
1   cup chopped onion
2   cloves garlic, minced
2   16-ounce cans tomatoes, cut up
1   cup beef broth
1   4-ounce can diced green chilies *or* ⅓ cup chopped, pickled jalapeño peppers
2   tablespoons chili powder
1   tablespoon brown sugar
2   teaspoons dried oregano, crushed

1 teaspoon ground cumin
½ teaspoon salt
3 cups hot cooked rice *or*
   pinto beans
   Dairy sour cream *or*
   shredded cheddar
   cheese (optional)

Partially freeze meat. Thinly slice across the grain into bite-size strips or cut into ½-inch cubes. In a Dutch oven brown *half* of the meat in hot oil. Remove from pan. Brown remaining meat with the onion and garlic, adding more oil, if necessary. Drain off fat. Return all meat, onion, and garlic to pan.

Stir in the *undrained* tomatoes, the beef broth, green chili peppers or jalapeño peppers, chili powder, brown sugar, oregano, cumin, and salt. Bring mixture to boiling; reduce heat. Cover and simmer for 1 hour or till meat is tender.

Serve with rice or beans. If desired, top with sour cream or cheddar cheese. Makes 6 servings.

Nutrition information per serving: 366 calories, 30 g protein, 42 g carbohydrate, 8 g total fat (2 g saturated), 59 mg cholesterol, 856 mg sodium, 865 mg potassium

New Mexico

POSOLE

Corn is a sacred food to Native Americans. They've developed hundreds of uses for it, including this stew of meat, chili, and the dried, hulled kernels known as hominy. It's a dish for celebrations, served on feast days and on New Year's Day for good luck.

1½ pounds lean, boneless pork,
    cut into 1-inch cubes
2 tablespoons cooking oil
1 medium onion, chopped
   (½ cup)
2 cloves garlic, minced
4 cups chicken broth
1½ teaspoons dried oregano,
    crushed
¼ teaspoon ground cumin
2 14½-ounce cans hominy,
   drained
1 4-ounce can chopped green
   chilies
   Sliced radishes
   (optional)
   Shredded cabbage
   (optional)
   Sliced green onion
   (optional)

In a large saucepan or Dutch oven brown *half* of the pork cubes in hot oil; remove meat and set aside. Brown the remaining meat with the onion and garlic; cook till meat is brown. Return all of the meat to saucepan. Stir in the chicken broth, oregano, and cumin. Bring to boiling; reduce heat. Cover and simmer for 40 minutes.

Stir in the hominy and green chilies. Cover and simmer for 30 minutes more. Skim off fat. Ladle into bowls. If desired, serve with sliced radishes, shredded cabbage, and sliced green onion. Makes 6 to 8 servings.

Nutrition information per serving: 306 calories, 31 g protein, 18 g carbohydrate, 12 g total fat (3 g saturated), 66 mg cholesterol, 798 mg sodium, 540 mg potassium

Texas

SHREDDED BEEF BURRITO

*This burrito filling has all
the flavors of a typical Texas chili:
oregano, cumin, garlic, chili powder,
and beef. The tortilla is another link
to the Lone Star State.*

1 pound boneless beef chuck,
   1 inch thick
1 4-ounce can diced green
   chilies
¼ cup salsa
¼ cup chopped onion
2 cloves garlic, minced
½ teaspoon chili powder
½ teaspoon dried oregano,
   crushed
½ teaspoon ground cumin
¼ teaspoon salt
¼ teaspoon crushed red
   pepper
8 7-inch flour tortillas
   (see recipe, page 156, *or*
   use purchased)
1 medium green *or* red sweet
   pepper, cut into thin
   strips (optional)
½ cup chopped tomato
   (optional)
1 6-ounce container frozen
   avocado dip, thawed, *or*
   ½ cup dairy sour cream
   (optional)

Trim fat from meat. Cut the meat
into 1-inch cubes. In a medium
saucepan combine beef, *undrained*
chilies, salsa, onion, garlic, chili
powder, oregano, cumin, salt, and
red pepper. Add ½ cup *water*. Bring
to boiling; reduce heat. Cover and

simmer about 2 hours or till meat is
very tender, stirring occasionally to
break cubes of meat into shreds.
Cook, uncovered, for 15 to 20
minutes or till excess liquid is evaporated and mixture is desired
consistency.

Stack tortillas and wrap tightly
in foil. Heat in a 350° oven for 10
minutes to soften.

For serving, immediately fill
each warm tortilla with about ⅓ cup
beef mixture. If desired, top with
pepper strips, chopped tomato, and
avocado dip or sour cream. Fold in
bottom and sides. Serves 4.

Note: This meat mixture can be
used for tacos, chimichangas, or on
a hamburger bun.

*Nutrition information per serving:
428 calories, 31 g protein, 39 g carbohydrate,
16 g total fat (6 g saturated), 71 mg cholesterol, 796 mg sodium, 552 mg potassium*

Arizona

CHICKEN WITH PEPPERS AND CILANTRO PESTO

*Before the advent of canned foods, some
of the pepper crop was preserved to
ensure a supply during the barren
southwestern winter. So they could be
peeled and frozen, peppers were roasted
indoors on a stove-top comal (griddle)
or outdoors in a* horno, *(a beehive-
shaped mud oven).*

1 large red sweet pepper
4 large skinless, boneless
   chicken breast halves
   (1 pound total)
¼ cup Cilantro Pesto
   (see recipe, page 160)
2 teaspoons cooking oil
¼ teaspoon paprika
½ cup dairy sour cream
   (optional)

To roast the pepper, halve it; remove stem, seeds, and membranes. Place the pepper halves, cut sides down, on a foil-lined baking sheet. Bake in a 425° oven 20 to 25 minutes or till skin is bubbly and browned. Place pepper in a new brown paper bag. Seal; let stand 20 to 30 minutes or till cool. Peel skin from pepper. Cut lengthwise into ½-inch strips. Set aside.

Place each chicken breast half between 2 pieces of clear plastic wrap. Pound lightly to ¼-inch thickness. Remove plastic wrap. Spread *1 tablespoon* Cilantro Pesto on boned side of each breast half. Place several pepper strips crosswise on one end of each breast half. Roll up chicken, jelly-roll style, starting from end near pepper strips. Secure rolls with wooden toothpicks.

Place chicken rolls in a shallow baking dish or pan. Brush lightly with oil; sprinkle with paprika. Bake in a 375° oven for 25 to 30 minutes or till no longer pink. If desired, serve with sour cream and additional Cilantro Pesto. Serves 4.

Nutrition information per serving:
245 calories, 28 g protein, 3 g carbohydrate, 13 g total fat (1 g saturated), 74 mg cholesterol, 143 mg sodium, 334 mg potassium

New Mexico

PIÑON PINE MUFFINS

Southwestern Native Americans have been eating pine nuts for centuries. They roast them as a snack, use them whole in cooking, or grind them into meal for baking.

1¼ cups all-purpose flour
⅓ cup whole wheat flour
2 tablespoons sugar
2 teaspoons baking
   powder
¼ teaspoon salt
1 beaten egg
¾ cup milk
¼ cup cooking oil
½ cup toasted chopped pine
   nuts *or* almonds
½ cup shredded Swiss cheese
   or cheddar cheese
   (2 ounces)
¼ cup sliced green onion

In a large mixing bowl stir together all-purpose flour, whole wheat flour, sugar, baking powder, and salt. Make a well in the center of the flour mixture. In a medium bowl combine egg, milk, and cooking oil. Stir in pine nuts, cheese, and green onion. Add all at once to flour mixture. Stir just till moistened (batter should be lumpy).

Lightly grease muffin cups; fill ¾ full. Bake in a 400° oven about 20 minutes or till golden. Remove from pans; serve warm. Makes 10 to 12 muffins.

Nutrition information per serving:
195 calories, 6 g protein, 19 g carbohydrate, 11 g total fat (2 g saturated), 28 mg cholesterol, 92 mg sodium, 108 mg potassium

New Mexico

BLUE CORNMEAL MUFFINS

Corn was so important to Native Americans in the Southwest that each color was associated with special qualities. In ceremonies, blue corn was the western direction. The color blue was also thought to have medicinal properties. A paste of blue cornmeal was prescribed as a balm for aching joints.

2   cups all-purpose flour
¾   cup yellow cornmeal
⅔   cup sugar
4   teaspoons baking powder
½   teaspoon salt
¾   cup blue cornmeal
2   beaten eggs
1   8¾-ounce can cream-style corn
¾   cup milk
½   cup oil

Using two mixing bowls, place *1 cup* of the flour in each bowl. In the first bowl, stir in the yellow cornmeal, *⅓ cup* sugar, *2 teaspoons* baking powder, and *¼ teaspoon* salt. In the second bowl, stir in the blue cornmeal, the remaining sugar, remaining baking powder, and remaining salt.

Combine eggs, corn, milk, and oil; mix well. Divide in half. Stir *half* of the liquid mixture into each bowl. Stir just till moistened (batter should be lumpy).

Lightly grease muffin cups or line with paper bake cups. Fill muffin cups ⅔ full using half blue cornmeal batter and half yellow cornmeal batter (spoon the batters side by side into the muffin cups). Bake in a 400° oven for 15 to 20 minutes or till golden. Remove from pans; serve warm. Makes about 18 muffins.

Nutrition information per muffin:
199 calories, 4 g protein, 30 g carbohydrate, 7 g total fat (1 g saturated), 24 mg cholesterol, 182 mg sodium, 68 mg potassium

Texas

TEXAS COLESLAW

Yes, like almost everything on a Texas menu, this salad is hot. It has to be to stand up to true five-alarm barbecue, which it accompanies as a side dish.

2   cups finely shredded green cabbage
2   cups finely shredded red cabbage
1   cup shredded jicama
½   cup chopped yellow sweet pepper
½   cup chopped green pepper
½   cup raisins
½   cup dairy sour cream *or* plain yogurt
½   cup mayonnaise *or* salad dressing
1   tablespoon finely chopped jalapeño pepper
1   teaspoon sugar
½   teaspoon ground cumin
¼   teaspoon salt
¼   teaspoon pepper
½   of a medium avocado, seeded, peeled, and chopped

In a large mixing bowl stir together the green cabbage, red cabbage, jicama, yellow pepper, green pepper, and raisins.

For dressing, stir together the sour cream, mayonnaise, jalapeño pepper, sugar, cumin, salt, and pepper. Pour dressing over cabbage mixture; toss to coat. Cover and chill for 1 to 24 hours. Gently stir chopped avocado into coleslaw. Makes 6 servings.

Nutrition information per serving:
296 calories, 3 g protein, 21 g carbohydrate, 24 g total fat (5 g saturated), 19 mg cholesterol, 238 mg sodium, 514 mg potassium

---

Arizona

NAVAJO FRY BREAD

If you visit a Navajo reservation, you will have the opportunity to try this puffy fried bread. However, other Native Americans besides the Navajo prepare it, so it's also generically referred to as Indian fry bread. Topped with ground beef, shredded lettuce, and the like, it's called an Indian taco.

1½   cups all-purpose flour
1   package active dry yeast
1   5-ounce can evaporated milk
½   cup sugar
¼   cup water
¼   cup shortening
1   teaspoon salt
2   eggs
2½   to 3 cups all-purpose flour
     Cooking oil for frying
     Powdered sugar

Combine *1½ cups* of the flour and the yeast. In a saucepan heat and stir milk, sugar, water, shortening, and salt till warm (120° to 130°) and shortening almost melts. Add to the flour mixture along with the eggs. Beat with an electric mixer on low speed for 30 seconds, scraping bowl constantly. Beat on high speed for 3 minutes. Using a wooden spoon, stir in as much of the remaining flour as you can.

Turn out onto a lightly floured surface. Knead in enough of the remaining flour to make a moderately stiff dough that is smooth and elastic (6 to 8 minutes total). Shape into a ball. Place in a lightly greased bowl, turn once to grease surface. Cover and refrigerate several hours or overnight. (Dough can be refrigerated up to 3 days and fried as needed, but is best the first day.)

Remove dough from refrigerator; let stand at room temperature for 30 minutes. Punch dough down. Turn out onto a lightly floured surface. Cover and let rest for 10 minutes. Roll dough to ⅛- to ¼-inch thickness. Cut into 3x4-inch rectangles.

Heat cooking oil to 365°. Carefully fry 2 rectangles at a time about 1½ to 2 minutes or till golden, turning once. Drain on paper towels. Sprinkle with powdered sugar while still warm; serve immediately. Makes about 20 rectangles.

Nutrition information per rectangle:
184 calories, 4 g protein, 27 g carbohydrate, 7 g total fat (2 g saturated), 23 mg cholesterol, 122 mg sodium, 57 mg potassium

Arizona

FLOUR TORTILLAS

*In the wheat-growing Mexican state of
Sonora, the preference is to make
tortillas out of wheat flour rather than
ground corn. As Arizona is just over the
border to the north, it too is partial to
flour. Arizona tortillas tend to be very
large, a foot in diameter or even more.*

2 **cups all-purpose flour**
1 **teaspoon salt**
1 **teaspoon baking powder**
2 **tablespoons shortening *or*
    lard**
½ **cup warm water**

In a medium mixing bowl combine
flour, salt, and baking powder. Cut
in shortening or lard till thoroughly
combined. Gradually add water
and toss together till dough can be
gathered into a ball (if necessary,
add more water, 1 tablespoon at a
time). Knead dough 15 to 20 times.
Let dough rest 15 minutes.

For 8-inch tortillas, divide
dough into 12 equal portions;
shape each portion into a ball. (For
10-inch tortillas, divide dough into
8 equal portions; shape each portion into a ball.)

On a lightly floured surface, use
a rolling pin to flatten each ball into
an 8-inch (or 10-inch) circle. Stack
rolled-out tortillas between pieces
of waxed paper.*

Carefully peel off top sheet of
waxed paper. Place tortilla, paper
side up, on a medium-hot, ungreased skillet or griddle. As tortilla begins to heat, carefully peel
off remaining sheet of waxed

paper. Cook tortilla about 30 seconds or till puffy. Turn and cook
about 30 seconds more or till edges
curl up slightly. Wrap the tortillas
in foil if using immediately.*
Makes twelve 8-inch or eight 10-
inch tortillas.

***Note:** To freeze tortillas, stack
them, alternating each tortilla with
2 layers of waxed paper. Wrap the
stack in a moisture- and vapor-
proof bag, foil, or freezer wrap.
Seal tightly and freeze. Thaw completely before using.

*Nutrition information per 8-inch tor-
tilla: 95 calories, 2 g protein, 16 g carbohydrate, 2 g total fat (0 g saturated), 0 mg cholesterol, 205 mg sodium, 22 mg potassium*

New Mexico

CORN TORTILLAS

*While the corn tortilla is considered
the sandwich bread of Mexico,
in fact southwestern Native Americans
were making a similar flat cake when
the Spanish explorers arrived.*

2 **cups Masa Harina
    tortilla flour**
1¼ **cups warm water**

In a medium mixing bowl combine
tortilla flour and water. Stir mixture together with your hands till
dough is firm but moist (if necessary, add more water, 1 tablespoon
at a time). Let dough rest for 15
minutes.

Divide the dough into 12 equal portions and shape each portion into a ball.

Using a tortilla press or rolling pin, flatten each ball between 2 pieces of waxed paper into a 6-inch circle.

Carefully peel off top sheet of waxed paper. Place tortilla, paper side up, on a medium-hot, ungreased skillet or griddle. As tortilla begins to heat, carefully peel off remaining sheet of waxed paper. Cook, turning occasionally, for 2 to 2½ minutes or till tortilla is dry and light brown (tortilla should still be soft). Wrap tortillas in foil if using immediately.* Makes twelve 6-inch tortillas.

*Note: To freeze tortillas, stack them, alternating each tortilla with 2 layers of waxed paper. Wrap the stack in a moisture- and vapor-proof bag, foil, or freezer wrap. Seal tightly and freeze. Thaw completely before using.

Nutrition information per tortilla: 69 calories, 2 g protein, 14 g carbohydrate, 1 g total fat (0 g saturated), 0 mg cholesterol, 1 mg sodium, 56 mg potassium

New Mexico

BLUE CORNMEAL PANCAKES WITH FRESH BERRIES

The Hopis made pancakes out of blue cornmeal on sandstone slabs, which they heated from below. To retain the revered blue color, the corn received a special alkali treatment.

1	cup all-purpose flour
⅓	cup blue cornmeal *or* yellow cornmeal
2	tablespoons sugar
1½	teaspoons baking powder
½	teaspoon baking soda
¼	teaspoon salt
1	beaten egg
1⅓	cups buttermilk
2	tablespoons cooking oil
¾	cup fresh blueberries
	Margarine *or* butter
	Maple syrup *or* maple-flavored syrup
	Fresh raspberries (optional)

In a mixing bowl stir together flour, cornmeal, sugar, baking powder, baking soda, and salt. In another bowl combine egg, buttermilk, and oil. Add to flour mixture all at once. Stir mixture just till blended but still lumpy. Fold in blueberries.

Pour about ¼ cup of the batter onto a hot, lightly greased griddle or heavy skillet. Cook till pancakes are golden brown, turning to cook second side when pancakes have bubbly surfaces and slightly dry edges. Serve warm with margarine and syrup and, if desired, fresh raspberries. Makes 12 pancakes.

Nutrition information per pancake: 189 calories, 3 g protein, 29 g carbohydrate, 7 g total fat (1 g saturated), 19 mg cholesterol, 143 mg sodium, 109 mg potassium

New Mexico

REFRIED BEANS

Along with the chili pepper, the speckled pinto bean is New Mexico's number one vegetable by action of the state legislature. In Spanish, beans are frijoles. *When cooked beans are pan-fried, then mashed, they are the famous* frijoles refritos.

1   pound dry pinto beans
2   tablespoons bacon
      drippings *or* cooking oil
1½ teaspoons salt
2   cloves garlic, minced

In a Dutch oven combine pinto beans and 6 cups *water*. Bring to boiling; reduce heat. Simmer for 2 minutes; remove from heat. Cover and let stand for 1 hour. (*Or,* soak beans in water overnight in a covered pan.) Drain beans.

In the same Dutch oven combine drained beans and 4 cups additional *water*. Bring to boiling. Cover; simmer for 2 hours or till beans are very tender. *Do not drain.*

Add bacon drippings or cooking oil, salt, and garlic. Using a potato masher, mash bean mixture completely. Cook, uncovered, for 10 to 15 minutes or till thick, stirring often. Makes 8 to 10 servings.

Nutrition information per serving:
208 calories, 10 g protein, 33 g carbohydrate, 4 g total fat (2 g saturated), 4 mg cholesterol, 421 mg sodium, 603 mg potassium

Texas

LAYERED BLACK BEAN SALAD

While black beans are more popular in southern Mexico than in the American Southwest, they do appear in many of the region's dishes, including soups and salads.

2½ cups shredded lettuce
1   15-ounce can black beans,
      rinsed and drained
1   to 2 tablespoons snipped
      fresh cilantro
½   cup chopped red onion
½   cup chopped green
      pepper
½   cup chopped red sweet
      pepper
2   to 4 tablespoons chopped
      fresh *or* canned green
      chilies
¾   cup dairy sour cream
1   tablespoon lime juice
1   clove garlic, minced
¼   teaspoon salt
¾   cup chopped tomato
1   small avocado, seeded,
      peeled, and chopped

In a deep 2-quart bowl, place *1½ cups* of the lettuce. Layer black beans, cilantro, onion, green pepper, red pepper, and green chilies. Top with remaining lettuce.

For dressing, stir together sour cream, lime juice, garlic, and salt. Spread dressing over top of salad, sealing to edge of bowl. Cover and chill for 2 to 24 hours.

Before serving, sprinkle the chopped tomato and chopped avocado over salad. Toss to coat the vegetables. Makes 4 to 6 servings.

Nutrition information per serving: 277 calories, 10 g protein, 28 g carbohydrate, 16 g total fat (7 g saturated), 19 mg cholesterol, 218 mg sodium, 759 mg potassium

---

SPICY CORN SOUFFLÉ

Southerners who moved west brought their regional dishes with them. This corn soufflé is actually like a traditional spoon bread fired up with local seasonings like cumin, oregano, cinnamon, and hot pepper.

¼ cup chopped onion
¼ cup finely chopped red *or* green sweet pepper
1 clove garlic, minced
3 tablespoons margarine *or* butter
3 tablespoons all-purpose flour
½ teaspoon oregano, crushed
¼ teaspoon ground cumin
¼ teaspoon ground cinnamon
⅛ teaspoon ground red pepper
⅛ teaspoon ground coriander
¼ teaspoon salt
½ cup milk
1 cup shredded cheddar cheese (4 ounces)
1 8¾-ounce can cream-style corn
3 egg yolks
3 egg whites

In a medium saucepan cook onion, red or green pepper, and garlic in margarine till tender. Stir in flour, oregano, spices, and salt. Add milk all at once. Cook and stir till thickened and bubbly. Remove from heat. Add cheese and stir till melted. Stir in corn. In a medium bowl beat egg yolks with a fork till combined. Gradually add corn mixture, stirring constantly. Set aside.

In a large bowl beat egg whites till stiff peaks form (tips stand straight). Gently fold about *1 cup* of the beaten egg whites into the corn mixture to lighten it. Gradually pour corn mixture over remaining beaten egg whites, folding to combine. Pour into an ungreased 1½-quart soufflé dish. Bake in a 350° oven about 40 minutes or till a knife inserted near center comes out clean. Serve immediately. Makes 4 servings.

Nutrition information per serving: 335 calories, 15 g protein, 20 g carbohydrate, 23 g total fat (9 g saturated), 192 mg cholesterol, 616 mg sodium, 249 mg potassium

Texas

PICO DE GALLO SALSA

It's not clear why this salsa, or the well-known jicama salad of the same name, is called "rooster's beak." Perhaps because a rooster pecks his food into little pieces, the size of ingredients used for both.

2   medium tomatoes, peeled and finely chopped
2   tablespoons finely chopped onion
2   tablespoons snipped fresh cilantro *or* parsley
1   serrano pepper, finely chopped
    Dash sugar

In a medium mixing bowl stir together the chopped tomatoes, onion, cilantro or parsley, serrano pepper, and sugar. Cover and chill for several hours or overnight, stirring occasionally.

Store, tightly covered, in the refrigerator up to 3 days. Use as a dip for chips or as a topping for main dishes. Makes 1¼ cups.

Nutrition information per tablespoon: 4 calories, 0 g protein, 1 g carbohydrate, 0 g total fat (0 g saturated), 0 mg cholesterol, 1 mg sodium, 33 mg potassium

Texas

CILANTRO PESTO

The musky, smoky character of cilantro can be an acquired taste for palates unfamiliar with it. In the Southwest, though, it's as common an ingredient as parsley is everywhere else.

1½ cups firmly packed, fresh cilantro leaves
½   cup firmly packed parsley sprigs with stems removed
½   cup grated Parmesan cheese *or* asiago cheese
¼   cup pine nuts *or* slivered almonds
2   cloves garlic, quartered
¼   teaspoon salt
¼   cup olive oil *or* cooking oil

In a blender container or food processor bowl combine cilantro, parsley, Parmesan or asiago cheese, pine nuts or almonds, garlic, and salt. Cover and blend or process with several on-off turns till a paste forms, stopping the machine several times and scraping the sides. With machine running, gradually add the oil and blend or process to the consistency of soft butter.

Divide into 4 portions (about ¼ cup each) and place in small airtight containers. Refrigerate for 1 or 2 days or freeze up to 1 month. Bring to room temperature for serving. Use as directed in recipe. Makes about 1 cup.

Nutrition information per tablespoon: 55 calories, 2 g protein, 1 g carbohydrate, 5 g total fat (1 g saturated), 2 mg cholesterol, 93 mg sodium, 34 mg potassium

Arizona

AVOCADO SALSA

Avocados were served by Montezuma to the Spanish explorers. They were so plentiful that an old name for them was poor man's butter. This is like a chunky guacamole.

½ cup chopped avocado
1 tablespoon lime juice
1 teaspoon olive oil
¼ teaspoon salt
⅛ teaspoon pepper
½ cup chopped, peeled, and
     seeded tomato
⅓ cup finely chopped red
     onion
2 to 3 tablespoons finely
     chopped fresh *or*
     pickled jalapeño
     peppers
2 tablespoons finely chopped
     fresh cilantro

In a mixing bowl combine avocado and lime juice; toss to coat well. Stir in oil, salt, and pepper. Add tomato, onion, jalapeño pepper, and cilantro. Mix well.

Cover and chill for 2 to 24 hours before serving. Serve with tortilla chips or as a meat accompaniment. Makes 6 servings.

Nutrition information per serving:
48 calories, 1 g protein, 3 g carbohydrate, 4 g total fat (1 g saturated), 0 mg cholesterol, 134 mg sodium, 178 mg potassium

New Mexico

MEXICAN HOT CHOCOLATE

The Aztecs thought that chocolate was an aphrodisiac. Viewed as very macho, it was reserved for men of the noble classes. Happily, hot chocolate is now an equal opportunity beverage in Mexico and throughout the Southwest.

6 cups milk
½ cup sugar
3 squares (3 ounces)
     unsweetened
     chocolate, chopped
1 teaspoon ground
     cinnamon
2 beaten eggs
2 teaspoons vanilla
     Whipped cream

In a large saucepan combine *1 cup* of the milk, the sugar, chocolate, and cinnamon. Cook and stir over medium-low heat till chocolate is melted. Gradually stir in remaining milk. Cook and stir till milk is very hot, almost boiling. *Do not boil.*

Gradually stir *1 cup* of the hot milk mixture into eggs, then transfer entire mixture to saucepan. Cook and stir for 2 minutes over low heat. Remove from heat and stir in vanilla. Beat with a rotary beater till very frothy.

Pour hot chocolate into mugs and dollop with whipped cream. Makes six 8-ounce servings.

Nutrition information per serving:
286 calories, 12 g protein, 33 g carbohydrate, 14 g total fat (8 g saturated), 89 mg cholesterol, 144 mg sodium, 496 mg potassium

Texas

CARAMEL FLAN WITH MANGOES

In New Mexico and Texas, it isn't unusual to see this Spanish baked custard made with sweetened condensed milk rather than regular milk and eggs. There was a time when these dairy foods were hard to come by in rural areas. Even though they are now widely available, the recipe has yet to catch up.

⅓ cup sugar
3 beaten eggs
1½ cups milk
⅓ cup sugar
1 teaspoon vanilla
    Fresh mango slices *or* other fresh fruit

In a heavy, medium skillet place ⅓ cup sugar. Cook over medium-high heat till sugar begins to melt *(do not stir);* shake skillet occasionally to heat sugar evenly. Reduce heat to low and cook till sugar is melted and golden brown; stir as necessary after sugar begins to melt. Pour caramelized sugar into an 8-inch quiche dish. Tilt dish to coat bottom. Let stand 10 minutes.

Combine eggs, milk, ⅓ cup sugar, and vanilla. Beat till well combined. Place quiche dish in a 13x9x2-inch baking pan on the oven rack. Pour egg mixture into prepared quiche dish. Pour boiling water into the baking pan around quiche dish to a depth of ¾ inch. Bake in a 325° oven for 20 to 25 minutes or till a knife inserted near the center comes out clean.

Serve warm or chilled. Loosen edge of dish with a spatula or knife, slipping point of spatula down sides to let air in. Invert onto a serving plate. Garnish with mango slices. Makes 6 servings.

Nutrition information per serving:
171 calories, 5 g protein, 30 g carbohydrate, 4 g total fat (2 g saturated), 111 mg cholesterol, 63 mg sodium, 137 mg potassium

New Mexico

BIZCOCHITOS

When children return from church on Christmas day in New Mexico, these anise-flavored sugar cookies, shaped like fleurs-de-lis (stylized irises), are given to them as a special holiday treat.

1 cup margarine *or* butter
2¼ cup all-purpose flour
1 teaspoon anise seed, finely crushed, *or* several drops anise flavoring
1 egg
1 cup sugar
1 tablespoon brandy *or* milk
1 teaspoon baking powder
1 teaspoon vanilla
¼ teaspoon salt
2 tablespoons sugar
1 teaspoon ground cinnamon (optional)

Beat margarine or butter with an electric mixer on high speed for 30 seconds. Add about *half* of the flour, the aniseseed, egg, sugar, brandy or milk, baking powder, vanilla, and salt. Beat till thoroughly combined. Beat in remaining flour. Divide dough in half. Cover and chill for 3 hours.

On a lightly floured surface, roll half of the dough at a time to ⅛-inch thickness. Cut with a fleur-de-lis- shape cookie cutter (or other desired shape). Place on an ungreased cookie sheet.

If desired, combine the 2 tablespoons sugar with the cinnamon. Sprinkle sugar or sugar-cinnamon mixture lightly onto cookies. Bake in a 375° oven for 6 to 8 minutes or till edges are firm and bottoms are very lightly browned. Cool cookies on a wire rack. Makes 36 to 48 cookies.

Nutrition information per cookie: 101 calories, 1 g protein, 12 g carbohydrate, 5 g total fat (1 g saturated), 6 mg cholesterol, 68 mg sodium, 12 mg potassium

New Mexico

BUÑUELOS

These fritters belong to the greater family of southwestern breads that include tortillas, Indian fry bread, and sopapillas (deep-fried dough "pillows"). Along with cups of steaming hot chocolate, they are a winter favorite, particularly on Christmas Eve when they are served dipped in a wine syrup.

2   **cups all-purpose flour**
1   **teaspoon baking powder**
½   **teaspoon salt**
¼   **teaspoon cream of tartar**
2   **tablespoons shortening**
2   **beaten eggs**
⅓   **cup milk**
  Cooking oil for frying
  Sugar, Cinnamon Sugar, *or* Cinnamon-Sugar Syrup

In a mixing bowl stir together flour, baking powder, salt, and cream of tartar. Cut in shortening till thoroughly combined. Make a well in center of flour mixture.

In a small mixing bowl combine eggs and milk. Add to flour mixture all at once. Stir just till dough clings together.

On a lightly floured surface knead dough about 2 minutes or till smooth. Divide dough into 24 equal portions; shape each portion into a ball. Cover dough and let rest for 15 to 20 minutes.

In a heavy 10-inch skillet heat ¾ inch oil to 375°. Meanwhile, on a lightly floured surface, roll each ball into a 4-inch circle.

Fry 1 circle at a time in hot oil for 1 to 1½ minutes on each side or till golden. Drain on paper towels. Sprinkle with sugar or Cinnamon Sugar, or drizzle with Cinnamon-Sugar Syrup. Make and serve the same day. Makes 24 buñuelos.

Cinnamon Sugar: In a mixing bowl stir together ½ cup *sugar* and 1 teaspoon ground *cinnamon*.

Cinnamon-Sugar Syrup: In a small saucepan combine ½ cup *sugar*, ¼ cup packed *brown sugar*, ¼ cup *water*, 1 tablespoon *corn syrup*, and 3 inches *stick cinnamon* or dash ground *cinnamon*. Bring to boiling. Reduce heat and boil gently, without stirring, about 20 minutes or till thick. Discard cinnamon stick. Makes about ⅔ cup syrup.

Nutrition information per buñuelos: 112 calories, 2 g protein, 12 g carbohydrate, 6 g total fat (1 g saturated), 18 mg cholesterol, 67 mg sodium, 18 mg potassium

Arizona

SANGRITA

*The proper way to enjoy this
southwestern Bloody Mary is as
follows: alternate sips of* Sangrita *and
tequila, then bite a lime wedge to
cleanse the palate. The drink is aptly
named, given its deep red color
—from the Spanish word for* blood.

6   medium tomatoes
     (about 2 pounds),
     peeled, seeded, and
     coarsely cut up, *or* one
     28-ounce can
     tomatoes
⅓ cup lime juice
1   slice of a medium onion
1   jalapeño pepper, seeded
     and cut up
1   teaspoon sugar
     Several dashes bottled
     hot pepper sauce
1   cup orange juice
⅓ cup tequila
     Ice cubes
     Celery stalks (optional)
     Lime wedges (optional)

In a blender container place fresh
tomatoes or *undrained* canned tomatoes, lime juice, onion, jalapeño
pepper, sugar, and hot pepper
sauce. Cover and blend till smooth.

Strain mixture through a sieve
lined with cheesecloth. Transfer to
a serving pitcher. Stir in orange
juice and tequila. Serve over ice
cubes. If desired, garnish with celery stalks and lime wedges. Makes
seven to nine 4-ounce servings.

Nutrition information per serving:
*69 calories, 1 g protein, 10 g carbohydrate, 0
g total fat (0 g saturated), 0 mg cholesterol,
12 mg sodium, 324 mg potassium*

New Mexico

TORTILLA TORTE

*In New Mexico, enchiladas
are stacked like a torte, with filling
in between each layer, rather than
filled and rolled. While this recipe
is new, the procedure is classic.*

1   12-ounce package
     (2 cups) semisweet
     chocolate pieces
2   8-ounce cartons dairy sour
     cream
10 8-inch flour tortillas
     (see recipe, page 156,
     or use purchased)
½ cup dairy sour cream
2   tablespoons powdered
     sugar

In a medium saucepan melt chocolate over low heat, stirring constantly. Stir in the 2 cartons sour
cream. Remove from heat; cool.

Place 1 tortilla on a serving
plate. Spread a scant *⅓ cup* of the
chocolate mixture atop. Repeat
with remaining tortillas and chocolate mixture. Cover and chill for
several hours or overnight.

Before serving, in a small mixing bowl stir together the ½ cup
sour cream and the powdered
sugar. Garnish torte with sour
cream mixture. Serves 8 to 10.

Nutrition information per serving:
*505 calories, 8 g protein, 56 g carbohydrate,
31 g total fat (17 g saturated), 31 mg cholesterol, 254 mg sodium, 316 mg potassium*

$\mathscr{F}$lavors from the West

California

GOAT CHEESE, TOMATO, AND OREGANO BOBOLI PIZZA

Goat cheese appeared on the menus of a few California restaurants in the early 1970s. Its inclusion was part of a great experiment by young chefs to interpret classic French cuisine using the bounty of fresh foods available locally. Since then, goat cheese has become inseparably linked with this new cooking style.

1   16-ounce (12-inch) Italian
    bread shell (Boboli)
1   tablespoon olive oil *or*
    cooking oil
1   clove garlic, minced
⅛   teaspoon pepper
2   medium tomatoes, thinly
    sliced
½   of a medium onion, thinly
    sliced and separated
    into rings

3   tablespoons sliced pitted
    ripe olives
4   ounces chèvre
    (goat cheese)
1   tablespoon snipped fresh
    oregano *or* 1 teaspoon
    dried oregano, crushed
2   tablespoons toasted
    pine nuts

Place Italian bread shell on a lightly greased baking sheet. In small mixing bowl combine olive oil or cooking oil, garlic, and pepper. Brush generously over the bread shell. Bake in a 400° oven for 5 minutes.

Arrange tomato slices, without overlapping them, in a circular pattern on top of the bread shell; top with rhe sliced onion and the ripe olives.

Crumble or dollop the chèvre over the tomato slices; sprinkle with oregano. Bake in the 400° oven about 8 minutes more or till warm and cheese softens. Remove pizza from the oven; sprinkle with pine nuts. Cut into wedges. Makes 12 servings.

Nutrition information per serving:
159 calories, 7 g protein, 18 g carbohydrate, 7 g total fat (2 g saturated), 9 mg cholesterol, 274 mg sodium, 75 mg potassium

California

CIOPPINO

The men who fished commercially in San Francisco Bay were primarily Italians from Genoa. They prepared this seafood stew with their catch. Cioppino is still closely associated with the city's Fisherman's Wharf area. Most of the restaurants there offer it on their menus.

8 fresh *or* frozen clams in shells
8 ounces fresh *or* frozen fish fillets (red snapper, perch, sea bass, *or* halibut)
8 ounces fresh *or* frozen peeled and deveined shrimp
½ cup sliced fresh mushrooms
⅓ cup chopped green *or* red sweet pepper
¼ cup chopped onion
2 cloves garlic, minced
1 tablespoon olive oil *or* cooking oil
1 16-ounce can tomatoes, cut up
⅓ cup dry red *or* white wine
¼ cup water
2 tablespoons snipped parsley
2 tablespoons tomato paste
1 tablespoon lemon juice
1½ teaspoons snipped fresh basil *or* ½ teaspoon dried basil, crushed
1½ teaspoons snipped fresh oregano *or* ½ teaspoon dried oregano, crushed
1 teaspoon sugar
¼ teaspoon salt
⅛ teaspoon crushed red pepper

Thaw clams, if frozen. Scrub clam shells under cold running water using a stiff brush. Combine 8 cups *water* and 3 tablespoons *salt*. Add clams; soak 15 minutes. Drain and rinse. Discard water. Repeat the soaking, draining, and rinsing steps two more times.

Partially thaw fish and shrimp, if frozen. Remove and discard fish skin, if present. Cut fish into 1½-inch pieces; set aside. Cover and refrigerate fish pieces and shrimp till needed.

In a large saucepan cook mushrooms, green or red sweet pepper, onion, and garlic in hot oil till tender but not brown. Stir in *undrained* tomatoes, wine, water, parsley, tomato paste, lemon juice, basil, oregano, sugar, salt, and crushed red pepper. Bring to boiling; reduce heat. Simmer, covered, 20 minutes.

Add clams, fish pieces, and shrimp. Simmer, covered, for 5 to 10 minutes or till clams open, fish flakes easily, and shrimp are opaque. Discard any unopened clams. Makes 4 servings.

Nutrition information per serving: 202 calories, 25 g protein, 11 g carbohydrate, 5 g total fat (1 g saturated), 110 mg cholesterol, 527 mg sodium, 805 mg potassium

Utah

MORMON FISH CHOWDER

The Mormons, in establishing the Mormon Trail, traveled 1,400 miles from Nauvoo, Illinois, to the Salt Lake Valley. Their cooking was simple and satisfying, and reflected their midwestern and eastern way of cooking.

1½ pounds fresh *or* frozen
   haddock fillets *or* other
   fish fillets
4 ounces salt pork, diced, *or*
   3 strips bacon, diced
1 cup chopped onion
4 cups cubed, peeled
   potatoes (6 medium)
2 cups water
¾ teaspoon salt
¼ teaspoon pepper
2 cups milk
1 12-ounce can evaporated
   milk
2 tablespoons all-purpose
   flour

Thaw fish, if frozen. Cut fish into
1-inch pieces. Set aside. In a Dutch
oven cook salt pork or bacon slowly till golden brown. Drain, reserving *1 tablespoon* drippings in pan; set
salt pork or bacon aside.

Add onion to pan; cook till tender but not brown. Stir in potatoes,
water, salt, and pepper. Bring to
boiling; reduce heat. Simmer, covered, about 15 minutes or till potatoes are tender. Add fish. Simmer,
covered, about 3 minutes or till fish
just flakes when tested with a fork.

Combine milk and evaporated
milk. Slowly stir milk mixture into
flour till smooth; add to fish mixture. Cook and stir till thickened
and bubbly. Add cooked salt pork
or bacon; heat through. Makes
6 servings.

Nutrition information per serving:
384 calories, 30 g protein, 41 g carbohydrate,
11 g total fat (5 g saturated), 88 mg choles-
terol, 503 mg sodium, 1,080 mg potassium

California

ALMOND-AVOCADO SPREAD

Almond trees were planted in
the gardens of the Spanish missions in
California in the eighteenth century,
although almonds weren't successful as
a crop for at least another hundred
years. Avocados arrived in California in
the mid-1800s, but didn't flourish
until after the turn of the century.

1 large ripe avocado, seeded,
   peeled, and mashed
1 tablespoon lime juice
¼ teaspoon chili powder
¼ teaspoon seasoned salt
¼ cup toasted chopped
   almonds
2 tablespoons diced green
   chilies
2 slices bacon, crisp-cooked,
   drained, and crumbled
3 medium shrimp, peeled,
   cooked, and chopped
2 tablespoons toasted sliced
   or slivered almonds
   Toasted tortilla wedges

Mix avocado, lime juice, chili powder, salt, and ¼ teaspoon *pepper*. Stir
in the ¼ cup almonds, chilies, and
bacon. Cover surface with plastic
wrap; chill up to 4 hours. To serve,
sprinkle with shrimp and remaining almonds. If desired, garnish
with whole shrimp. Serve with tortilla wedges. Makes 1 cup.

Nutrition information per table-
spoon: 50 calories, 2 g protein, 2 g carbohy-
drate, 4 g total fat (1 g saturated), 10 mg
cholesterol, 57 mg sodium, 120 mg potassium

Idaho

POTATO SKINS WITH MUSHROOM FILLING

In the early 1870s, when Luther Burbank first tried to sell seedlings for what was to become the famous Idaho Russet potato, few farmers were interested. He finally found a buyer, but only for a fraction of his asking price.

3   medium baking potatoes, baked
2   tablespoons margarine *or* butter, melted
1½ cups chopped fresh mushrooms
¼   cup sliced green onion
¼   cup finely chopped red sweet pepper
1   garlic clove, minced
1   tablespoon margarine *or* butter
2   tablespoons finely chopped walnuts
2   tablespoons snipped parsley
1   slightly beaten egg yolk
     Dash ground red pepper

Cut potatoes in half lengthwise. Scoop out pulp, leaving ¼- to ½-inch-thick shells. Brush with the 2 tablespoons margarine. Sprinkle with salt. Place cut side up on a baking sheet. Bake in a 425° oven about 10 minutes or till crisp. Cook mushrooms, onion, sweet pepper, and garlic in remaining margarine

till tender and most liquid evaporates. Remove from heat. Stir in walnuts, parsley, egg yolk, and red pepper. Fill potato with mushroom mixture. Bake 5 to 7 minutes or till hot. Makes 6 appetizers.

Nutrition information per appetizer: 142 calories, 3 g protein, 16 g carbohydrate, 8 g total fat (1 g saturated), 35 mg cholesterol, 102 mg sodium, 277 mg potassium

Idaho

MARSALA-MARINATED TROUT

There must be something special about Idaho's rivers and streams. Almost all of the rainbow trout available in markets across the country are farmed from these waters.

4   8- to 10-ounce fresh *or* frozen pan-dressed rainbow trout *or* lake perch
½   cup dry marsala *or* other white wine
1   tablespoon lemon juice
½   teaspoon dried thyme, crushed
½   cup sliced fresh mushrooms
½   cup chopped carrot
⅓   cup chopped onion
1   clove garlic, minced
2   tablespoons cooking oil
¼   cup chicken broth

Thaw fish, if frozen. Place fish in a shallow baking dish. Sprinkle with salt and pepper.

For marinade, stir together the marsala, lemon juice, and thyme; pour over fish. Cover and marinate in the refrigerator for 2 hours. Drain fish, reserving marinade. Pat fish dry.

In a 12-inch skillet cook mushrooms, carrot, onion, and garlic in hot oil till tender but not brown. Push to the edges of the skillet. Add fish and cook 4 minutes on each side. Add marinade and broth. Cover, simmer about 4 minutes or till fish flakes easily with a fork. Remove fish and vegetables.

Simmer marinade mixture till it is reduced to ¼ cup; spoon over fish. Makes 4 servings.

Nutrition information per serving: *263 calories, 31 g protein, 4 g carbohydrate, 12 g total fat (2 g saturated), 83 mg cholesterol, 95 mg sodium, 870 mg potassium*

Colorado

ROCKY MOUNTAIN TROUT

Pioneer families that settled near water depended on fish to supplement their meager diet until they could plant crops or a vegetable garden. The clear waters of Rocky Mountain streams are particularly renowned for their trout.

4   8- to 10-ounce fresh *or* frozen pan-dressed rainbow trout
¼   cup finely chopped red onion

¼   cup finely chopped green pepper
2   teaspoons tarragon vinegar *or* white wine vinegar
1   teaspoon snipped fresh basil
¼   teaspoon salt
¼   teaspoon cumin
⅛   teaspoon pepper
1   tablespoon grated Parmesan cheese
2   tablespoons cooking oil
     Whole tiny new potatoes (optional)
     Fresh basil sprigs (optional)

Thaw fish, if frozen. For stuffing, in a mixing bowl stir together the onion, green pepper, vinegar, basil, salt, cumin, and pepper. Add Parmesan cheese; mix well.

Rinse fish and pat dry with paper towels. Brush the outsides and cavities of fish with oil. Spoon one-fourth of the stuffing mixture into each fish cavity.

Brush a wire grill basket with cooking oil. Place fish in basket. Grill fish on an uncovered grill directly over medium-hot coals for 7 to 11 minutes or till fish flakes easily with a fork, turning once.

If desired, serve with new potatoes and garnish with basil sprigs. Makes 4 servings.

Nutrition information per serving: *234 calories, 30 g protein, 1 g carbohydrate, 12 g total fat (2 g saturated), 84 mg cholesterol, 201 mg sodium, 737 mg potassium*

California

STIR-FRIED SEAFOOD WITH LINGUINE

Californians have enjoyed stir-fries since the first Chinese chop suey parlors opened their doors after the 1849 gold rush. Customers at these restaurants thought they were eating authentic Chinese dishes, but actually the food was modified to appeal to western tastes. Chop suey doesn't exist in China.

1	pound fresh *or* frozen sea scallops
½	pound fresh *or* frozen peeled and deveined medium shrimp
10	ounces linguine
2	cups fresh pea pods *or* one 6-ounce package frozen pea pods, thawed
⅔	cup chicken broth
¼	cup dry sherry
3	tablespoons soy sauce
4	teaspoons cornstarch
1	teaspoon toasted sesame oil
¼	teaspoon crushed red pepper
1	tablespoon cooking oil
4	cloves garlic, minced
6	green onions, bias-sliced into 1-inch pieces (¾ cup)
⅓	cup dried tomatoes (oil-packed), drained and cut into thin strips
3	tablespoons finely shredded Parmesan cheese

Thaw scallops and shrimp, if frozen. Cook linguine according to package directions; drain. Cut any large scallops in half. In a medium bowl combine the scallops and shrimp; set aside. Cut pea pods diagonally in half. For sauce, in a small bowl stir together chicken broth, sherry, soy sauce, cornstarch, sesame oil, and crushed red pepper. Set sauce aside.

Pour cooking oil into a wok or 12-inch skillet. (Add more oil as necessary during cooking.) Preheat over medium-high heat. Stir-fry garlic in hot oil for 15 seconds. Add green onions and, if using, fresh pea pods; stir-fry for 2 minutes. Remove vegetables from the wok.

Add *half* of the scallop mixture to the hot wok. Stir-fry for 2 to 3 minutes or till scallops are opaque and shrimp turn pink.

Remove from wok. Repeat with the remaining scallop mixture. Transfer entire scallop mixture to wok; push from center of wok. Add sauce to center of wok. Cook and stir till thickened and bubbly.

Add cooked vegetables, linguine, thawed pea pods, if using, and tomatoes. Stir all ingredients together to coat with sauce. Cook and stir about 1 minute more or till heated through. Transfer to a large serving dish. Top with cheese. Makes 6 servings.

Nutrition information per serving: 368 calories, 26 g protein, 46 g carbohydrate, 8 g total fat (2 g saturated), 86 mg cholesterol, 850 mg sodium, 580 mg potassium

California

CRAB LOUIS

Who is Louis? He may have been San Francisco chef Louis Coutard, but no one is quite sure. Whoever the creator, he gave his name to this dressing for crab salad. It's pronounced Louie not Lewis, by the way.

¼ cup whipping cream
½ cup mayonnaise *or* salad
   dressing
¼ cup sliced green onion
2 tablespoons chili sauce
1 teaspoon prepared
   horseradish
½ teaspoon finely shredded
   lemon peel
1 teaspoon lemon juice
⅛ teaspoon salt
   Dash ground red pepper
1 to 2 tablespoons milk
   (optional)
   Red-tip leaf lettuce leaves
4 cups shredded Chinese
   cabbage *and/or* romaine
½ cup shredded carrot

12 ounces coarsely flaked,
   cooked crabmeat (2¼ cups)
   or three 4-ounce
   packages frozen,
   crab-flavored,
   salad-style fish
1½ cups red *and/or* yellow
   baby pear tomatoes,
   halved
2 hard-cooked eggs, sliced
1 medium avocado, seeded,
   peeled, and sliced
   lengthwise
   Paprika
   Lemon wedges

For dressing, in a small bowl beat whipping cream till soft peaks form. Fold in mayonnaise or salad dressing, green onion, chili sauce, horseradish, lemon peel, lemon juice, salt, and ground red pepper. Cover dressing, and chill for 2 to 24 hours. (If necessary, thin dressing with 1 to 2 tablespoons milk before serving.)

To serve, line 4 salad plates with lettuce leaves. Toss together shredded Chinese cabbage or romaine and shredded carrot; pile atop lettuce leaves. Arrange crabmeat atop the shredded cabbage mixture. Arrange tomatoes, egg slices, and avocado slices around crabmeat. Drizzle with chilled dressing. Sprinkle with paprika. Garnish the salad with lemon wedges. Makes 4 servings.

Nutrition information per serving: 493 calories, 24 g protein, 14 g carbohydrate, 40 g total fat (9 g saturated), 228 mg cholesterol, 677 mg sodium, 1,056 mg potassium

California

FRESH TUNA WITH FETTUCCINE

Some 300 species of fish and shellfish are harvested from California waters, including tuna, swordfish, sole, and many varieties of rockfish.

1   pound fresh *or* frozen tuna
     or swordfish steaks
     (1 inch thick)
½   cup chopped onion
2   cloves garlic, minced
1   tablespoon olive oil *or*
     cooking oil
2   14½-ounce cans diced
     tomatoes
2   tablespoons snipped fresh
     basil *or* 1½ teaspoons
     dried basil, crushed
2   tablespoons tomato paste
¼   teaspoon salt
¼   teaspoon crushed red
     pepper
1   9-ounce package frozen
     artichoke hearts,
     thawed and cut into
     quarters
2   tablespoons capers,
     drained
3   cups hot cooked spinach
     fettuccine
     Fresh oregano (optional)

Thaw fish, if frozen. Cut fish into 1-inch cubes, discarding any skin and bones. Set aside.

For sauce, in a large skillet cook onion and garlic in hot olive oil or cooking oil till onion is tender but not brown. Stir in the *undrained* tomatoes, basil, tomato paste, salt, and crushed red pepper. Bring to boiling. Reduce heat and simmer,

uncovered, about 20 minutes or till very thick. Add fish cubes. Cover and cook about 6 minutes or till fish flakes easily with a fork.

Gently stir artichokes and capers into sauce; heat through. Serve sauce over fettuccine. If desired, garnish with oregano. Serves 4.

Nutrition information per serving:
411 calories, 35 g protein, 46 g carbohydrate, 10 g total fat (2 g saturated), 42 mg cholesterol, 637 mg sodium, 1,078 mg potassium

California

VEAL WITH SHERRY AND OLIVES

Spanish priests carried olive cuttings from Mexico into what is now southern California in the early eighteenth century. Olive trees were planted in the orchards of their missions.

1   pound boneless veal leg
     top round steak *or* lean
     boneless pork, cut into
     thin bite-size strips
3   tablespoons margarine *or*
     butter
1   cup thinly bias-sliced
     carrot
3   green onions, bias-sliced
     into 1-inch pieces
     (¼ cup)
3   tablespoons all-purpose
     flour
1   teaspoon instant chicken
     bouillon granules
¼   teaspoon coarsely cracked
     black pepper

2 cups half-and-half *or* light cream
¾ cup sliced pitted ripe olives
¼ cup dry sherry
3 cups hot cooked spinach fettuccine
2 tablespoons snipped fresh parsley

In a large skillet cook and stir *half* the veal or pork at a time in margarine or butter about 3 minutes or till brown. Remove veal or pork from skillet, reserving drippings.

In the same skillet, cook and stir carrots and green onions for 3 to 4 minutes or till crisp-tender. Stir in flour, bouillon granules, and pepper. Add half-and-half or light cream all at once. Cook and stir till thickened and bubbly. Cook and stir for 1 minute more.

Stir in cooked veal, olives, and dry sherry; heat through. Spoon veal mixture over pasta. Sprinkle with parsley. Makes 4 servings.

Nutrition information per serving: 578 calories, 35 g protein, 44 g carbohydrate, 29 g total fat (11 g saturated), 133 mg cholesterol, 644 mg sodium, 694 mg potassium

Wyoming

COWPUNCHER STEW

In the dining halls of large western ranches, eating was the main order of business for the hands. There was little conversation during meals that typically included dishes like cowpuncher stew. After supper, however, if the cook permitted, the crew might hang around to swap some tales.

1½ pounds beef stew meat, cut in 1-inch cubes
3 tablespoons all-purpose flour
2 tablespoons cooking oil
1½ cups strong coffee
2 tablespoons molasses
1 clove garlic, minced
1 teaspoon Worcestershire sauce
½ teaspoon dried oregano, crushed
⅛ teaspoon ground red pepper
4 carrots, cut in ½-inch slices
4 small onions, quartered
3 medium potatoes, peeled and cut up
3 tablespoons all-purpose flour

Coat beef cubes with a mixture of 3 tablespoons flour and ½ teaspoon *salt*. In a Dutch oven brown *half* of the meat at a time in hot oil. Return all meat to pan. Stir in the coffee, molasses, garlic, Worcestershire sauce, oregano, red pepper, and ½ teaspoon *salt*. Cover; simmer 1½ hours or till meat is nearly tender,

Add the carrots, onion, potatoes, and 1½ cups *water*. Simmer, covered, about 30 minutes or till vegetables are tender. Combine the 3 tablespoons flour and ¼ cup cold *water*; stir into the stew mixture. Cook and stir till mixture is thickened and bubbly. Cook and stir for 1 minute more. Makes 6 servings.

Nutrition information per serving: 359 calories, 31 g protein, 32 g carbohydrate, 12 g total fat (4 g saturated), 86 mg cholesterol, 445 mg sodium, 814 mg potassium

Montana

MARINATED VENISON LOIN WITH FRIED GRAPES

Before the great surge of settlers moved in, deer, bear, and elk were abundant on the frontier. The hunter lucky enough to shoot one could feed his family for a long time.

1	5- to 6-pound loin end saddle of venison
2	medium onions, quartered
2	medium tomatoes, cut up
6	juniper berries, crushed
1	to 2 bay leaves
¾	cup red wine
¼	cup margarine *or* butter, melted
¼	cup whipping cream
2	tablespoons cranberry jelly *or* currant jelly
2	tablespoons catsup
1	teaspoon prepared mustard
¼	cup dairy sour cream
	Fried Grapes
	Fresh Grapes (optional)
	Parsley (optional)

Wash venison and pat dry. Trim off excess fat. Place in a roasting pan, bone side down. Sprinkle with salt and pepper. Place onions, tomatoes, juniper berries, and bay leaves around venison. Pour wine and melted margarine or butter over venison. Insert a meat thermometer into the thickest portion of the meat. Roast in a 375° oven about 1 hour or till thermometer registers 140° (medium-rare); baste with pan juices every 20 minutes. Transfer meat to a platter; cover and let stand about 15 minutes.

Meanwhile, for sauce, strain pan juices into a saucepan (should be about 1 cup). Cook mixture down till it measures ½ cup. Stir in whipping cream. Cook and stir till thickened and bubbly. Stir in jelly, catsup, and mustard. Cook and stir till jelly is dissolved. Stir in sour cream and heat through. (*Do not boil.*) Spoon sauce over venison and garnish with Fried Grapes and, if desired, fresh grapes and parsley. Makes 12 servings.

Fried Grapes: Rinse 1½ cups *grapes* and remove stems. Toss with ⅓ cup *all-purpose flour* to coat well. Dip the grapes in 1 beaten *egg*, then in ¾ cup *fine dry bread crumbs*. In a large skillet fry grapes in 2 tablespoons hot *margarine or butter* and 1 tablespoon *cooking oil* about 5 minutes or till coating is golden, turning frequently.

Nutrition information per serving: 336 calories, 33 g protein, 17 g carbohydrate, 14 g total fat (4 g saturated), 138 mg cholesterol, 206 mg sodium, 507 mg potassium

Nevada

MINER'S CAMP PIE

This stew must have fed a miner whose claim panned out. According to one report from an 1849 camp, potatoes sold for $30 a bushel, an unheard of amount at the time.

1	pound lamb shoulder, trimmed and cut in ¾-inch cubes
1	tablespoon cooking oil
1⅓	cups beef broth
⅓	cup dry red wine *or* beef broth
2	cloves garlic, minced
1	teaspoon dried marjoram, crushed
½	teaspoon dried thyme, crushed
1	bay leaf
¼	teaspoon salt
¼	teaspoon pepper
2	cups peeled potatoes, cut into ½-inch cubes
1½	cups whole small fresh mushrooms
1	cup sliced carrots
1	cup onion wedges
¼	cup all-purpose flour
1	3-ounce package cream cheese, cubed
¼	cup snipped parsley
1	cup all-purpose flour
½	teaspoon onion salt
¼	cup margarine *or* butter
2	tablespoons shortening
1	egg, beaten

In a large saucepan brown *half* of the meat at a time in hot oil. Drain fat. Return all meat to pan. Add ⅔ cup of the broth, the wine, garlic, marjoram, thyme, bay leaf, salt, and pepper. Bring to boiling; reduce heat. Cover and simmer for 30 minutes. Stir in potatoes, mushrooms, carrots, and onion. Return to boiling; reduce heat. Cover and simmer about 30 minutes or till tender. Discard bay leaf. Combine the ¼ cup flour and remaining broth. Stir into meat mixture. Cook and stir till thickened and bubbly. Stir in cubed cream cheese and parsley. Stir gently till cheese melts. Keep warm.

Meanwhile, for pastry, in a bowl combine the 1 cup flour and onion salt. Cut in margarine and shortening till mixture resembles coarse crumbs. Stir in beaten egg till well blended. Form into ball. Roll pastry into a rectangle 1 inch larger than a 2-quart rectangular baking dish or a circle 1 inch larger than diameter of a 1½-quart casserole. Transfer meat mixture into the baking dish or casserole. Place pastry atop. Cut slits in pastry. Seal and flute edge. Bake in a 375° oven about 20 minutes or till golden. Serves 4.

Nutrition information per serving: *715 calories, 29 g protein, 60 g carbohydrate, 38 g total fat (12 g saturated), 138 mg cholesterol, 853 mg sodium, 916 mg potassium*

California

CHICKEN WITH BLACK BEAN SAUCE

In the 1850s Chinese arrived in California by the thousands to build the transcontinental railroad. Later they opened restaurants and worked as cooks in mining camps and in private homes. West Coast cuisine reflects continued immigration from Asia even today.

4   large skinless, boneless chicken breast halves (1 pound total)
⅓   cup water
1   tablespoon soy sauce
2   teaspoons cornstarch
½   teaspoon sugar
½   teaspoon instant chicken bouillon granules
1   tablespoon cooking oil
2   cloves garlic, minced
1   pound fresh asparagus, cut into 2-inch pieces (3 cups), *or* one 10-ounce package frozen cut asparagus, thawed
1   medium onion, cut into thin wedges (¾ cup)
1   tablespoon fermented black beans, chopped
3   cups hot cooked rice

Rinse chicken and pat dry. Cut into ¾-inch pieces. For sauce, in a small bowl stir together the water, soy sauce, cornstarch, sugar, and chicken bouillon granules. Set sauce mixture aside.

Pour cooking oil into a wok or large skillet. (Add more oil as necessary during cooking.) Preheat over medium-high heat. Stir-fry garlic in hot oil for 15 seconds. If using fresh asparagus, stir-fry for 1 minute. Add thawed asparagus (if using), onion, and black beans; stir-fry about 3 minutes more or till the vegetables are crisp-tender. Remove vegetables from the wok.

Add *half* of the chicken to the hot wok. Stir-fry for 2 to 3 minutes or till no pink remains. Remove the chicken from the wok. Repeat with remaining chicken. Return all chicken to the wok. Push the chicken from the center of the wok. Stir sauce. Add the sauce to the center of the wok. Cook and stir till thickened and bubbly.

Return the cooked vegetables to the wok. Stir all ingredients together to coat with sauce. Cook and stir about 1 minute more or till heated through. Serve immediately over hot cooked rice. Makes 4 servings.

Nutrition information per serving: 420 calories, 35 g protein, 51 g carbohydrate, 8 g total fat (2 g saturated), 72 mg cholesterol, 588 mg sodium, 629 potassium

California

CALIFORNIA CHICKEN SALAD WITH JALAPEÑO DRESSING

Californians have always loved spicy flavors, a heritage of the early cooking that developed on the huge Spanish colonial land-grant ranchos. They've also been quick to integrate the new with the old. Exotics like kiwi fruit, once grown only in China and New Zealand and now a major California crop, are commonplace in markets throughout the state.

4   large skinless, boneless
    chicken breast halves
    (about 1 pound total)
2   tablespoons lemon juice
1   jalapeño pepper, finely
    chopped
1   tablespoon cooking oil
½   teaspoon lemon-pepper
    seasoning
12 ounces asparagus spears
    Boston *or* Bibb lettuce
    leaves
1   5-ounce can baby corn,
    drained
2   kiwi fruit *or* carambola
    (star fruit), sliced
2   apricots, nectarines, *or*
    peaches, pitted and cut
    into wedges
    Jalapeño Dressing

Rinse chicken; pat dry. Combine the lemon juice, jalapeño pepper, cooking oil, and lemon-pepper seasoning; brush over both sides of chicken breasts. Grill chicken on an uncovered grill directly over *medium* coals for 12 to 15 minutes or till no longer pink, turning once.

Cool chicken about 5 minutes or till cool enough to handle. (*Or*, broil chicken 4 to 5 inches from heat for 12 to 15 minutes, turning once.)

Meanwhile, cook the asparagus, covered, in a small amount of boiling water for 4 to 8 minutes or till crisp-tender.

To serve, line 4 salad plates with lettuce leaves. Diagonally cut the chicken breast halves into slices; reassemble halves atop lettuce leaves. Divide asparagus spears, baby corn, kiwi fruit or carambola, and apricots, nectarines, or peaches among salad plates. Pour Jalapeño Dressing over salads. Serves 4.

Jalapeño Dressing: Using a blender container or food processor bowl combine ½ cup *mayonnaise or salad dressing*, 2 tablespoons *honey*, 1 tablespoon *lime juice or lemon juice*, 1 coarsely chopped (not seeded) *jalapeño pepper*, ¼ teaspoon *dry mustard*, and ¼ teaspoon *paprika*. Cover and blend or process till smooth. Cover and chill.

Nutrition information per serving: *475 calories, 30 g protein, 24 g carbohydrate, 30 g total fat (5 g saturated), 89 mg cholesterol, 392 mg sodium, 677 mg potassium*

Utah

SPLIT PEA AND SAUSAGE SOUP

A typical meal for Mormons traveling westward in the mid-1800s might have included a big kettle of split pea soup, whole wheat bread with comb honey, and a lettuce salad with whipped cream dressing.

1½	cups green split peas
6	cups chicken broth
1	clove garlic, minced
1	tablespoon snipped fresh oregano *or* ¾ teaspoon dried oregano, crushed
⅛	teaspoon pepper
1	bay leaf
½	pound bulk pork sausage
1	cup chopped carrot
¾	cup chopped onion
¾	cup peeled potato, cut in ¼-inch cubes
½	cup chopped celery

Rinse peas. In a large saucepan or kettle combine split peas, broth, garlic, oregano, pepper, and bay leaf. Bring to boiling; reduce heat. Cover and simmer for 1 hour, stirring occasionally.

Meanwhile, form pork sausage into twenty-five ½- to ¾-inch balls; place in a 13x9x2-inch baking pan. Bake in a 400° oven for 10 to 15 minutes or till no pink remains. Remove from pan; place on paper towels to drain.

Stir carrot, onion, potato, celery, and sausage balls into soup. Return to boiling; reduce heat. Cover and simmer for 20 minutes. Uncover; simmer 10 to 15 minutes more or till desired consistency and vegetables are tender. Discard bay leaf. Makes 5 servings.

Nutrition information per serving: 480 calories, 27 g protein, 56 g carbohydrate, 16 g total fat (6 g saturated), 23 mg cholesterol, 1,224 mg sodium, 1,433 mg potassium

Wyoming

CHICKEN POTPIES

Life became easier once pioneers established their homesteads, and the meagerness of the meals of those early days disappeared. Familiar dishes like meat pies made with fresh-killed poultry and vegetables from home gardens began to appear on the dinner table.

	Pastry for Double-Crust Pie (see recipe, page 213)
1	10-ounce package frozen peas and carrots
½	cup chopped onion
½	cup chopped fresh mushrooms
¼	cup margarine *or* butter
⅓	cup all-purpose flour
½	teaspoon salt
½	teaspoon dried sage, marjoram, *or* thyme, crushed
⅛	teaspoon pepper
2	cups chicken broth
¾	cup milk
3	cups cubed cooked chicken *or* turkey
¼	cup snipped parsley
¼	cup chopped pimiento

Prepare pastry; set aside. Cook peas and carrots according to package directions; drain. In a saucepan cook onion and mushrooms in margarine or butter till tender. Stir in flour, salt, herb, and pepper. Add chicken broth and milk all at once. Cook and stir till thickened and bubbly. Stir in drained peas and carrots, chicken or turkey, parsley, and pimiento; heat till bubbly. Pour chicken mixture into six 10-ounce round casseroles. (*Or,* use a 2-quart rectangular baking dish.)

Roll pastry into a 15x10-inch rectangle. Cut into six 5-inch circles, and place atop the 10-ounce casseroles. (*Or,* roll pastry into a 13x9-inch rectangle. Place over the 2-quart rectangular baking dish.) Flute edges of pastry and cut slits in the top for steam to escape. Bake in a 450° oven for 12 to 15 minutes or till pastry is golden brown. Makes 6 servings.

Nutrition information per serving: 631 calories, 31 g protein, 46 g carbohydrate, 35 g total fat (8 g saturated), 62 mg cholesterol, 788 mg sodium, 506 mg potassium

California

COBB SALAD

Patrons of the Brown Derby Restaurant in Los Angeles, where this salad originated in 1936, never needed to ask how the restaurant got its name. The original site on Wilshire Boulevard was built in the shape of a gargantuan hat.

6 cups shredded red Swiss chard *or* shredded lettuce
3 cups chopped cooked chicken
1½ cups chopped, seeded tomatoes (2 medium)
¾ cup crumbled blue cheese (3 ounces)
6 slices bacon, crisp-cooked, drained, and crumbled
3 hard-cooked eggs, chopped
1 small head Belgian endive
1 medium avocado, seeded, peeled, and cut into wedges
Brown Derby French Dressing

Place the shredded Swiss chard or lettuce in 6 salad bowls. Evenly divide the chicken, tomatoes, blue cheese, bacon, and eggs among the bowls.

Separate the Belgian endive into leaves. Place a few endive leaves and avocado wedges in each bowl. Serve with Brown Derby French Dressing. Makes 6 servings.

Brown Derby French Dressing: In a screw-top jar combine ½ cup *olive oil or salad oil*, ⅓ cup *red wine vinegar*, 1 tablespoon *lemon juice*, 1 teaspoon *Worcestershire sauce*, ½ teaspoon *salt*, ½ teaspoon *sugar*, ½ teaspoon *dry mustard*, ½ teaspoon *pepper*, and 1 clove *garlic*, minced. Cover and shake well. Shake before serving. Makes about 1 cup.

Nutrition information per serving: 496 calories, 32 g protein, 11 g carbohydrate, 36 g total fat (9 g saturated), 181 mg cholesterol, 597 mg sodium, 726 mg potassium

Nevada

MARINATED GRILLED LAMB

*Most Basques came to the West from
the mountains between Spain and
France in answer to a call from
American sheep ranchers for herders.
Not surprisingly, lamb in every form
was part of their cooking.*

1   5- to 7-pound leg of lamb,
    boned and butterflied
1   cup dry red wine
⅓   cup soy sauce
⅓   cup Dijon-style mustard
2   tablespoons olive oil

Remove fell (paper-thin, reddish
pink layer), if present, from outer
surface of leg of lamb. Trim excess
fat from lamb. Place lamb in a plastic bag set in a deep bowl.

For marinade, in a mixing bowl
combine wine, soy sauce, Dijon-
style mustard, and olive oil. Pour
marinade over lamb; seal bag.
Marinate in the refrigerator for 8 to
24 hours, turning bag occasionally
to distribute marinade. Drain lamb;
discard marinade.

To keep the lamb flat during
cooking, insert two 18-inch wood-
en or metal skewers through meat
at right angles, making a cross.

In a covered grill arrange *medium* coals around a drip pan. Test
for *medium-slow* heat over the drip
pan. Place lamb on the grill rack
over the drip pan but not over the
coals. Lower the grill hood. Grill
about 1¼ hours for medium doneness. Remove skewers. Let stand
for 15 minutes.

To serve, thinly slice lamb
across the grain. Makes 12 to 16
servings.

Nutrition information per serving:
*257 calories, 35 g protein, 1 g carbohydrate,
11 g total fat (4 g saturated), 109 mg cholesterol, 399 mg sodium, 437 mg potassium*

Colorado

HUNTER'S LEG OF LAMB

*Despite the range wars that were
common occurrences between cattlemen
and sheepherders, Colorado ranches still
managed to develop a fine reputation for
high-quality beef and lamb.*

1   4- to 6-pound leg of lamb,
    boned and butterflied
¾   cup dry red wine
⅓   cup Worcestershire sauce
1   6-ounce package dried
    apricots, chopped
½   cup water
1   6-ounce package long
    grain and wild rice mix
1   cup finely chopped onion
1   teaspoon lemon-pepper
    seasoning
¼   cup snipped fresh basil *or*
    1 tablespoon dried
    basil, crushed
    Watercress (optional)

Remove fell (paper-thin, pinkish
red layer), if present, from outer
surface of lamb. Place lamb in a 3-
quart rectangular baking dish. Stir
together the red wine and the

Worcestershire sauce; pour over lamb. Cover and marinate in refrigerator for 6 hours or overnight. Turn meat over once or spoon marinade over meat occasionally.

Remove meat from dish, reserving marinade. In a small bowl combine chopped apricots and water. Bring to boiling. Remove from heat; cover and let stand 5 minutes.

Prepare the rice mix according to the package directions, adding chopped onion to mix. In a large bowl stir together the cooked rice and onions, undrained apricots, basil, and lemon-pepper seasoning. Mix well.

Trim fat. Place meat, boned side up, between 2 pieces of plastic wrap; pound meat with a meat mallot to an even thickness. Spread *half* of the rice mixture over roast. Roll up; tie securely.

Place roast, seam side down, on a rack in a shallow roasting pan. Insert a meat thermometer into thickest portion of meat. Roast in a 325° oven for 1¾ to 2½ hours or till thermometer registers 150°. Baste lamb with reserved marinade several times during cooking. (Do not brush during the last 5 minutes.) Let stand 15 minutes before carving. Meanwhile, put remaining rice mixture in a 1-quart casserole; cover. Bake with lamb during the last 25 to 30 minutes of meat's roasting and standing time. Remove strings. If desired, garnish with watercress. Makes 10 servings.

Nutrition information per serving: *320 calories, 32 g protein, 27 g carbohydrate, 8 g total fat (3 g saturated), 91 mg cholesterol, 539 mg sodium, 700 mg potassium*

California

GREEN GODDESS DRESSING

In the early part of this century, George Arliss starred in a San Francisco production of The Green Goddess, *a play by William Archer. In honor of the actor, the famed Palace Hotel created this dressing.*

¾	**cup packed parsley leaves**
⅓	**cup mayonnaise *or* salad dressing**
⅓	**cup dairy sour cream *or* plain yogurt**
1	**green onion, cut up**
1	**tablespoon vinegar**
1	**teaspoon anchovy paste *or* 1 anchovy fillet, cut up**
¼	**teaspoon dried basil, crushed**
⅛	**teaspoon garlic powder**
⅛	**teaspoon dried tarragon, crushed**
1	**to 2 tablespoons milk**

In a blender container or food processor bowl combine parsley, mayonnaise, sour cream, green onion, vinegar, anchovy paste, basil, garlic powder, and tarragon. Cover and blend or process till smooth. Cover and store in the refrigerator for up to 2 weeks.

Before serving, stir in some milk to make the dressing the desired consistency. Makes about 1 cup.

Nutrition information per tablespoon: *45 calories, 0 g protein, 1 g carbohydrate, 5 g total fat (1 g saturated), 5 mg cholesterol, 39 mg sodium, 30 mg potassium*

California

PASTA WITH ARTICHOKE SAUCE

Castroville, some 100 miles south of San Francisco, describes itself as the artichoke center of the world. In fact, more artichokes are grown in the Mediterranean area, but California produces all of the commercial crop in the United States.

½	cup chopped onion
1	clove garlic, minced
1	tablespoon olive oil *or* cooking oil
2	tablespoons all-purpose flour
1	tablespoon snipped fresh basil *or* oregano *or* 1 teaspoon dried basil *or* oregano, crushed
⅛	teaspoon salt
1¼	cups milk
1	13¾-ounce can artichoke hearts, drained and cut up
2	tablespoons finely shredded asiago cheese *or* Parmesan cheese
4	ounces spinach fettucine, carrot fettucine, *or* whole wheat fettuccine, cooked and drained Coarsely ground pepper

For sauce, in a saucepan cook onion and garlic in hot oil till tender but not brown. Stir in flour, basil or oregano, and salt. Add milk all at once. Cook and stir till thickened and bubbly. Cook and stir for 1 minute more. Stir in artichoke hearts and cheese; heat through.

To serve, spoon sauce over hot fettuccine. Sprinkle with pepper. Makes 4 servings.

Nutrition information per serving: 238 calories, 10 g protein, 35 g carbohydrate, 7 g total fat (2 g saturated), 9 mg cholesterol, 211 mg sodium, 420 mg potassium

California

AVOCADO AND FRUIT SALAD

In 1911 a nurseryman from southern California traveled throughout Mexico looking for avocado stock that would adapt to the California soil and climate. All but one of the cuttings he brought back failed to flourish. The one that survived was named fuerte, *Spanish for "strong." That tree was the start of California's avocado industry.*

¼	cup walnut oil *or* salad oil
¼	cup raspberry vinegar Boston *or* Bibb lettuce leaves
2	medium red grapefruit, peeled and sectioned
1	medium avocado, seeded, peeled, and sliced lengthwise
1	medium papaya, seeded, peeled, and sliced lengthwise
2	tablespoons toasted chopped walnuts
½	cup raspberries (optional)

For dressing, in a screw-top jar combine walnut oil or salad oil and raspberry vinegar. Cover and shake well. Chill for at least 1 hour.

Line 4 salad plates with Boston or Bibb lettuce leaves. Place grapefruit sections in center. Fan avocado and papaya slices on opposite sides of grapefruit. Sprinkle with toasted walnuts.

If desired, sprinkle the salads with raspberries. Shake dressing well; pour over each salad. Makes 4 servings.

Nutrition information per serving: *290 calories, 3 g protein, 22 g carbohydrate, 24 g total fat (3 g saturated), 0 mg cholesterol, 8 mg sodium, 679 mg potassium*

California

CAESAR SALAD WITH BAGEL CROUTONS

Like so many California dishes, this one has its roots in Mexico, although by way of Italy. It was the creation of Caesar Cardini for his restaurant in Tijuana, which is just across the border from San Diego.

1	egg
⅓	cup chicken broth
2	anchovy fillets *or* 1 teaspoon anchovy paste
3	tablespoons olive oil
1	teaspoon finely shredded lemon peel
2	tablespoons lemon juice
1	teaspoon Dijon-style mustard
¼	teaspoon white wine Worcestershire sauce
1	clove garlic, halved
10	cups torn romaine lettuce
1	cup Bagel Croutons
¼	cup grated Parmesan cheese
	Whole black peppercorns

For dressing, in a blender container or food processor bowl combine the egg, chicken broth, anchovy fillets or paste, olive oil, lemon peel, the lemon juice, mustard, and Worcestershire sauce. Cover and blend or process till smooth. Transfer the dressing to a small saucepan. Cook and stir over low heat for 8 to 10 minutes or till thickened. Do not boil. Transfer to a bowl. Cover surface with plastic wrap; chill for 2 to 24 hours.

To serve, rub the inside of a wooden salad bowl with the cut sides of the garlic clove; discard garlic clove. Add romaine, Bagel Croutons, and Parmesan cheese to salad bowl. Pour dressing over salad. Toss lightly to coat. Transfer to individual salad plates. Grind peppercorns over each serving. Makes 6 servings.

Bagel Croutons: Split 2 *onion bagels.* With the cut side down, slice each bagel half into ¼-inch-thick half moons. In a large skillet combine 3 tablespoons *margarine or butter,* 1 tablespoon *olive oil,* and 2 small cloves *garlic,* minced. Cook and stir till margarine or butter melts. Remove from heat. Stir bagel pieces into margarine mixture. Spread pieces in a single layer in a shallow baking pan. Bake in a 300° oven for 10 minutes. Stir; bake 10 to 15 minutes more or till dry and crisp. Cool croutons. Store in an airtight container for up to 1 week. Makes about 2 cups.

Nutrition information per serving: *241 calories, 7 g protein, 14 g carbohydrate, 18 g total fat (3 g saturated), 40 mg cholesterol, 343 mg sodium, 336 mg potassium*

Idaho

TWICE-BAKED POTATOES

Idaho homesteaders used potatoes as a cash crop in the mid-1800s. They sold the tubers to miners who rushed to the state looking for lead, gold, and silver.

2   large baking potatoes
      (10 to 12 ounces each)
½   cup sour cream dip with
      toasted onion
¼   cup finely shredded
      cheddar cheese
      (1 ounce)
¼   cup finely shredded
      zucchini
¼   cup finely shredded carrot
⅛   teaspoon salt
⅛   teaspoon white pepper *or*
      black pepper
1   to 2 tablespoons milk
      (optional)

Scrub potatoes thoroughly with a brush. Pat dry, and prick with a fork. Bake in a 425° oven for 40 to 60 minutes or till tender.

Cut potatoes in half lengthwise. Gently scoop out potato, leaving a thin shell. Place the potato pulp in a small mixing bowl.

With an electric mixer on low speed or a potato masher, beat or mash potato pulp. Add the sour cream dip, cheddar cheese, zucchini, carrot, salt, and pepper; beat till smooth. (If necessary to reach desired consistency, stir in 1 to 2 tablespoons milk.)

Spoon mashed potato mixture into potato shells. Place in a 1½-quart rectangular baking dish. Bake in a 425° oven for 20 to 25 minutes or till lightly browned. Serves 4.

Nutrition information per serving: 261 calories, 6 g protein, 41 g carbohydrate, 9 g total fat (5 g saturated), 20 mg cholesterol, 140 mg sodium, 735 mg potassium

California

PASTA SALAD WITH CHÈVRE AND TOMATOES

In recent years, California chefs have developed a cuisine inspired in part by the foods of Mediterranean countries. They recognize that California's warm, gentle climate mirrors that of southern France and Italy, as does the wonderful abundance of fresh ingredients available to them.

1½   cups tricolor corkscrew
      macaroni
1   6-ounce jar marinated
      artichoke hearts
2   ounces sliced salami, cut
      into strips
⅓   cup sliced pitted ripe
      olives
2   tablespoons olive oil *or*
      salad oil
2   tablespoons red wine
      vinegar
1   tablespoon snipped fresh
      basil *or* 1 teaspoon
      dried basil, crushed

1 tablespoon snipped fresh oregano *or* 1 teaspoon dried oregano, crushed

4 ounces chèvre (goat cheese), cut into chunks, *or* crumbled feta cheese

½ cup halved red *and/or* yellow cherry tomatoes

Cook macaroni according to package directions; drain. Rinse with cold water; drain again.

Meanwhile, drain the artichoke hearts, reserving the marinade. Coarsely chop the artichokes.

In a large mixing bowl combine cooked macaroni, artichokes, salami, and ripe olives.

For dressing, in a screw-top jar combine the reserved artichoke marinade, olive or salad oil, wine vinegar, basil, and oregano. Cover and shake well. Pour over pasta mixture and toss lightly to coat. Cover and chill for 4 to 24 hours.

To serve, toss in chèvre or feta cheese and tomatoes. Makes 4 to 6 servings.

Nutrition information per serving: 387 calories, 14 g protein, 38 g carbohydrate, 21 g total fat (7 g saturated), 22 mg cholesterol, 570 mg sodium, 274 mg potassium

California

SUMMER RATATOUILLE

The Asian twist to this classic French eggplant casserole is very typical of current California cooking, which has become an increasingly cross-cultural mélange.

2 tablespoons olive oil *or* cooking oil

1 small onion, cut into wedges

2 Japanese eggplants, cut into ¼-inch-thick slices

1 cup sliced fresh shiitake mushrooms *or* other mushrooms

1 small zucchini *or* yellow summer squash, halved lengthwise and cut into ¼-inch-thick slices (1 cup)

½ cup red *and/or* yellow sweet pepper strips

2 cloves garlic, minced

2 medium tomatoes, cut into wedges

3 tablespoons snipped fresh basil *or* 2 teaspoons dried basil, crushed

¼ teaspoon salt

¼ teaspoon coarsely ground pepper

⅓ cup finely shredded asiago cheese *or* Parmesan cheese

Heat olive oil or cooking oil in a large skillet. Add onion, eggplant, mushrooms, zucchini or yellow summer squash, sweet pepper strips, and garlic. Cook and stir over medium heat about 10 minutes or till vegetables are tender. Add tomatoes, basil, salt, and pepper. Cook, stirring occasionally, for 5 minutes more. Sprinkle with cheese. Makes 4 to 5 servings.

Nutrition information per serving: 173 calories, 6 g protein, 18 g carbohydrate, 10 g total fat (3 g saturated), 6 mg cholesterol, 299 mg sodium, 568 mg potassium

COWBOY BEANS

*No range cook would start out
on the trail without a good supply of
dried beans. In fact, mealtime
was often referred to as bean time.*

½   **pound dry pinto beans
(1¼ cups)**
½   **cup chopped smoked ham
or salt pork**
1   **cup chopped onion**
1   **8-ounce can tomato sauce**
1   **4-ounce can diced green
chilies**
¼   **cup packed brown sugar**
1   **to 1½ teaspoons chili
powder**
½   **teaspoon salt**
½   **teaspoon dry mustard**

Rinse beans. In a large saucepan combine beans and 4 cups *water*. Bring to boiling; reduce heat. Simmer for 2 minutes. Remove from heat. Cover and let stand for 1 hour. *(Or,* skip boiling the water and soak beans overnight in a covered bowl.)

Drain and rinse beans. In the same pan combine beans and 4 cups *fresh water*. Bring to boiling; reduce heat. Cover and simmer about 1¼ hours or till beans are tender, stirring occasionally. Drain beans, reserving liquid.

In a 1-quart casserole combine the beans, ham, and onion. Stir together ½ *cup* of the bean liquid, tomato sauce, chili peppers, brown sugar, chili powder, salt, and mustard. Stir into bean mixture. Bake,

covered, in a 325° oven about 1 hour. Uncover and bake about 45 minutes more or to desired consistency, stirring occasionally. Makes 6 servings.

Nutrition information per serving: *198 calories, 12 g protein, 37 g carbohydrate, 1 g total fat (0 g saturated), 6 mg cholesterol, 788 mg sodium, 721 mg potassium*

SOURDOUGH BREAD

*Like their Alaska counterparts,
California miners during the gold
rushes of 1849 and later kept a bubbling
crock of sourdough starter to use for
baking. San Francisco is still famous
for its sourdough bread, which has a
unique flavor that no one has been able
to duplicate anywhere else.*

1   **cup Sourdough Starter
(see recipe, page 187)**
5½   **to 6 cups all-purpose flour**
1   **package active dry yeast**
1½   **cups water**
3   **tablespoons sugar**
3   **tablespoons margarine *or*
butter**
1   **teaspoon salt
Cornmeal**

Bring Sourdough Starter to room temperature. In a large mixing bowl combine *2½ cups* of the flour and yeast; set aside. In a saucepan heat and stir water, sugar, margarine or butter, and salt *just till warm* (120° to 130°) and margarine almost melts. Add to flour mixture. Add Sourdough Starter. Beat with an electric mixer on low to medium speed for 30 seconds, scraping bowl. Beat on high speed for 3 minutes. Stir in as much of the remaining flour as you can.

On a lightly floured surface, knead in enough of the remaining flour to make a moderately stiff dough that is smooth and elastic (6 to 8 minutes total). Shape into a ball. Place dough in a lightly greased bowl, turning once to grease the surface. Cover and let rise in a warm place till double (45 to 60 minutes).

Punch dough down. Turn out onto a lightly floured surface. Divide in half. Cover and let rest for 10 minutes. Meanwhile, lightly grease a large baking sheet. Sprinkle with cornmeal. Shape *each* half of dough into a ball. Place on prepared baking sheet. Flatten slightly to 6 inches in diameter. With a sharp knife, make crisscross slashes about ¼ inch deep across the tops of the loaves. Cover and let rise in a warm place till *nearly* double (about 30 minutes).

Bake in a 375° oven for 30 to 35 minutes or till bread tests done (if necessary, cover loosely with foil the last 15 minutes of baking to prevent overbrowning). Cool on a wire rack. Makes 2 loaves (24 servings).

Nutrition information per serving:
144 calories, 4 g protein, 28 g carbohydrate, 2 g total fat (0 g saturated), 0 mg cholesterol, 102 mg sodium, 45 mg potassium

SOURDOUGH STARTER

1	package active dry yeast
2½	cups warm water (105° to 115°)
2	cups all-purpose flour
1	tablespoon sugar *or* honey

In a bowl dissolve yeast in *½ cup* of the warm water. Stir in the remaining water, flour, and sugar or honey. Stir till smooth. Cover bowl with 100 percent cotton cheesecloth. Let stand at room temperature (75° to 85°) 5 to 10 days or till the mixture has a sour, fermented aroma, stirring 2 or 3 times each day. (Fermentation time depends upon the room temperature; a warmer room hastens fermentation.)

When fermented, transfer starter to a 1-quart jar. Cover with cheesecloth; refrigerate. Do not cover jar with a tight-fitting lid. If starter isn't used within 10 days, stir in 1 teaspoon *sugar or honey*. Repeat every 10 days till used.

To use starter, bring desired amount to room temperature. For every 1 cup used, stir ¾ cup *all-purpose flour*, ¾ cup *water*, and 1 teaspoon *sugar or honey* into the remaining amount. Cover and let stand at room temperature at least 1 day or till bubbly. Then refrigerate for later use. Makes about 2 cups.

California

STUFFED ARTICHOKES

California's artichoke industry got its start at the end of the nineteenth century. The first commercial acreage was developed by Italian immigrants who settled in the coastal area south of San Francisco. The thistly plant thrived in the foggy, damp climate. Today, about 12,000 acres are under cultivation in four counties.

4   small artichokes
      (about 8 ounces each)
1   tablespoon lemon juice
4   dried tomato halves
      (not oil-packed)
¾   cup finely chopped
      zucchini
⅓   cup fine dry bread crumbs
⅓   cup grated Parmesan
      cheese *or* Romano
      cheese
¼   cup crumbled feta cheese
2   tablespoons margarine *or*
      butter, melted
2   teaspoons snipped fresh
      oregano *or* ½ teaspoon
      dried oregano, crushed
⅛   teaspoon pepper

Wash artichokes; trim stems and remove loose outer leaves. Cut off 1 inch from each top; snip off the sharp leaf tips. Brush the cut edges with lemon juice.

In a large saucepan or Dutch oven bring a large amount of water to boiling. Add artichokes. Return to boiling; reduce heat. Cover and simmer for 20 to 30 minutes or till a leaf pulls out easily. Drain artichokes upside down on paper towels. Spread leaves apart.

When cool enough to handle, use a spoon to remove center leaves (cone) and choke; discard.

Meanwhile, place dried tomatoes in a small bowl. Add enough boiling water to cover tomatoes; soak for 10 to 15 minutes or till softened. Drain and pat dry. Finely chop tomatoes; set aside.

In a medium mixing bowl combine zucchini, bread crumbs, Parmesan or Romano cheese, feta cheese, melted margarine or butter, oregano, pepper, and chopped tomatoes. Add enough water to moisten.

Place artichokes upright in a 2-quart square baking dish. Spoon zucchini mixture into artichoke centers and between leaves. Bake, loosely covered with foil, in a 350° oven about 25 minutes or till heated through. Makes 4 servings.

Nutrition information per serving:
278 calories, 13 g protein, 34 g carbohydrate, 12 g total fat (5 g saturated), 20 mg cholesterol, 599 mg sodium, 870 mg potassium

California

WESTERN PEPPER JELLY

When westerners put up their pickles and preserves, they revised their treasured recipes to include regional flavors and ingredients like spicy jalapeños. This jelly is offered as a condiment for meat, or as an hors d'oeuvre spread on crackers and topped with cheese.

2 medium cooking apples, cored and coarsely chopped (2 cups)
1 medium green pepper, coarsely chopped (¾ cup)
6 to 8 jalapeño peppers, halved
5 cups sugar
1½ cups cider vinegar
½ of a 6-ounce package (1 foil pouch) liquid fruit pectin
¼ cup finely chopped green pepper
¼ cup finely chopped red sweet pepper
1 small banana pepper, finely chopped

In a 4- or 5-quart Dutch oven combine apples, coarsely chopped green pepper, jalapeño peppers, sugar, vinegar, and ¼ cup *water.* Bring to boiling; reduce heat. Boil gently, uncovered, for 10 minutes.

Strain mixture through a sieve, pressing with back of a spoon to remove all liquid (you should have about 4 cups). Discard pulp. Return liquid to Dutch oven; bring to boil. Add pectin; bring to a full, rolling boil. Boil hard for 1 minute, stirring occasionally. Remove from heat. Stir in the finely chopped green pepper, red sweet pepper, and banana pepper.

Pour into hot, sterilized half-pint jars, leaving ¼-inch headspace. Wipe the rims and adjust the lids. Process in boiling-water canner for 5 minutes (start timing after water boils). Remove and cool on a wire rack till set. (Jelly will take 2 to 3 days to set. Chopped pepper pieces will float to top on standing.) Makes about 5 half-pints.

Note: If you would like to use antique canning jars, ladle the hot jelly into sterilized jars, leaving ½-inch headspace. Adjust lids; cool and then store in refrigerator.

Nutrition information per tablespoon: 47 calories, 0 g protein, 13 g carbohydrate, 0 g total fat (0 g saturated), 0 mg cholesterol, 0 mg sodium, 15 mg potassium

Montana

KOLACHES

For the Bohemians who settled in Montana, these yeast-raised sweet rolls were a fragrant reminder of home. There are a number of traditional fillings, including one made of ground poppy seed, milk, and honey.

3¾ to 4¼ cups all-purpose
 flour
1 package active dry yeast
1 cup milk
¾ cup margarine *or* butter
½ cup sugar
½ teaspoon salt
4 egg yolks
1 teaspoon finely shredded
 lemon peel
 Apricot Filling
2 tablespoons margarine *or*
 butter, melted, *or* milk
 Powdered sugar

In a large mixing bowl stir together *2 cups* of the flour and the yeast. Set mixture aside.

In a medium saucepan heat and stir the 1 cup milk, the ¾ cup margarine or butter, sugar, and salt *just till warm* (120° to 130°) and margarine almost melts. Add to the flour mixture. Add the egg yolks. Beat with an electric mixer on low to medium speed for 30 seconds, scraping the sides of the bowl constantly. Then beat on high speed for 3 minutes. Using a wooden spoon, stir in the lemon peel and as much of the remaining flour as you can.

Turn dough out onto a lightly floured surface. Knead in enough of the remaining flour to make a moderately soft dough that is smooth and elastic (3 to 5 minutes total). Place dough in a greased bowl, turning once to grease the surface. Cover and let rise in a warm place till double (1 to 1½ hours). Meanwhile, prepare desired filling. Set aside to cool.

Punch down dough. Turn the dough out onto a lightly floured surface. Divide in half. Cover and let rest for 10 minutes. Grease baking sheets. Shape *each* half of dough into 12 balls, pulling the edges under to make smooth tops. Place the balls 3 inches apart on the prepared baking sheets. Flatten each ball to 2½ inches in diameter. Cover; let rise till *nearly* double (about 35 minutes).

Using your thumb or two fingers, make an indentation in the center of each dough circle. Spoon about *2 teaspoons* filling into each indentation. Lightly brush the 2 tablespoons melted margarine or milk around the edges of rolls.

Bake in a 375° oven for 10 to 12 minutes or till rolls are golden brown. Remove rolls from baking sheets and cool on a wire rack. Lightly sift powdered sugar over the tops. Makes 24 kolaches.

Apricot Filling: In a small saucepan combine 1 cup snipped dried *apricots* and enough *water* to come 1 inch above the apricots. Bring to boiling. Reduce heat. Cover and simmer for 10 to 15 minutes or till apricots are very soft. Drain, reserving *2 tablespoons* cooking liquid.

In a blender container or food processor bowl place apricots, reserved liquid, ¼ cup *sugar*, 1 teaspoon *lemon juice*, and ¼ teaspoon ground *nutmeg*. Cover and blend or process till smooth, stopping to scrape down the sides as necessary. Makes 1 cup.

Nutrition information per kolache: *188 calories, 3 g protein, 26 g carbohydrate, 8 g total fat (1 g saturated), 36 mg cholesterol, 108 mg sodium, 124 mg potassium*

California

DATE PINWHEEL COOKIES

Date palms need the hot, dry climate of the desert to survive, so it's not surprising that those planted by the Spanish missionaries along the California coast did poorly. Early in this century, experiments with an Algerian variety in the state's inland valleys finally proved successful.

Date Filling
½   **cup margarine *or* butter**
½   **cup shortening**
3   **cups all-purpose flour**
½   **cup sugar**
½   **cup packed brown sugar**
1   **egg**
3   **tablespoons milk**
1   **teaspoon vanilla**
½   **teaspoon baking soda**
¼   **teaspoon salt**

Prepare Date Filling; set aside.

Beat margarine or butter and shortening with an electric mixer about 30 seconds or till softened. Add about *half* of the flour. Then add the sugars, egg, milk, vanilla, baking soda, and salt. Beat till thoroughly combined, scraping the sides of the bowl occasionally. Beat or stir in the remaining flour. Cover and chill about 1 hour or till easy to handle.

To shape, divide the dough in half. Place each half of the dough between 2 sheets of waxed paper. Using a rolling pin, roll each half into a 12x10-inch rectangle. Remove top sheets of waxed paper.

Spread Date Filling over each half of the dough. From a long side, roll up each half jelly-roll style, removing bottom sheet of paper as you roll. Moisten and pinch edges to seal each roll. Wrap each in waxed paper or plastic wrap. Chill for 4 to 48 hours.

Grease a cookie sheet; set aside. Cut the dough into ¼-inch-thick slices. Place slices 2 inches apart on the prepared cookie sheet. Bake in a 375° oven for 10 to 12 minutes or till done. Remove cookies from cookie sheet and cool on a wire rack. Makes about 84 cookies.

Date Filling: In a saucepan snip one 8-ounce package (1⅓ cups) pitted whole *dates*. Stir in ½ cup *water* and ⅓ cup *sugar*. Bring to boiling, then reduce heat. Cook and stir about 2 minutes or till thickened. Then stir in 2 tablespoons *lemon juice* and ½ teaspoon *vanilla*. Set the filling aside to cool. Makes about 2 cups.

Nutrition information per cookie: 56 calories, 1 g protein, 8 g carbohydrate, 2 g total fat (0 g saturated), 2 mg cholesterol, 22 mg sodium, 27 mg potassium

California

CREAMY FRESH APRICOT TART

Apricots were reportedly grown in Virginia in the seventeenth century, but even that gentle climate was too harsh for the delicate fruit. Commercial orchards were successfully established in the Santa Clara Valley near San Jose as early as 1792. Today the Golden State leads the nation and the world in apricot production.

1¼ cups all-purpose flour
¼   cup sugar
½   cup ground toasted pistachio nuts *or* almonds
½   cup cold margarine *or* butter
2   beaten egg yolks
1   tablespoon water
½   cup sugar
3   tablespoons cornstarch
2   cups milk
3   beaten egg yolks
1   tablespoon margarine *or* butter
1   teaspoon vanilla
8   fresh whole apricots, pitted and quartered
3   tablespoons chopped toasted pistachio nuts *or* toasted slivered almonds

For pastry, stir together the flour, the ¼ cup sugar, and ground nuts. Cut in the ½ cup margarine till pieces are the size of small peas. Combine the 2 egg yolks and water; gradually stir the egg yolk mixture into the flour mixture. Using your fingers, gently knead dough just till a ball forms. If necessary, chill 30 to 60 minutes or till easy to handle.

On a lightly floured surface roll dough from center to edges, forming a 12-inch circle. Wrap pastry around a rolling pin; unroll pastry onto a 10-inch tart pan with a removable bottom. Ease pastry into tart pan, being careful not to stretch it. Press pastry into the fluted sides of the tart pan and trim edges. Using the tines of a fork, prick bottom and sides of pastry generously.

Line pastry shell with a double thickness of foil. Bake in a 375° oven 10 minutes. Remove foil. Bake 8 to 10 minutes more or till golden. Completely cool pastry shell in pan.

Meanwhile, for filling, in a saucepan mix the ½ cup sugar and the cornstarch; stir in milk. Cook and stir over medium heat till mixture is bubbly. Cook and stir 2 minutes more. Remove from heat. Gradually stir about *1 cup* of the milk mixture into the 3 egg yolks. Stir egg yolk mixture into milk mixture in saucepan. Bring to a gentle boil; reduce heat. Cook and stir 2 minutes. Remove from heat. Stir in the 1 tablespoon margarine and vanilla. Cover surface with plastic wrap; cool to room temperature *(do not stir)*. Spread filling in cooled pastry shell. Arrange apricot quarters, cut sides up, in a circle atop filling. Press fruit gently into filling till flush with filling surface. Cover; chill 1 to 3 hours. Before serving, sprinkle with toasted nuts. Serves 8.

Nutrition information per serving: 418 calories, 9 g protein, 46 g carbohydrate, 23 g total fat (4 g saturated), 138 mg cholesterol, 145 mg sodium, 356 mg potassium

California

GRAPEFRUIT MERINGUE PIE

California is a main producer of citrus fruit, including oranges, lemons, and grapefruit. The citrus industry faced a unique crisis after the San Francisco earthquake of 1906: so much lumber was needed to rebuild the city that none was left to make crates for boxing citrus fruit.

1	cup sugar
3	tablespoons all-purpose flour
3	tablespoons cornstarch
	Dash salt
1½	cups water
3	eggs
2	tablespoons margarine *or* butter
1½	teaspoons finely shredded grapefruit peel
⅓	cup grapefruit juice
	Pastry for Single-Crust Pie (see recipe, page 30)
	Meringue for Pie

For filling, in a medium saucepan combine sugar, flour, cornstarch, and salt. Gradually stir in water. Cook and stir over medium-high heat till thickened and bubbly. Reduce heat; cook and stir for 2 minutes more. Remove from heat.

Separate egg yolks from whites; set whites aside to come to room temperature for meringue. Beat egg yolks slightly. Gradually stir *1 cup* of the hot filling into yolks; return all to saucepan. Bring to a gentle boil. Cook and stir 2 minutes more. Remove from heat. Stir in margarine or butter and grapefruit peel. Gradually stir in grapefruit juice, gently mixing well. Pour hot filling into Baked Pastry Shell.

Immediately spread meringue over *hot* pie filling, carefully spreading to edge of pastry to seal and prevent shrinkage.

Bake in a 350° oven for 15 minutes. Cool for 1 hour on a wire rack. Cover and chill. Makes 8 servings.

Meringue for Pie: Let the 3 *egg whites* stand at room temperature for 30 minutes. In a large mixing bowl combine the egg whites, ½ teaspoon *vanilla*, and ¼ teaspoon *cream of tartar*. Beat with an electric mixer on medium speed about 1 minute or till soft peaks form (tips curl). Gradually add 6 tablespoons *sugar*, 1 tablespoon at a time, beating on high speed about 4 minutes more or till mixture forms stiff, glossy peaks and sugar dissolves.

Nutrition information per serving: 430 calories, 7 g protein, 60 g carbohydrate, 19 g total fat (4 g saturated), 80 mg cholesterol, 306 mg sodium, 70 mg potassium

Utah

PIONEER FRUIT CANDY

A shortage of food was a familiar hardship to the first Mormon settlers in Utah. To be prepared for any emergency, Mormons still follow the practice of stockpiling a year's worth of provisions. Canned and preserved foods, like the dried fruits used for this candy, are pantry staples.

1⅓ cups raisins
¾ cup dried figs
⅔ cup pitted dates
½ cup chopped pitted prunes
1 teaspoon finely shredded orange peel
½ cup finely chopped walnuts
1 tablespoon frozen orange juice concentrate, thawed
8 ounces chocolate *or* white candy coating, chopped
1 tablespoon shortening

Finely chop first four ingredients. *Or,* process in a food processor.

Mix fruit, orange peel, walnuts, and juice concentrate. Shape into balls about 1-inch in diameter. Chill several hours or overnight.

In a saucepan melt candy coating and shortening over low heat, stirring constantly. Dip candies in chocolate to coat evenly. Place on waxed paper. Let harden on a wire rack. Makes about 42 candies.

Nutrition information per candy: 76 calories, 1 g protein, 13 g carbohydrate, 3 g total fat (1 g saturated), 0 mg cholesterol, 1 mg sodium, 107 mg potassium

California

CALIFORNIA ALMOND SHORTBREAD COOKIES

Virtually all of this country's almonds are from California. While attempts were made to grow the nut elsewhere, few states could provide the proper climatic conditions for the trees to thrive. Almonds are also California's largest food export.

2 cups all-purpose flour
½ cup sugar
½ cup ground toasted almonds
1 cup butter
¾ cup semisweet chocolate pieces
1½ teaspoons shortening
About 40 blanched whole almonds

In a bowl combine flour, sugar, and ground almonds. Cut in butter till mixture resembles fine crumbs and starts to cling. Shape into a ball and knead till smooth. Divide the dough in half.

On an ungreased cookie sheet pat or roll *half* of the dough into a 9x5-inch rectangle. Repeat with other half of dough.

Bake in a 325° oven for 20 to 25 minutes or till bottom of the dough just starts to turn brown. Cool about 5 minutes. While the shortbread is still warm, cut each rectangle into 3x1 inch sticks; cool on a wire rack.

In a small heavy saucepan melt chocolate and shortening together over low heat, stirring occasionally. Dip half of each cookie into chocolate mixture. Place an almond in the center of each glazed half. Place cookies on waxed paper and let stand till chocolate is set. (*Or,* refrigerate cookies about 5 minutes or till chocolate is set.) Makes about 40 cookies.

Nutrition information per cookie:
110 calories, 1 g protein, 10 g carbohydrate, 7 g total fat (4 g saturated), 12 mg cholesterol, 48 mg sodium, 45 mg potassium

California

POACHED FIGS WITH CRÈME ANGLAISE

California provides all of America's commercially grown figs. The first variety planted in the state came to be known as the Black Mission as it was brought here by the Spanish padres. Along with the amber-colored Calimyrna, it is still one of the most popular.

⅔ cup whipping cream
1 egg yolk
⅓ cup sugar
½ teaspoon vanilla
1 cup port
4 light *or* 8 dark fresh whole figs *or* 2 large pears, cored and halved
Fresh mint sprigs

For crème anglaise, in a small, heavy saucepan bring the cream just to boiling, stirring frequently. Remove saucepan from heat.

In a bowl combine about *2 tablespoons* of the hot cream, the egg yolk, and sugar. Beat with an electric mixer on high speed 2 to 3 minutes or till thick and lemon-colored.

Gradually stir about *half* of the remaining cream mixture into the egg yolk mixture. Transfer the egg yolk mixture to the saucepan. Cook and stir over medium heat about 5 minutes or till mixture *nearly* returns to boiling. Remove from heat. Stir in vanilla. Cover surface with plastic wrap. Chill in the refrigerator till serving time.

To poach figs or pears, in a skillet bring port to boiling; add figs or pears. Return to boiling; reduce heat. Cover; simmer over low heat about 5 minutes or till tender. Using a slotted spoon, remove fruit from port. Return port to boiling; cook over medium heat 4 to 5 minutes or till liquid is reduced to about ½ cup. Chill fruit and port separately.

To serve, spoon crème anglaise onto 4 dessert plates. Place figs or pear half in the center of each plate. Drizzle with the port. Garnish with fresh mint. Makes 4 servings.

Nutrition information per serving:
381 calories, 2 g protein, 44 g carbohydrate, 16 g total fat (10 g saturated), 108 mg cholesterol, 23 mg sodium, 320 mg potassium

California

CAPPUCCINO

San Francisco has always been known as a coffee-drinking town. The coffeehouses in the North Beach section, home to much of the city's Italian population, were famous as gathering places in the 1950s for poets, writers, and artists.

1½ **cups half-and-half, light cream,** *or* **milk**
2 **cups brewed espresso coffee**
   Unsweetened cocoa powder *or* **ground cinnamon**

In a saucepan heat half-and-half till almost boiling. Remove from heat and beat with a rotary beater or wire whisk till foamy. To each of 4 coffee cups add *½ cup* of espresso coffee and *½ cup* of half-and-half. Sprinkle with cocoa powder. Makes four 8-ounce servings.

Nutrition information per serving: *121 calories, 3 g protein, 4 g carbohydrate, 10 g total fat (6 g saturated), 33 mg cholesterol, 39 mg sodium, 185 mg potassium*

flavors from the Pacific Northwest & Beyond

PHEASANT IN ORANGE-HONEY SAUCE

For the early immigrants to the Northwest, there were no crops to harvest nor animals to spare for butchering. They depended on hunting and gathering for their food. Fortunately, there was an abundance of choices, including wild game birds.

1	2½- to 3-pound pheasant *or* broiler-fryer chicken, quartered
1	tablespoon margarine *or* butter
1	tablespoon oil
1	cup chopped onion
¼	cup frozen orange juice concentrate, thawed
¼	cup water
2	tablespoons snipped parsley
1	tablespoon lemon juice
1	teaspoon grated fresh gingerroot *or* ¼ teaspoon ground ginger
¼	teaspoon salt
¼	teaspoon pepper
¼	teaspoon ground nutmeg
2	tablespoons honey
	Kale (optional)

Rinse the poultry; pat dry with paper towels.

In a 12-inch skillet heat margarine or butter and oil; add poultry and onion. Cook over medium heat about 10 minutes or till browned, turning occasionally to brown evenly. Turn meaty side up. Combine the orange juice concentrate, water, parsley, lemon juice, gingerroot or ginger, salt, pepper, and nutmeg; add to skillet. Bring to boiling; reduce heat and simmer, covered, 35 to 40 minutes or till poultry is tender.

Transfer poultry to a platter; cover and keep warm. Increase heat and boil juices gently about 5 minutes or till reduced to 1 cup. Stir in honey. Serve over poultry. If desired, garnish with kale. Makes 4 servings.

Nutrition information per serving: *416 calories, 36 g protein, 20 g carbohydrate, 21 g total fat (6 g saturated), 111 mg cholesterol, 223 mg sodium, 587 mg potassium*

Alaska

SALMON IN PHYLLO WITH MUSTARD-CREAM SAUCE

In the last century, salmon was so plentiful in the Columbia River that it was harvested during low tide with nets pulled by teams of horses. Five species of salmon return to Pacific waters each year, including the chinook, which reaches sixty pounds or more.

1 pound skinless salmon fillets
¼ cup dairy sour cream
2 tablespoons snipped fresh dill *or* 1 teaspoon dried dillweed
8 sheets frozen phyllo dough (18x14-inch rectangles), thawed
⅓ cup margarine *or* butter, melted
Mustard Cream Sauce
Green onion strips (optional)

Cut salmon into 4 portions. Spread *1 tablespoon* of the sour cream over one side of each fish portion. Sprinkle with dill or dillweed, dash *salt*, and dash *pepper*. Set aside.

Unfold phyllo dough; cover with a damp towel or clear plastic wrap. Lay 1 sheet of phyllo dough flat. Brush with some of the melted margarine or butter. Top with another sheet of phyllo dough. Brush with more melted margarine or butter. Add 2 more sheets of dough, making a total of 4 sheets, brushing each sheet with margarine or butter.

Fold the rectangle of dough in half crosswise to form a 9x14-inch rectangle; brush top with margarine or butter. Cut in half crosswise, making 2 smaller rectangles, each about 9x7 inches. Place a salmon fillet upside down on each dough rectangle. Fold the top portion of the dough up over the salmon; then bring bottom portion over salmon, brushing dough with margarine and pressing lightly. Bring the dough edges together and seal.

Repeat with remaining phyllo dough, margarine or butter, and salmon for a total of 4 salmon-phyllo bundles.

Arrange bundles on a baking sheet. Brush tops with margarine. Bake in a 375° oven for 15 to 18 minutes or till phyllo dough is golden and fish flakes easily with a fork. Serve with Mustard Cream Sauce. If desired, garnish bundles with long green onion strips. Serves 4.

Mustard Cream Sauce: Combine ⅓ cup *dry white wine* and 3 tablespoons finely chopped *shallots*. Bring to boiling; reduce heat. Simmer, uncovered, for 8 to 10 minutes or till the liquid is reduced to about 3 tablespoons, stirring occasionally.

Combine 1 cup *light cream* and 4 teaspoons *all-purpose flour*. Stir into wine mixture with ⅛ teaspoon *white pepper*. Cook and stir over medium heat till bubbly. Stir in 1 tablespoon *Dijon-style mustard*. Cook and stir for 1 minute more.

Nutrition information per serving:
626 calories, 29 g protein, 29 g carbohydrate, 42 g total fat (13 g saturated), 120 mg cholesterol, 534 mg sodium, 499 mg potassium

Oregon

PEAR, PROSCIUTTO, AND BLUE CHEESE APPETIZERS

Washington and Oregon, along with California, produce virtually all of the nation's commercial pear crop. The first Bartlett pear tree was planted in Oregon in 1854 in the Rogue River Valley. That valley is also the birthplace of Oregon's acclaimed blue cheese.

3   to 4 ounces very thinly sliced prosciutto
1   ripe pear, cored and cut into 12 wedges
½   cup crumbled blue cheese
2   tablespoons soft-style cream cheese
2   teaspoons milk

Cut prosciutto lengthwise into 12 strips (each about 6x1½ inches). Combine blue cheese, cream cheese, and milk.

Spread about *½ tablespoon* of the blue cheese mixture on a prosciutto strip. Wrap the strip around one pear wedge. Repeat with remaining ingredients.

To serve, place seam side down on a lettuce-lined platter. Chill up to 2 hours. Makes 12 appetizers.

Nutrition information per appetizer:
48 calories, 3 g protein, 2 g carbohydrate, 3 g total fat (2 g saturated), 11 mg cholesterol, 181 mg sodium, 59 mg potassium

Alaska

GRILLED ELK BURGERS

Elk was hunted by northwestern Native Americans and by immigrants in the early years. Although no longer a necessity, hunting is still a favorite form of recreation in the Northwest.

1   beaten egg
3   tablespoons catsup
1   teaspoon Worcestershire sauce
¼   cup soft bread crumbs
1   small onion, finely chopped (¼ cup)
1   teaspoon prepared horseradish
1½   pounds ground elk *or* ground buffalo
6   hamburger buns, split and toasted
     Assorted condiments

In a bowl combine the egg, catsup, and Worcestershire sauce. Stir in the bread crumbs, onion, horseradish, and ½ teaspoon *salt*. Add the ground meat; mix well. Shape into six ¾-inch-thick burgers.

Grill over *medium-hot* coals till no pink remains, turning once (15 to 18 minutes). Serve burgers on toasted buns with assorted condiments. Makes 6 servings.

Nutrition information per serving:
292 calories, 31 g protein, 27 g carbohydrate, 6 g total fat (2 g saturated), 131 mg cholesterol, 419 mg sodium, 407 mg potassium

Washington

FRESH HERB AND CHÈVRE SPREAD

*Although California gets the lion's
share of attention for its justly
famous goat cheeses, the Puget Sound
area of Washington produces
a fine local product.*

1	8-ounce package cream cheese, softened
8	ounces chèvre (goat cheese)
2	tablespoons finely chopped green onion
1	tablespoon snipped fresh tarragon *or* 1 teaspoon dried tarragon, crushed
1	tablespoon snipped fresh rosemary *or* ½ teaspoon dried rosemary, crushed
¼	teaspoon ground white pepper
2	dried tomato halves (oil-packed)
	Fresh tarragon *or* rosemary (optional)
	Assorted crackers

Beat together the cream cheese,
chèvre, green onion, tarragon,
rosemary, and white pepper.

Pat tomatoes with paper towels
to remove excess oil. Finely chop
tomatoes; stir into cheese mixture.

If desired, press cheese mixture
into a 2- to 2½-cup mold lined with
plastic wrap. Cover and chill for
several hours or overnight.

Unmold onto a serving platter.
(*Or*, chill spread in a bowl and
spoon onto a serving platter to
serve.) If desired, garnish with
fresh tarragon or rosemary. Serve
with crackers. Makes 2 cups.

*Nutrition information per table-
spoon: 46 calories, 2 g protein, 5 g carbohydrate, 4 g total fat (3 g saturated), 11 mg
cholesterol, 49 mg sodium, 26 mg potassium*

Oregon

BASQUE LAMB SHANKS

*Before the turn of the century, Basque
sheepherders came from Spain to settle
in the mountainous areas of the West.
Their families followed later. Retired
sheepherders and their wives opened
boardinghouses that became famous
for their home cooking.*

3	or 4 lamb shanks (about 3½ pounds total)
1	tablespoon cooking oil
2	14½-ounce cans stewed tomatoes
½	cup chopped onion
½	cup water
½	teaspoon dried thyme, crushed
½	teaspoon dried basil, crushed
¼	teaspoon salt
¼	teaspoon pepper
1	15-ounce can garbanzo beans, drained
3	cups hot cooked rice *or* couscous

In a Dutch oven brown lamb shanks on all sides in hot oil. Drain off fat. Add *undrained* tomatoes, onion, water, thyme, basil, salt, and pepper. Bring to boiling, reduce heat. Cover and simmer for 1½ hours or till lamb is tender. Skim excess fat from pan juices. Stir in garbanzo beans and heat through.

Serve over hot cooked rice or couscous. Makes 4 to 6 servings.

Nutrition information per serving: 546 calories, 39 g protein, 62 g carbohydrate, 16 g total fat (6 g saturated), 108 mg cholesterol, 603 mg sodium, 889 mg potassium

Alaska

CHILLED SALMON STEAKS WITH LEMON-DILL DRESSING

The Indians of the Northwest would offer prayers of thanksgiving in celebration of the arrival of the first salmon in the spring. The combination of salmon and dill is not Native American, but typically Scandinavian. Danes, Swedes, and Norwegians immigrated to the Oregon Territory from the Midwest.

1½ cups water
¼   cup lemon juice
1   medium onion, sliced
10 whole black peppercorns
3   sprigs parsley
2   bay leaves
6   fresh *or* frozen salmon steaks, cut 1 to 1¼ inches thick (about 2 pounds)
¾   cup mayonnaise *or* salad dressing
3   tablespoons buttermilk
2   tablespoons snipped fresh dill *or* 2 teaspoons dried dillweed
1   tablespoon snipped fresh chives
½   teaspoon finely shredded lemon peel
2   teaspoons lemon juice
    Fresh dill (optional)
    Lemon wedges (optional)

In a 12-inch skillet combine water, lemon juice, onion, peppercorns, parsley, bay leaves, and ½ teaspoon *salt*. Bring to boiling; add salmon steaks. Cover; simmer 8 to 12 minutes (12 to 18 minutes for frozen) or till fish flakes easily with a fork.

Remove salmon from skillet; discard poaching liquid. Cover; refrigerate salmon 2 hours or till chilled.

For dressing, in a small mixing bowl combine mayonnaise or salad dressing, buttermilk, dill, chives, lemon peel, and lemon juice. Cover and chill about 1 hour. Serve salmon steaks topped with dressing. If desired, garnish salmon with dill and lemon wedges. Makes 6 servings.

Nutrition information per serving: 458 calories, 32 g protein, 4 g carbohydrate, 34 g total fat (5 g saturated), 115 mg cholesterol, 419 mg sodium, 510 mg potassium

Washington

MARINATED VENISON CHOPS

Dr. John McLoughlin, chief agent of the Hudson's Bay Company outpost in Fort Vancouver in the early nineteenth century, fancied the pleasures of the table. His dinners were formal, complete with bagpipe accompaniment, and often showcased wild game like venison.

4	boneless venison chops *or* steaks, cut ¾ inch thick (about 1 pound)
¼	cup red wine vinegar
2	tablespoons cooking oil
¼	cup catsup
2	teaspoons Worcestershire sauce
1	teaspoon sugar
1	clove garlic, minced
½	teaspoon dry mustard
¼	teaspoon salt
	Dash pepper
	Fresh mint *or* basil sprigs

Place venison chops or steaks in a plastic bag set in a deep bowl or shallow baking dish. For marinade, combine the wine vinegar, cooking oil, catsup, Worcestershire sauce, sugar, garlic, dry mustard, salt, and pepper. Pour marinade over meat in the plastic bag; close bag. Refrigerate for 6 hous or overnight, turning bag occasionally.

Drain venison, reserving marinade; pat dry. Place marinated chops on the rack of an unheated broiler pan. Broil 4 inches from heat for 6 to 8 minutes; brush with marinade. Turn and continue broiling to desired doneness. (Allow about 10 minutes total time for medium-rare, 12 minutes for medium, and 14 minutes for well-done.)

Place broiled chops on a serving platter. Heat remaining marinade to boiling and skim off fat; serve with chops. Makes 4 servings.

Nutrition information per serving: 217 calories, 26 g protein, 6 g carbohydrate, 10 g total fat (2 g saturated), 95 mg cholesterol, 393 mg sodium, 397 mg potassium

Alaska

HALIBUT STEAKS WITH THYME AND TOMATO COULIS

More halibut is fished from Alaskan waters than anywhere else. The size of the catch is enormous, measured in the millions of pounds, even though the season is very short. The Native Americans liked to steam halibut gently in stone-lined cooking pits with seaweed.

4	fresh *or* frozen halibut steaks, cut 1 inch thick (about 1½ pounds total)
1	shallot, finely chopped
1	tablespoon olive oil *or* cooking oil
1	tablespoon margarine *or* butter, melted
1	teaspoon snipped fresh thyme *or* ¼ teaspoon dried thyme, crushed
	Tomato Coulis

Thaw fish, if frozen. In a small mixing bowl stir together shallot, olive oil or cooking oil, melted margarine or butter, and thyme.

Place the fish on the greased unheated rack of a broiler pan; sprinkle with salt and pepper. Broil 4 inches from the heat for 7 minutes; turn fish. Brush each fish steak with some of the thyme mixture. Broil 3 to 5 minutes more or till fish flakes easily with a fork.

Spoon Tomato Coulis onto 4 plates. Top with fish. Serves 4.

Tomato Coulis: In a medium saucepan cook ¼ cup chopped *onion* and 1 clove *garlic*, minced, in 1 tablespoon *olive oil or cooking oil* till onion is very tender. Stir in 1 pound ripe fresh *tomatoes*, peeled, seeded, and coarsely chopped (2½ cups); ¼ teaspoon *salt*; and ⅛ teaspoon *pepper*. Bring to boiling. Reduce heat; simmer, uncovered, for 15 to 20 minutes or till sauce is slightly reduced and thickened.

Transfer tomato mixture to a blender container or food processor bowl. Cover and blend or process till puréed. Return purée to saucepan and stir in 1 tablespoon snipped *parsley*. Cook and stir over medium heat till heated through.

Nutrition information per serving: 286 calories, 33 g protein, 7 g carbohydrate, 13 g total fat (2 g saturated), 49 mg cholesterol, 252 mg sodium, 985 mg potassium

Hawaii

MAHIMAHI WITH HONEY-GINGER GLAZE

Until recently, mahimahi was best enjoyed in the islands where it was served as fresh as possible. Improvements in refrigeration and transportation now allow mainland fanciers of this tropical fish to savor its sweet, moist flesh.

4   **4-ounce skinless mahimahi fillets (about 1 inch thick)**
3   **tablespoons honey**
3   **tablespoons sherry vinegar**
1   **teaspoon grated gingerroot**
½   **teaspoon finely shredded orange peel**
2   **cloves garlic, minced**
1   **tablespoon cooking oil**
½   **teaspoon cornstarch**
    Lemon wedges (optional)
    Endive (optional)

Place mahimahi in a shallow dish. For marinade, stir together honey, sherry vinegar, gingerroot, orange peel, and garlic. Pour marinade over fish. Turn fish to coat with marinade. Cover; marinate for 30 minutes, turning fish occasionally.

Drain fish, reserving marinade. In a large skillet cook fish in hot oil over medium-high heat about 6 minutes. Turn fish and cook about 6 minutes more or till fish flakes easily when tested with a fork. Remove fish from skillet; keep warm.

For glaze, in the same skillet stir together the reserved marinade and cornstarch. Scrape bottom of pan to loosen browned bits. Bring mixture to boiling. Cook and stir over medium-high heat about 1 minute or till glaze thickens. Spoon glaze over fish fillets. If desired, garnish with lemon wedges and endive. Makes 4 servings.

Nutrition information per serving: 191 calories, 19 g protein, 15 g carbohydrate, 6 g total fat (1 g saturated), 88 mg cholesterol, 76 mg sodium, 312 mg potassium

Washington

GRILLED VEAL CHOPS WITH WALLA WALLA ONION MARMALADE

The Walla Walla Valley in southeastern Washington is a major agricultural area. Probably its most famous crop is the Walla Walla onion, which is almost a third again as sweet as a regular onion. Locals say they prefer to eat the onions raw, like apples. They're that good.

2   large Walla Walla onions *or* other onions, thinly sliced and separated into rings (2 cups)
1   teaspoon grated gingerroot
2   tablespoons margarine *or* butter
1½ cups chicken broth
1   tablespoon white wine vinegar
½   teaspoon coarsely cracked black pepper
½   cup dry white wine
1   cup whipping cream
4   veal loin chops, cut ¾ inch thick
    Italian parsley (optional)

For onion marmalade, cook onions and gingerroot in margarine till tender but not brown. Add *1 cup* of the chicken broth, the vinegar, pepper, and ½ teaspoon *salt*. Cook, uncovered, over high heat about 15 minutes or till liquid evaporates.

Add remaining broth and the wine. Return to boiling and simmer, uncovered, about 5 minutes or till liquid is reduced by two-thirds. Stir whipping cream into onion mixture. Cook and stir over medium heat about 15 minutes or till thickened.

Meanwhile, grill veal chops on an uncovered grill directly over *medium-hot* coals for 5 minutes. Turn and grill for 5 to 7 minutes more or to desired doneness. Serve onion marmalade with veal chops. If desired, garnish with Italian parsley. Makes 4 servings.

Nutrition information per serving: 541 calories, 28 g protein, 8 g carbohydrate, 42 g total fat (20 g saturated), 176 mg cholesterol, 695 mg sodium, 468 mg potassium

Hawaii

GINGER-ORANGE SHRIMP STIR-FRY

Chinese and Japanese laborers moved to the Pacific Northwest to work on the railroads and to cook in the lumber camps. After the railroads were built, many of these workers stayed on. Asian ingredients and cooking techniques are very much a part of this region's cuisine.

1   pound fresh *or* frozen peeled and deveined medium shrimp
3   tablespoons soy sauce
½   teaspoon finely shredded orange peel
2   tablespoons orange juice
2   teaspoons cornstarch
1   teaspoon sugar

½ teaspoon crushed red
pepper *or* ⅛ teaspoon
black pepper
2 tablespoons cooking oil
1 teaspoon grated gingerroot
4 green onions, bias-sliced
into 1-inch pieces
2 medium red sweet
peppers, cut into
¾-inch pieces
3 oranges, peeled and
sectioned
3 cups hot cooked rice

Thaw shrimp, if frozen. For sauce, in a bowl stir together soy sauce, orange peel, orange juice, cornstarch, sugar, and crushed red pepper or black pepper. Set aside.

Pour *1 tablespoon* of the cooking oil into a wok or large skillet. Preheat over medium-high heat. Stir-fry gingerroot for 15 seconds. Add green onions and red sweet peppers. Stir-fry about 3 minutes or till crisp-tender. Remove vegetables from wok.

Add remaining oil to wok. Add *half* of the shrimp to the hot wok. Stir-fry 2 to 3 minutes or till shrimp turn pink; remove. Repeat with remaining shrimp.

Return all shrimp to wok. Push shrimp from center of wok. Stir sauce; add to center of wok. Cook and stir till thickened and bubbly.

Stir vegetables into the sauce; cook and stir about 1 minute more or till heated through. Stir in oranges. Serve immediately with hot cooked rice. Makes 4 servings.

Nutrition information per serving:
416 calories, 23 g protein, 62 g carbohydrate, 8 g total fat (1 g saturated), 152 mg cholesterol, 948 mg sodium, 499 mg potassium

PINEAPPLE SALSA

Pineapples are thought to be as Hawaiian as the hula. They aren't. The fruit didn't appear in the islands until the end of the eighteenth century and didn't prove successful commercially until James Dole organized the Hawaiian Pineapple Company on Oahu in 1901.

⅔ cup fresh *or* canned
chopped pineapple
⅓ cup fresh *or* canned
chopped peaches
⅓ cup chopped green *or* red
sweet pepper
2 tablespoons sliced green
onion
2 tablespoons lime juice
1 teaspoon snipped fresh
cilantro *or* parsley

In a medium bowl combine pineapple, peaches, green or red sweet pepper, and green onion. Add lime juice and cilantro or parsley, tossing to coat. Serve with chicken, turkey, or fish. Makes 4 servings.

Nutrition information per serving:
24 calories, 0 g protein, 6 g carbohydrate, 0 g total fat (0 g saturated), 0 mg cholesterol, 1 mg sodium, 89 mg potassium

Washington

GEODUCK CLAM CHOWDER

Northwesterners know to say gooey-duck when they order this huge (about three-pound) bizarre-looking Pacific clam. A large water-spouting neck, or siphon, protrudes from its shell like a periscope, providing a clue for clam diggers. The body meat is sliced for steaks, the neck ground for chowder.

2   medium potatoes, peeled
    and chopped (2 cups),
    or 2 cups loose-pack
    frozen hash brown
    potatoes
1   cup chicken broth
½   cup chopped onion
½   cup chopped celery
1¼ cups milk
2   tablespoons all-purpose
    flour
⅛   teaspoon pepper
¾   cup ground *or* minced
    geoduck clams *or*
    one 6½-ounce can
    minced clams
2   slices bacon, crisp-cooked
    and crumbled
    Snipped chives (optional)

In a medium saucepan combine chopped potatoes or frozen hash brown potatoes, chicken broth, onion, and celery. Bring to boiling, reduce heat. Cover and simmer about 10 minutes or till potatoes are tender. *Do not drain.* Slightly mash the potatoes.

In a small mixing bowl stir together the milk, flour, and pepper. Stir into potato mixture. Cook and stir till thickened and bubbly.

Stir in *undrained* clams; heat through. Sprinkle each serving with bacon and, if desired, chives. Makes 4 to 6 side-dish servings.

Nutrition information per serving:
214 calories, 14 g protein, 31 g carbohydrate, 4 g total fat (2 g saturated), 25 mg cholesterol, 375 mg sodium, 749 mg potassium

Washington

PUMPKIN SOUP

When pumpkin seeds from England arrived at the Hudson's Bay Company, they were not for human consumption. They were ordered to provide food for the pigs!

¼   cup chopped onion
1   tablespoon margarine *or*
    butter
1   14½-ounce can chicken
    broth
½   cup finely chopped, peeled
    potato *or* loose-pack,
    frozen, hash brown
    potatoes
½   cup loose-pack frozen corn
¼   cup finely chopped red *or*
    green sweet pepper
½   of a 16-ounce can (1 cup)
    pumpkin
¼   teaspoon salt
⅛   teaspoon pepper
1   cup half-and-half, light
    cream, *or* milk
    Sliced green onion *or*
    chives (optional)

In a large saucepan cook onion in hot margarine or butter till tender but not brown. Stir in chicken broth, finely chopped potato or frozen hash brown potatoes, corn, and red or green sweet pepper. Cover and simmer about 15 minutes or till vegetables are tender.

Stir pumpkin, salt, and pepper into broth mixture. Slowly add half-and-half, light cream, or milk, stirring constantly. Heat through. Ladle soup into individual bowls. If desired, garnish with sliced green onion or chives. Makes 4 side-dish servings.

Nutrition information per serving: *178 calories, 6 g protein, 17 g carbohydrate, 11 g total fat (5 g saturated), 23 mg cholesterol, 523 mg sodium, 406 mg potassium*

Oregon

MUSHROOM MEDLEY AU GRATIN

Thousands of varieties of wild mushrooms grow in the damp forests of Oregon and Washington, although only relatively few are safe to forage for and eat. Asian shiitake and oyster mushrooms are also cultivated.

2   tablespoons grated Parmesan cheese
2   tablespoons fine dry bread crumbs
2   teaspoons margarine *or* butter, softened
8   ounces shiitake mushrooms
4   ounces oyster mushrooms
16 ounces button mushrooms, sliced
1   clove garlic, minced

2   tablespoons margarine *or* butter
2   tablespoons all-purpose flour
2   teaspoons Dijon-style mustard
½   teaspoon dried thyme, crushed
¼   teaspoon salt
⅔   cup milk
    Kale (optional)

In a small bowl combine Parmesan cheese, bread crumbs, and the 2 teaspoons margarine; set aside.

Separate caps and stems from shiitake and oyster mushrooms. Reserve stems to use in stocks or discard. Slice mushroom caps.

In a large skillet cook button mushrooms and garlic in the 2 tablespoons margarine or butter over medium-high heat about 4 minutes or till tender and most of the liquid has evaporated. Remove mushrooms, reserving drippings. Add shiitake and oyster mushrooms; cook for 7 to 8 minutes or till tender and most of the liquid has evaporated. Stir in flour, mustard, thyme, and salt. Add milk all at once. Cook and stir till thickened and bubbly. Cook and stir 1 minute more. Stir in button mushrooms.

Transfer to a 1-quart casserole. Sprinkle with crumb mixture. Bake in a 350° oven about 20 minutes or till bubbly. If desired, serve atop kale. Makes 4 servings.

Nutrition information per serving: *200 calories, 7 g protein, 22 g carbohydrate, 10 g total fat (2 g saturated), 5 mg cholesterol, 386 mg sodium, 677 mg potassium*

Oregon

GOOSEBERRY RELISH

Attempts by colonists in New England to plant gooseberry seeds from Europe failed because of disease. Indigenous varieties were found to carry white pine blight, so cultivation wasn't pursued. A new hybrid of the English and American strains was eventually developed and is under cultivation in Washington and Oregon.

2   cups gooseberries
1   cup packed brown sugar
¼   cup vinegar
2   tablespoons port wine *or* sweet marsala
1   teaspoon finely shredded orange peel
¼   teaspoon ground cinnamon
⅛   teaspoon ground cloves
⅛   teaspoon ground allspice
⅛   teaspoon ground nutmeg

Remove tops and stems from gooseberries; rinse and drain. In a 2-quart saucepan stir together berries, brown sugar, vinegar, wine, and orange peel. Bring to boiling; reduce heat. Simmer, uncovered, for 5 minutes, stirring frequently.

Stir cinnamon, cloves, allspice, and nutmeg into the hot gooseberry mixture. Simmer, uncovered, for 5 minutes more, stirring often.

Serve warm or chilled on ham, pork, or chicken. To store, cool to room temperature. Cover and chill for up to 2 weeks. Makes 1½ cups.

Nutrition information per tablespoon: 42 calories, 0 g protein, 11 g carbohydrate, 0 g total fat (0 g saturated), 0 mg cholesterol, 3 mg sodium, 60 mg potassium

Alaska

SOURDOUGH PANCAKES

Miners working in the goldfields of Alaska depended on sourdough starter to leaven bread. These rugged settlers came to be called sourdoughs themselves because the starter was so much a part of their lives in the wilderness.

1¼   cups Sourdough Starter (see recipe, page 187)
1   cup all-purpose flour
1   tablespoon sugar
1   teaspoon baking powder
½   teaspoon baking soda
¼   teaspoon salt
1   beaten egg
2   tablespoons cooking oil

Bring Sourdough Starter to room temperature. In a mixing bowl stir together flour, sugar, baking powder, baking soda, and salt. In another mixing bowl combine Sourdough Starter, egg, and cooking oil. Add to flour mixture all at once. Stir mixture just till blended but still slightly lumpy.

For each pancake, pour about ¼ cup batter onto a hot lightly greased griddle or heavy skillet. (*Or,* for each silver-dollar-size pancake pour about *1 tablespoon* batter onto hot griddle.)

Cook till pancakes are golden brown, turning to cook second sides when pancakes have bubbly surfaces and slightly dry edges. Makes 8 to 10 pancakes.

Nutrition information per pancake: *179 calories, 5 g protein, 30 g carbohydrate, 4 g total fat (1 g saturated), 27 mg cholesterol, 167 mg sodium, 46 mg potassium*

BANANA-MACADAMIA NUT MUFFINS

The hard-shell macadamia nut isn't native to the islands, but was brought there in 1881 from Australia where it grows wild. The nut was named for Dr. John MacAdam, an Australian scientist, who was so enamored of its rich, addictive flavor that he became one of its most vocal promoters.

1¾   cups all-purpose flour
⅓   cup chopped macadamia nuts
⅓   cup packed brown sugar

2   teaspoons baking powder
¼   teaspoon baking soda
¼   teaspoon salt
¼   teaspoon ground nutmeg
1   beaten egg
¾   cup mashed banana
½   cup orange juice
⅓   cup cooking oil
    Streusel Topping

In a large mixing bowl combine the flour, nuts, brown sugar, baking powder, baking soda, salt, and nutmeg. Make a well in the center of the dry ingredients.

Combine the egg, the mashed banana, orange juice, and cooking oil; add all at once to flour mixture. Stir just till moistened (batter should be lumpy). Lightly grease muffin cups or line them with paper bake cups; fill ⅔ full. Sprinkle muffins with the Streusel Topping.

Bake in a 400° oven about 20 minutes or till golden. Remove from pan; serve warm. Makes 12 to 14 muffins.

Streusel Topping: In a small mixing bowl stir together 2 tablespoons *all-purpose flour* and 2 tablespoons *sugar*. Cut in 1 tablespoon *margarine or butter* till mixture resembles coarse crumbs. Stir in ⅓ cup chopped *macadamia nuts.*

Nutrition information per muffin: *231 calories, 3 g protein, 26 g carbohydrate, 13 g total fat (2 g saturated), 18 mg cholesterol, 86 mg sodium, 139 mg potassium*

Oregon

OATMEAL-PRUNE MUFFINS

Cuttings for prune trees were brought to the Willamette Valley by French settlers in the mid-1850s. Pioneer cooks used them in preserves, baked goods, puddings, and stuffings.

1⅓ cups all-purpose flour
¾ cup rolled oats
2 teaspoons baking powder
½ teaspoon baking soda
¼ teaspoon salt
1 beaten egg
¾ cup milk
½ cup packed brown sugar
¼ cup cooking oil
½ teaspoon vanilla
1 cup snipped, dried, pitted prunes

Grease eighteen 1¾-inch or twelve 2½-inch muffin cups or line them with paper bake cups; set aside. In a bowl stir together flour, oats, baking powder, soda, and salt. Make a well in the center of the dry mixture.

In a bowl combine the egg, milk, brown sugar, oil, and vanilla. Add egg mixture all at once to the dry mixture. Stir just till moistened (batter should be lumpy). Fold prunes into the batter.

Spoon *half* of the batter into the prepared 1¾-inch muffin cups, filling each ¾ full. *Or,* divide all of the batter among the 2½-inch muffin cups. Bake in a 400° oven for 10 to 12 minutes for 1¾-inch muffins or 16 to 18 minutes for 2½-inch muffins or till done. Cool in muffin cups on a wire rack 5 minutes; remove muffins from cups. Repeat with remaining batter. Serve warm. Makes thirty-six 1¾-inch or twelve 2½-inch muffins.

Nutrition information per muffin: 58 calories, 1 g protein, 9 g carbohydrate, 2 g total fat (1 g saturated), 6 mg cholesterol, 49 mg sodium, 55 mg potassium

Washington

WILTED SPINACH AND DUNGENESS CRAB SALAD

The Dungeness crab represents Washington state much as the cod does Massachusetts. Although found in Pacific waters from Alaska to California, it was named for the Dungeness Bay of Washington's Olympic Peninsula.

1½ pounds fresh *or* frozen cooked crab claws *or* 12 ounces fresh *or* frozen cooked crabmeat
6 cups torn fresh spinach
1 cup sliced fresh mushrooms

¼ cup sliced green onion
3 slices bacon
¼ cup white wine vinegar
1 tablespoon sugar
¼ teaspoon salt
1 11-ounce can mandarin
    orange sections, drained
¼ cup toasted sliced almonds

Thaw crabmeat, if frozen. Drain well. In a large bowl combine spinach, mushrooms, and green onion. Set aside.

In a 12-inch skillet cook bacon till crisp. Drain bacon on paper towels, reserving drippings in skillet. Crumble bacon; set aside.

Stir wine vinegar, sugar, and salt into drippings. Heat to boiling. Add spinach mixture and crabmeat to skillet, tossing 30 to 60 seconds or till spinach is just wilted. Remove from heat.

Gently stir in the orange sections. Sprinkle with the almonds and bacon. Serve immediately. Makes 4 servings.

Nutrition information per serving:
307 calories, 25 g protein, 15 g carbohydrate, 17 g total fat (6 g saturated), 79 mg cholesterol, 659 mg sodium, 1,041 mg potassium

Oregon

BLACKBERRY JAM

Oregon is the nation's blackberry patch. Most of the berries used commercially in the United States come from Oregon vines. Jams and preserves were one way for early settlers to extend the season for fresh fruit.

4 cups blackberries
4 cups sugar
¼ teaspoon finely shredded
    lemon peel *or* orange
    peel
½ of a 6-ounce package
    (1 foil pouch) liquid
    fruit pectin
2 tablespoons lemon juice

Crush blackberries. Measure *2 cups* berries. In a bowl combine berries, sugar, and lemon peel or orange peel. Let stand 10 minutes.

Combine pectin and lemon juice. Add to berry mixture; stir for 3 minutes.

Ladle at once into jars or freezer containers, leaving a ½-inch headspace. Seal, label, and let stand at room temperature about 2 hours or till jam is set. Store up to 3 weeks in the refrigerator or 1 year in the freezer. Makes 4 half-pints.

Nutrition information per tablespoon: 53 calories, 0 g protein, 14 g carbohydrate, 0 g total fat (0 g saturated), 0 mg cholesterol, 0 mg sodium, 22 mg potassium

Oregon

BLACKBERRY PIE WITH HAZELNUT GLAZE

Berry pies were favorite desserts for pioneer cooks. They knew that blackberry vines grew in logged-over areas, and during the summer months would set out, pails in hand, for a day of berry picking.

¾ cup sugar
¼ all-purpose flour
½ teaspoon finely shredded lemon peel
4 cups fresh *or* frozen unsweetened blackberries
Pastry for Double-Crust Pie (see recipe, page 213)
Hazelnut Glaze (optional)

In a large mixing bowl combine the sugar, flour, and lemon peel. Add fresh or frozen blackberries; toss gently till coated. (If using frozen blackberries, before adding let them stand 15 to 30 minutes or till the berries are *partially* thawed but still icy.)

Transfer berry mixture to a pastry-lined 9-inch pie plate. Add top crust; cut slits in top crust. Trim, seal, and flute edge. To prevent overbrowning, cover edge of pie with foil.

Bake in a 375° oven for 25 minutes for fresh berries (50 minutes for frozen berries). Remove foil.

Bake for 20 to 25 minutes more for fresh berries (20 to 30 minutes for frozen berries) or till top is golden. If desired, top hot pie with Hazelnut Glaze. Cool. Serves 8.

Hazelnut Glaze: In a small saucepan combine ⅓ cup packed *brown sugar* and 3 tablespoons *half-and-half or light cream*. Cook and stir over low heat till sugar melts. Stir in ⅓ cup chopped toasted *hazelnuts*. Pour over hot pie.

Nutrition information per serving: 450 calories, 5 g protein, 61 g carbohydrate, 21 g total fat (5 g saturated), 2 mg cholesterol, 139 mg sodium, 228 mg potassium

Washington

APPLE-CHERRY PIE

Apples from the Wenatchee Valley of Washington formed the basis of the state's gigantic apple industry. Washington is also well known for its cherries, like the dark, black-red, sweet Bing and the Royal Anne. The Bing cherry is a transplant from Oregon, however. It was developed in orchards near Portland in the mid-1800s.

2 cups fresh *or* frozen pitted tart red cherries
1 cup sugar
2 tablespoons all-purpose flour
1 teaspoon ground cinnamon
¼ teaspoon ground nutmeg

3   cups peeled, cored, and
    thinly sliced apples
    Pastry for Double-Crust
    Pie (see recipe, right)
2   tablespoons margarine *or*
    butter
1   tablespoon milk
½   teaspoon sugar
    Dash ground cinnamon

If using frozen cherries, let stand at room temperature 30 minutes or till partially thawed. Stir together the 1 cup sugar, the flour, the 1 teaspoon cinnamon, and the nutmeg; set aside.

In a large bowl combine cherries and apple slices. Add sugar mixture. Toss to coat. Transfer to pastry-lined 9-inch pie plate. Dot fruit with margarine or butter. Adjust top crust. Seal and flute edge. If desired, cut decorative shapes from dough scraps. Brush the back sides of the shapes with milk and arrange on the top crust. Cut slits in the top crust. Brush top crust with milk. Combine the ½ teaspoon sugar and the dash cinnamon; sprinkle over crust. Cover edge with foil.

Bake in a 375° oven for 25 minutes (50 minutes if using frozen cherries). Remove foil. Bake for 20 to 25 minutes more or till the top is golden and fruit is tender. Makes 8 servings.

Nutrition information per serving: 439 calories, 4 g protein, 61 g carbohydrate, 21 g total fat (5 g saturated), 0 mg cholesterol, 160 mg sodium, 136 mg potassium

PASTRY FOR DOUBLE-CRUST PIE

2   cups all-purpose flour
½   teaspoon salt
⅔   cup shortening *or* lard
6   to 7 tablespoons cold
    water

In a mixing bowl stir together flour and salt. Cut in shortening or lard till pieces are the size of small peas. Sprinkle *1 tablespoon* of the water over part of the mixture; gently toss with a fork. Push to side of bowl. Repeat till all is moistened. Divide dough in half. Form each half of dough into a ball.

On a lightly floured surface, flatten each ball of dough with your hands. Roll out dough from center to edges, forming a circle about 12 inches in diameter. Wrap pastry around a rolling pin. Unroll pastry onto a 9-inch pie plate. Ease pastry into pie plate, being careful not to stretch pastry. Trim pastry even with rim of pie plate.

For top crust, repeat rolling remaining dough. Cut slits to allow steam to escape. Fill pastry in pie plate with desired filling. Place the top crust on filling. Trim top crust to ½ inch beyond edge of plate. Fold the top crust under bottom crust; flute edge. Bake as directed in individual recipes.

Oregon

PEAR COBBLER

Harry and David Rosenberg thought that the Royal Riviera pears from their Bear Creek Orchards near Medford, Oregon, were something special. In 1934, they carefully packed some samples and hit the road. They returned with hundreds of orders, the start of their now world-famous mail-order company.

4	cups sliced, peeled pears
⅓	cup packed brown sugar
2	tablespoons water
1	tablespoon lemon juice
2	tablespoons water
1	tablespoon cornstarch
⅓	cup all-purpose flour
2	tablespoons finely crushed graham crackers
1	tablespoon finely chopped pecans
1	tablespoon brown sugar
¾	teaspoon baking powder
2	tablespoons margarine *or* butter
1	slightly beaten egg white
2	tablespoons milk
1½	teaspoons sugar
⅛	teaspoon ground cinnamon
	Half-and-half, light cream, *or* vanilla ice cream (optional)
	Red currants (optional)

In a large saucepan, bring pears, the ⅓ cup brown sugar, 2 tablespoons water, and lemon juice to boiling, stirring to dissolve sugar. Reduce heat. Cover and simmer for 5 minutes or till fruit is almost tender, stirring occasionally. Combine 2 tablespoons water and the cornstarch; add to pear mixture. Cook and stir till thickened and bubbly.

Meanwhile, for biscuit topping, in a mixing bowl stir together the flour, crushed graham crackers, pecans, the 1 tablespoon brown sugar, and baking powder. Cut in the margarine or butter till the mixture resembles coarse crumbs. In another mixing bowl combine egg white and milk. Add all at once to the flour mixture, stirring just till moistened.

Spoon the hot fruit mixture into a 2-quart square baking dish. Immediately spoon the biscuit topping into 6 mounds atop the hot fruit mixture. Combine the sugar and cinnamon. Sprinkle sugar-cinnamon mixture over the biscuit mounds.

Bake in a 400° oven for 12 to 15 minutes or till a wooden toothpick inserted in the center of a biscuit comes out clean. Serve warm If desired, serve with half-and-half, light cream, or ice cream. Serves 6.

Nutrition information per serving:
194 calories, 2 g protein, 36 g carbohydrate, 5 g total fat (1 g saturated), 0 mg cholesterol, 97 mg sodium, 207 mg potassium

BAKED CUSTARD WITH COFFEE SAUCE

The gospel and the muumuu weren't all that the missionaries brought to the Hawaiian islands. They get the credit for planting the first coffee trees along the Kona Coast of the Big Island.

6	eggs
3	cups milk
½	cup sugar
1½	teaspoons vanilla
¼	teaspoon salt
	Coffee Sauce

In a large mixing bowl use a rotary beater or wire whisk to lightly beat eggs just till mixed. Stir in milk, sugar, vanilla, and salt.

Place an ungreased 4½- or 5-cup ovenproof ring mold (about 8 inches in diameter) in a 13x9x2-inch baking pan. (*Or*, place eight 6-ounce custard cups or individual molds in a large roasting pan.) Set the baking or roasting pan on the oven rack. Pour the egg mixture into the mold(s). Pour boiling or very hot tap water into the pan around the mold to a depth of 1 inch. Bake in a 325° oven for 35 to 45 minutes or till a knife inserted near the center come out clean.

Remove mold(s) from water in pan. Cool custard in the mold(s) on a wire rack. Cover and chill in the refrigerator for at least 2 hours before serving.

To serve, prepare the sauce. Remove custard from mold(s). Serve sauce with chilled custard. Serves 8.

Coffee Sauce: In a saucepan combine ½ cup *water*, ¼ cup *light corn syrup*, 2 teaspoons *cornstarch*, and 1 teaspoon *instant coffee crystals*. Cook and stir over medium heat till mixture is bubbly. Cook and stir for 2 minutes more. Remove mixture from heat.

Stir in ¼ teaspoon *vanilla* and, if desired, 1 teaspoon *coffee liqueur*. Cover and chill sauce in the refrigerator till serving time.

Nutrition information per serving:
243 calories, 10 g protein, 34 g carbohydrate, 7 g total fat (3 g saturated), 222 mg cholesterol, 140 mg sodium, 196 mg potassium

Hawaii

FROSTY HAWAIIAN NÓG

The Smooth Cayenne variety, brought to Hawaii from Jamaica in 1886 for its superior flavor, is the foundation of the canned pineapple industry. While it was sweet and delicious, it didn't ship well fresh. Pineapple growers learned that canning was the best way to preserve the fruit.

3   cups buttermilk
1   8-ounce can crushed
      pineapple (juice pack),
      chilled
¼   cup sugar *or* honey
1   teaspoon vanilla
¼   teaspoon salt
5   ice cubes *or* 1 cup small
      ice cubes
      Pineapple leaves *or* fresh
      mint sprigs (optional)

In a blender container place butter-milk, *undrained* pineapple, sugar or honey, vanilla, and salt. Cover and blend about 30 seconds or till com-bined. With blender running, add ice cubes, one at a time, through opening in lid. Blend till mixture is nearly smooth and frothy.

Pour into 5 chilled mugs or tall glasses. If desired, garnish each serving with pineapple leaves or a sprig of mint. Makes about five 8-ounce servings.

Nutrition information per serving:
126 calories, 5 g protein, 24 g carbohydrate, 1 g total fat (1 g saturated), 5 mg choles-terol, 155 mg sodium, 278 mg potassium

Hawaii

CREAM CHEESE-MACADAMIA PIE

The macadamia is one tough nut to crack. In fact, it's shell is so difficult to remove that the nut was never popular in its native Australia. It didn't become viable commercially in Hawaii either for almost fifty years, until someone invented a machine that could crack the almost impenetrable casing.

2   3-ounce packages cream
      cheese, softened
½   cup sugar
4   eggs
2   teaspoons vanilla
¼   teaspoon salt
      Pastry for Single-Crust
      Pie (see recipe, page 30)
1¼   cups chopped macadamia
      nuts
¾   cup light corn syrup
3   tablespoons sugar
3   tablespoons margarine *or*
      butter, melted

In a mixing bowl beat cream cheese with an electric mixer on medium speed till smooth. Add the ½ cup sugar, *one* of the eggs, *1 tea-spoon* of the vanilla, and salt; beat just till combined. Spread cream cheese mixture onto bottom of a pastry-lined 9-inch pie plate. Sprinkle nuts over cream cheese mixture.

Use a rotary beater or wire whisk to lightly beat the remaining eggs just till mixed. Stir in the corn syrup, the 3 tablespoons sugar, margarine, and remaining vanilla.

Place the partially filled pie plate on a baking sheet on the oven rack. Slowly pour the syrup mixture over the nuts. To prevent overbrowning, cover the pie edge with foil.

Bake in a 375° oven for 20 minutes. Remove foil. Bake for 25 to 30 minutes more or till edges puff and center is nearly set. Cool completely Cover and chill to store. Serves 10.

Nutrition information per serving:
455 calories, 6 g protein, 44 g carbohydrate, 30 g total fat (8 g saturated), 104 mg cholesterol, 286 mg sodium, 97 mg potassium

HAWAIIAN UPSIDE-DOWN CAKE

This cake is a true showcase of Hawaiian agriculture. Sugar, pineapple, and macadamia nuts are Hawaii's top three crops, in that order. Coconut and ginger are other hallmarks of island cooking.

2   tablespoons margarine *or* butter
⅓   cup packed brown sugar
1   tablespoon rum *or*
      1 tablespoon water plus a few drops rum extract

1   8-ounce can pineapple slices, drained and halved
½   cup chopped toasted macadamia nuts
2   tablespoons flaked coconut, toasted
1⅓   cups all-purpose flour
⅔   cup sugar
2   teaspoons baking powder
¼   teaspoon ground ginger
⅔   cup milk
¼   cup margarine *or* butter, softened
1   egg
1   teaspoon vanilla
      Whipped cream (optional)

Melt the 2 tablespoons margarine or butter in a 9x1½-inch round baking pan. Stir in brown sugar and rum or water and rum extract. Arrange pineapple slices in pan; fill in the spaces with chopped macadamia nuts and coconut. Set pan aside.

Combine flour, sugar, baking powder, and ginger. Add milk, the ¼ cup margarine, egg, and vanilla. Beat for 1 minute. Spoon into pan.

Bake in a 350° oven 30 to 35 minutes or till a toothpick inserted near center comes out clean. Cool 5 minutes. Loosen sides; invert cake onto a plate. Serve warm; if desired, top with whipped cream. Serves 8.

Nutrition information per serving:
342 calories, 4 g protein, 45 g carbohydrate, 16 g total fat (3 g saturated), 28 mg cholesterol, 174 mg sodium, 142 mg potassium

Hawaii

PINEAPPLE DAIQUIRI ICE

Frozen daiquiris are refreshing tropical coolers. The drink was first concocted in Cuba and named after a town there. Hawaiian bartenders give it local flavor with island-grown fruits like pineapple, guava, or bananas.

2	20-ounce cans pineapple chunks (juice pack) *or* one 3- to 3½-pound pineapple, cleaned, cored, and cut into chunks
¾	cup sugar
¼	cup lime juice
¼	cup rum
	Pineapple leaves (optional)

If using canned pineapple, drain juice from *one* can of pineapple chunks. Combine drained, canned pineapple and *undrained*, canned pineapple, or fresh pineapple, with sugar, lime juice, and rum.

In a blender container or food processor bowl place about *one-third* of the pineapple mixture. Cover and blend or process till mixture is almost smooth. Repeat with remaining pineapple mixture, one-third at a time.

Freeze in a 2-quart ice-cream freezer according to manufacturer's directions. If desired, garnish each with pineapple leaves. Makes 12 servings.

Nutrition information per serving:
87 calories, 0 g protein, 20 g carbohydrate, 0 g total fat (0 g saturated), 0 mg cholesterol, 1 mg sodium, 58 mg potassium

Washington

APPLE-BERRY CIDER

Settlers in the Pacific Northwest who had a yen for the cider they so enjoyed back east pressed it from locally grown apples. The inclusion of berries picked from the bushes that grew wild throughout the Northwest gave the sweet drink a new taste.

8	cups apple cider *or* apple juice
1	10-ounce package frozen red raspberries *or* frozen sliced strawberries
4	inches stick cinnamon
1½	teaspoons whole cloves Cinnamon sticks (optional)
1	medium apple, cut into 8 wedges (optional)

In a large saucepan combine the apple cider or juice, raspberries or strawberries, the cinnamon, and the cloves. Bring to boiling and reduce heat. Cover and simmer for 10 minutes. Strain through a sieve lined with 100 percent cotton cheesecloth.

To serve, pour the cider into 8 heat-proof glasses or cups. If desired, garnish each serving with a cinnamon stick and apple wedge. Makes eight 8-ounce servings.

Nutrition information per serving: 163 calories, 0 g protein, 41 g carbohydrate, 0 g total fat (0 g saturated), 0 mg cholesterol, 8 mg sodium, 355 mg potassium

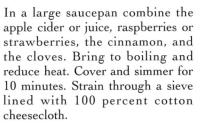

Oregon

HAZELNUT CRUNCH ICE CREAM

You say filbert, I say hazelnut. It's a regional difference: hazelnut in the East, filbert in the West. Or it was anyway, until the industry adopted hazelnut as the official market name. Oregon is the nation's largest producer of these tasty nuts. Washington is not far behind.

⅔ cup chopped hazelnuts (filberts)
¼ cup sugar
1 tablespoon margarine *or* butter
4 cups half-and-half *or* light cream
1½ cups sugar
1 tablespoon vanilla
2 cups whipping cream
 Cookies (optional)

In a small heavy skillet cook hazelnuts, the ¼ cup sugar, and margarine or butter over medium heat (*do not stir*) till sugar begins to melt, shaking skillet occasionally. Reduce heat to low and cook till sugar turns golden, stirring frequently with a wooden spoon. Immediately spread coated nuts on a baking sheet lined with greased foil. Cool and break into chunks. Set aside.

In a large mixing bowl combine half-and-half or light cream, the 1½ cups sugar, and vanilla. Stir till sugar dissolves. Stir in whipping cream and nut chunks. Freeze in a 4- or 5-quart ice cream freezer according to the manufacturer's directions. If desired, serve with cookies. Makes 2 quarts (16 to 20 servings).

Nutrition information per serving: 303 calories, 3 g protein, 26 g carbohydrate, 22 g total fat (11 g saturated), 63 mg cholesterol, 42 mg sodium, 123 mg potassium

A

Almonds
Almond-Avocado Spread, 167
California Almond Shortbread
Cookies, 194-95
Appetizers (See also Dips;
Spreads)
Bourbon-Pecan Pâté, 63
Buffalo Chicken Wings, 36
Guacamole, 137
Pear, Prosciutto, and Blue
Cheese Appetizers, 199
Pine Nut-Cheese Bites, 138
Shrimp with Cilantro-Lime
Cocktail Sauce, 138
Spicy Double Cheese
Straws, 65
Spicy Pecans, 62-63
Vegetable-Topped Cheese
Quesadilla, 136
Wisconsin Cheddar-Bacon
Puffs, 99
Apples
Apple-Berry Cider, 218-19
Apple-Cherry Pie, 212-13
Apple Strudel, 122
Baked Apples, 55
Beet and Apple Salad, 22
Berry-Apple Slump, 31
Chunky Applesauce, 27
Deep-Dish Apple Pie, 29
Dutch Apple Cake, 56
Huguenot Apple-Pecan
Torte, 93
Sausage-and-Apple-Stuffed
Iowa Chops, 110
Schnitz un Knepp, 38-39
Artichokes
Pasta with Artichoke
Sauce, 182
Stuffed Artichokes, 188
Avocados
Almond-Avocado Spread, 167
Avocado and Fruit Salad,
182-83
Avocado Salsa, 161
Guacamole, 137

B

Bananas
Banana-Cinnamon Waffles, 23
Banana-Macadamia Nut
Muffins, 209

Bananas Foster, 87
Cranberry-Banana Bread,
22-23
Beans
Black Bean and Chayote
Burritos, 149
Black Bean Soup, 79
Black-Eyed Pea Salad, 80-81
Boston Baked Beans, 18-19
Cincinnati Chili, 107
Cowboy Beans, 186
Creamy Navy Bean Soup, 40
Hoppin John, 80
Layered Black Bean Salad,
158-59
Red Beans and Rice, 77
Refried Beans, 158
Sweet-and-Sour Beans and
Carrots, 48-49
Beef (See also Corned Beef;
Sausage)
Beef Pot Roast, 100-101
Beer-Marinated Peppered
T-Bones, 102-3
Bierocks, 103
Chicken-Fried Steak, 102
Chimichangas, 148
Cincinnati Chili, 107
Cornish Beef Pasties, 104
Cowpuncher Stew, 173
Hamburgers, 106-7
Individual Beef Wellington, 41
Philadelphia Cheese Steak
Sandwich, 42-43
Picadillo, 140-41
Roast Beef with Peppered
Yorkshire Pudding, 39
Shredded Beef Burrito, 152
Texas Chili, 150-51
Texas-Style Beef Brisket, 139
Wine-and-Herb-Marinated
Rib Eye Roast, 101
Beets
Beet and Apple Salad, 22
Red Flannel Hash, 24
Beignets, 96
Beverages (Alcoholic)
Café Brûlot, 95
Cappuccino Eggnog, 98
Fish House Punch, 61
Hot Buttered Cider Sipper, 25
Mint Julep, 95
Sangrita, 164

Beverages (Nonalcoholic)
Apple-Berry Cider, 218-19
Café au Lait, 97
Cappuccino, 196
Frosty Hawaiian Nog, 216
Mexican Hot Chocolate, 161
Pink Rhubarb Punch, 132-33
Blackberries
Blackberry Jam, 211
Blackberry Jam Cake, 130-31
Blackberry Pie, 212
Blueberries
Berry-Apple Slump, 31
Spiced Blueberry Jam, 21
Breads (Quick)
Beaten Biscuits, 82
Black Walnut-Wild Raspberry
Bread, 126
Boston Brown Bread, 18
Buñuelos, 163
Corn Bread, 86
Corn Tortillas, 156-57
Cranberry-Banana Bread,
22-23
Flour Tortillas, 156
Spoon Bread, 83
Whole Wheat Popovers, 14
Breads (Yeast)
Anadama Bread, 16
Cinnamon Rolls, 50-51
Hot Cross Buns, 46
Kansas Whole Wheat-Honey
Bread, 119
Kolaches, 190
Lemony Moravian Sugar
Bread, 84
Navajo Fry Bread, 155
Parker House Rolls, 17
Sally Lunn, 86-87
Sourdough Bread, 186-87
Swedish Limpa Bread, 118
Walnut Potica, 123
Burgers
Grilled Elk Burgers, 199
Hamburgers, 106-7

C

Cabbage
Sausage and Kraut, 112
Sweet-and-Sour Red
Cabbage, 52
Texas Coleslaw, 154-55
Three-Pepper Slaw, 45

Index